Tom Fordyce and Ben Dirs

KARMA CHAMELEONS

MACMILLAN

First published 2010 by Macmillan

This edition published 2014 by Pan Books
an imprint of Pan Macmillan, a division of Macmillan Publishers Limited
Pan Macmillan, 20 New Wharf Road, London N1 9RR
Basingstoke and Oxford
Associated companies throughout the world
www.panmacmillan.com

ISBN 978-1-4472-7805-4

Visit **www.panmacmillan.com** to read more about all our books
and to buy them. You will also find features, author interviews and
news of any author events, and you can sign up for e-newsletters
so that you're always first to hear about our new releases.

KARMA CHAMELEONS

Also by Tom Fordyce and Ben Dirs

WE COULD BE HEROES

Ben Dedication

*For anyone who is uglier, balder, poorer
and more socially inadequate than me,
without whom I'd be a lot less happy.*

Tom Dedication

*To happiness hunters everywhere,
and to Murf for her unparalleled tracking skills.*

Contents

PROLOGUE

'Happy people exist, don't they?'

TOM

I was halfway up a hill on the second lap of the National Cross Country Championships, deep in a ding-dong battle against three skinny men with legs like pipe-cleaners, when the thought lodged immovably in my brain: I wasn't happy enough.

It wasn't the sleet blowing across London's Parliament Hill like a storm of tiny tacks, or the shin-deep mud that shackled my legs, or the sick feeling that was spreading from stomach to throat to teeth. I was used to that, and usually revelled in it. No. This was something else, something more fundamental. And it wouldn't go away.

The leaders accelerated over the brow of a hill, mottled arse-cheeks exposed by their flapping shorts like obscene semaphore. I tried to block out the distress signals. This sort of thing had always mattered to me – having someone to beat, a time to aim for, another race to win. The podium was out of reach, but I could still finish in the top third.

I slid down a steep slope and began the brutal climb at the start of the third lap. With each slippery stride, the self-doubt spread like mould. My mouth was full of mud, my head full of negativity. Something was horribly awry. I wanted to be somewhere else. And I wanted to be Ben Dirs.

It shouldn't have made any sense. Ben and I were bosom buddies for many reasons, but partly because we each filled the gaps the other had left. I did sit-ups; he did sit-downs. I scheduled; he shambled. I had decathlons for breakfast; he had Double Deckers.

While I was slogging round the National Cross Country Championships, he had also been busy – blowing his last £700 on the high times and low-life of Las Vegas. Not for him simple concepts like clean living and competition. Ben thought cardio was a small town in Sicily, and that a chest-press was something that got you thrown out of a lap-dancing club.

Vegas was his favourite week of the year, an annual extravaganza of decadence and duty-free cigarettes, of nights so unforgettably inebriated that he could never remember them, of outlandish tales featuring faked backstage passes for Barry Manilow shows and calamitous pursuits of the cutest of croupiers. Under normal circumstances I would have settled for vicarious kicks. On a night out with him the hours before 1 a.m. were always a joy, the ones after increasingly hazardous. Like the co-pilot on a plane spiralling out of control, you had to know when to grab the last parachute and leap to safety.

These, however, were no ordinary times. As I waited for him outside the Wetherspoons at Liverpool Street station a week after my cross-country crisis, I felt so unsettled that I could barely be bothered complaining that he was two hours late, or that we'd had to meet at a pub in a train station to reduce the chances of him getting lost en route.

The malaise hadn't ended with the race on Parliament Hill. There was more to this than mere sport. At night I'd been unable to sleep, beset by bouts of melancholic self-examination; during the day I'd struggled to get off the sofa, watching endless re-runs of programmes I hadn't cared about the first time around and flicking futile v-signs at the clamouring commercials in between. I'd always considered myself an upbeat individual, yet on a brief ten-minute cycle to the shops I'd called three different van-drivers something unpleasant and biologically unlikely. Why was I feeling this way?

Ben looked unwell, which was no great surprise. When required to rise before midday he had the ability to make police dogs whimper and horses rear up on their hind legs. 'Nightmare,' he coughed, red-eyed and bemused. 'Trains were all messed up. Some nutter lobbed himself under the fast one from Southend. Had to get a coach in and then walk from Bethnal Green. Went the wrong way out the station and ended up in Bow. I've just got off the bus.'

It was the classic Dirs travel tale. So many times had someone thrown themselves onto the tracks at Seven Kings as he was about to start his journey that I was beginning to suspect the existence of a shadowy suicide cult in the London-Essex borders. I'd been to Romford for nights out, and admittedly it was bad – but if you did want to kill yourself, you didn't have to go to the train station. Brush someone with your elbow in Brannigans and they would do it for you. By the time you made it to the station you were a mere £6 day single away from a better life – the sunlit uplands of Wickford, the land of milk and honey that is Rayleigh. Why end it all at that point?

Even considering his epic journey and the fact that he was up before 3 p.m. he seemed unexpectedly downbeat. After half an hour of stolid silence, a packet of scampi fries lay untouched in front of him. His lager, unsupped and unwanted, evaporated slowly alongside.

'Good times?' I said, leaning forward eagerly. 'Big nights? I wish I'd been there. Where'd you go – that place with actual canals running through it? Or the charming little local bar you were telling me about – what was it called again?'

'Hooters.' He shook his head mournfully. 'Didn't work. I felt miserable before I'd even left home. I got drunk and just felt worse.'

'In Vegas? How? Why this time?'

'The sun never stopped shining. There were ladies everywhere, and I was in one of the few places in the English-speaking world where my name didn't make people laugh themselves stupid. But I just felt rubbish, run down, clapped out. We saw Tony Bennett. Even he had more spring in his step than me, and I thought he'd been dead ten years.'

I grimaced. Earlier that morning I had made one final attempt to exercise my way back to contentment. Eight lengths into a 3,000m swim-set, I had abandoned it mid-stroke, climbed out of the pool and walked slowly back into the changing-room muttering 'No mas,' under my breath like a Speedo-sponsored Roberto Duran.

'I'll be honest with you,' said Ben. 'I'm a state. I wake up most mornings and feel ill. Too many fags, not enough exercise. By the time I feel better it's time to make myself ill again. I worked out the other day that I hadn't eaten a piece of fruit for two months. And I'm not sure Picnic bars really count.' He slumped forward until his forehead rested on the table. 'I should be happier than this.'

'Me too. I used to be able to find pleasure in almost anything. I was convinced I'd got it right. Not any more.'

'Last night I had a stand-up row with the telly. *Newsnight* was on. I'd been shouting at Paxman for five minutes before I realized what I was doing. That's not healthy.'

Maybe there was another problem. The previous November our year-long mission to be crowned world champions at something – anything – had finally drawn to an emotional conclusion. Nothing had quite felt right ever since.

In some ways it was to be expected. There's very little else in life that can match the high-octane drama of the World Wife-Carrying Championships, the medieval brutality of the World Shin-Kicking Championships or the gripping slow-motion spectacle that is the final of the World Snail-Racing. When I had been crowned the first ever World Ubogu champion (an idiosyncratic yet addictive sport involving the repetition of Victor Ubogu's surname as many times as possible in a single breath), I'd expected my life to be trans-formed for ever more. Instead, allegations of underhand tactics dogged me on the internet.

Strangers confronted me in pubs, wanting to take me on at Uboguing when I was ill-prepared and out of training. Rumours circulated of a breakaway organization from the World Ubogu Federation which, since Ben and I were both WUF's founding members and its joint chief executives, raised difficult questions about the loyalty of life president and inspiration, Mr Victor Ubogu. As the days slipped by without a single commercial endorsement or under-dressed groupie landing on my doormat, the pride and sense of achieve-ment had gradually been succeeded by disillusionment and emptiness.

'Let's take stock,' I said. 'I'm unhappy. You're unhappy. This can't go on.'

'Something needs to be done,' said Ben. 'I used to celebrate my birthdays. Now I mourn them.'

'If this was the Victorian era, we'd be considered middle-aged. If this was the Middle Ages, we'd be dead.'

'By our stage in life, Captain Cook had discovered Australia. Yuri Gagarin had been into space and back. Eric Bristow had won five world darts titles. But where are we?'

Was there consolation to be taken in our love lives? For very different reasons, I feared not. I'd been stepping out with a charming ladyfriend for two years but was so ambivalent about permanent allegiance that I had spurned her repeated offers of co-habitation in favour of sharing a rented house with a self-employed equine photographer called Rupert.

I was no emotional or intellectual Neanderthal. Rupert's regular Tuscan-influenced barbecues were a magnet for the brightest, most inquisitive minds in Hammersmith and Baron's Court. Almost nothing was off-limits at those glittering soirées. My reluctance to move in with Sarah was more about a mixture of logic and fear. Could you really guarantee that your favourite dish of today would still be your favourite in thirty years' time? What if her tastes changed too? Was there a more certain way to make a woman cry than compare her to a lightly grilled trout?

Ben had the opposite problem. Two years? If his dalliances stretched to two dates he considered it a success. Every time I saw him he had a fresh tale of woe to recount. The real problems started when even the recounting became impossible. Filled with the desire to direct her matchmaking urges somewhere more fruitful, Sarah had sent Dirsy on a blind date with one of her old friends from college. The first piece of feedback was promising. 'Serious sauce-pot,' read a text from Ben at 9.30 p.m. on the big night. 'Drinks like a prop forward. Smile that could detonate a bridge. It's on.'

The second update was less encouraging. The only part of the night Ben could remember the next day was leaving an exotic cabaret with her at five in the morning. Still, if they'd got that far, it must have been good, no?

No. A day later he had sent her a knockabout text, asking if she fancied another meet-up. Her reply had been unequivocal: 'Never contact me again.'

Sarah had tried phoning the friend. Again and again she found her calls directed to voicemail. Eventually another text came through. 'Moving overseas. Nothing to discuss. Goodbye.' 'I don't understand,' Ben had said mournfully. 'I thought it had potential.'

I looked down at the £1.29 Wetherspoons pints sitting on the table between us, and then around the pub. There was no natural daylight and only the most unnatural of smells, most of them coming from the Morning Mist air fresheners parked under every table. The barman had the complexion of a vampire. In the corner, an old boy wearing slippers sat alone with two bottles of Château Merde. What were we doing? Where were we going? Suddenly, it was all too clear.

'It doesn't have to be like this,' I said, something snapping inside. 'Feeling miserable. Confused. Bitter.'

'You're right. We might have got it wrong. But that doesn't mean everyone else has.'

At the bar, a large woman immersed in the horoscope pages of her celebrity gossip magazine absentmindedly picked her nose. The chalkboard offered Curry In A Hurry for £3.99 and six shots of bubblegum-flavoured vodka for a fiver. Stick or twist. There was no decision to make, not anymore.

'Happy people exist, don't they?'

'Of course. I've seen them.'

'Someone, somewhere, has the secret.' I sat up slowly. 'Let's go out there and discover what it is.'

A fresh start. A journey into the unknown. A two-man mission to find the one thing we all want more than anything else: happiness.

No more moping about. No more wishing the days away and then wondering where the years had gone. No more settling for second best and cynicism and the long slow slide into apathy and disappointment.

There was an unfamiliar stirring of excitement in my guts. 'Captain Cook. No one thought Australia existed, but he set out to find it. Gagarin. Saw the stars and took aim.'

'Bristow. Smashed Dave Whitcombe all over the Lakeside for a hat-trick of titles, but still went looking for more.'

'So why shouldn't we?'

I tried to keep calm. What we were suggesting would take time and great sacrifice. We would have to seek out sages, gather at the feet of gurus, meditate with mystics. Wherever there was the sweet smell of happiness and the promise of answers, there we must go.

Or must we? We were getting carried away. We couldn't just leave our lives behind and go gallivanting round the globe. All right, we didn't have mortgages to worry about – we didn't own so much as a doormat between us. House prices had spiralled so far out of our reach that a one-bedroom maisonette in the Bermondsey/Camberwell borders had taken on the unattainable glow of a maharaja's turreted palace. But there were our jobs as cricket text commentators. Our jobs that saw us unable to afford those bijou concrete boxes. Our jobs that owed us weeks of holiday time. Our jobs that would shortly be relocating hundreds of miles away to a part of the country that had plenty of rain and none of our friends.

There was nothing holding us back. There was everything pushing us forward.

'Tommy, it's time to roll the dice,' said Ben. 'We might end up with a one. I don't care. We're losing the game anyway. We might roll a six.'

'We might have to do things we'd never ordinarily do, hang out with people we'd never go near. We'll both have to change.'

'We both want to change. Farewell preconceptions, hello explorations.'

I looked at Ben. He looked at me. Something unusual stirred in his eyes – energy, vigour, the ability to focus. We picked up our pints and smiled for the first time in months.

'To the karma chameleons.'

'To happiness, wherever we may find it.'

We raised our glasses and touched them together. 'Is there a doctrine in the house?' I asked cheerily.

Ben winked. 'Get your toothbrush, Tommy. We're hitting the road again . . .'

1. MONEY

'To the palm tree, guv, Frond D . . .'

BEN

I've got a £400,000 yacht back in the marina and some Cristal champagne chilling on ice back at the bar. How can this possibly go wrong? Nice and cool, Dirsy, nice and cool.

'Choppy, isn't it?' I say to the peachy blonde girl looking wistfully out to sea, trying desperately not to sound like Tony Curtis in *Some Like It Hot*. She smiles almost imperceptibly. Strike that, she doesn't smile at all, just continues to look wistfully out to sea. I persevere: 'Of course, I know about these things – I've got a 40-footer back in the marina.' There is a sudden flicker of acknowledgement and my heart begins to take flight. Then she turns to me, comes over all inquisitive and says: 'I think I know you from somewhere – didn't you used to play badminton with my dad?'

Tom made me do it. The Cristal made me do it. Dubai made me do it. Preposterous, outrageous, insane Dubai, where anything is possible, or so I thought. We had to come here, too many people said so. Or at least my housemate said so.

'You're hunting for happiness?' said Dave. 'Well you're going to have to investigate money. What about Dubai?' The problem was, I didn't know anyone in Dubai. 'Yeah you do,' insisted Dave, 'remember Stef, used to work for Conti Catering, he's over there now.' I did remember Stef, dear old Stef, one of the finest potato-peelers Conti Catering had ever known.

'I'm looking for someone a bit more upmarket than a potato-peeler,' I said.

'Potato-peeling's in the past,' said Dave. 'He's minted now, got a massive boat and everything.'

And that's how we ended up in Dubai, the moral of the story being: never look down on the humble potato-peeler, or any menial kitchen worker for that matter – one day, he could be where you want to get to.

Since the invention of money, philosophers, gurus, religious men and drunk men down the pub have been wrestling with the link, or otherwise, between material gain and happiness. Indeed, money has been around for so long that it's impossible for us humans to imagine a world without it: we work for money, we live on money, we spend money, we give money, we save money, we waste money, we wage war with money, we wage war over money, we rule by money, we keep people in their place with money, we show off with money, and money is no less important for a poor man than it is for a rich man. In recent decades, studies and research papers have spewed forth from some of our finest academic institutions – Harvard, Princeton, Luton – all attempting to answer that age-old question: does money make us happy? Or does it only succeed in making us more miserable?

Dubai. It's as if God dropped his Meccano set in the middle of the desert and could only be bothered to clear half of it up. Buildings thrusting upwards at peculiar angles; twisted buildings, buildings that look like the sails of a ship, buildings that look like armadillos, even some buildings that look like buildings.

'It's like all the architects of the world have converged on this one place, unzipped their trousers and flopped their chaps on the table,' noted an awestruck Tom as we made our way from the airport.

And there in the middle of it all, seemingly stretching every sinew in an attempt to extricate itself from the absurdity below, is the Burj Khalifa, without doubt the most flabbergasting man-made object either of us had ever clapped eyes on. Standing 828m high, its 20-acre base planned like a 6-leaf desert flower, the Burj Khalifa is more than 300m higher than the previous highest building in the world, the Taipei 101, and is either the ultimate monument to the madness of the United Arab Emirates or one almighty middle-fingered salute to the naysayers, a 'fuck you, we'll be just fine'. Whichever it is, the logical next step in this round of architectural willy-waving is to erect a building in the shape of an almighty cock and balls, perhaps reaching 829m high by dint of some neon ejaculate exploding into the sky.

We met Stef in the Meridien Hotel in the Dubai Marina at noon, having flown through the night. 'First I'll show you around the boat,' said Stef, 'and then, if you like, we can do a bit of skiing.' I was so tired I thought I must be hearing things. Did he really just say skiing? 'It's got five slopes and a black run,' said Stef. 'Everything here's the biggest in the world, they can't handle it if it's not the biggest in the world . . .'

Stef's boat, while not the biggest in the world, had three double bedrooms, three toilets, two showers, a fully fitted kitchen, a living room, not to mention acres of space on top for sunbathing, boozing and generally messing about. But such luxury apparently has its downside, and I'm not just talking about the two-foot gap between the marina boardwalk and the boat, which I imagined after a Mojito or three would look more like fifteen yards.

'They say your two favourite days owning a boat are the day you buy it and the day you sell it,' said Stef as we supped on a beer on deck. 'It was way bigger than I should have bought and I couldn't even sail it at first, but I just went balls out. We've had some good times on it though, and I suppose buying it was symbolic of having made it to a certain extent. But I envy people who stay on it or go out on it and are able to say "bye!" and leave you to deal with the whole thing. Having the boat and certain possessions can actually weigh you down and once you're over the thrill of owning it it's luggage, crap you've got to deal with.'

Stef, who spent most of his formative years in Dubai, can remember when the marina wasn't a marina at all, just men fishing with nets off the sides of antique boats, and when the dunes of the Arabian Desert jutted right up against the waters of the Persian Gulf. But when he returned at the age of twenty-eight, the place was already slipping into turbo nutter mode.

'The happiest I've ever been was probably when I first came back here. I wanted to start my own business because I never found myself in a job I actually enjoyed, and I wasn't making very much money either. So the most happiness I got was at the beginning when I made 50 grand, and I thought, "I've got something in the bank now, I don't have to worry." I moved into internet marketing, I bought a property and it went up in price, then I sold it and put it back in the business and it went from there. Then all of a sudden I was earning more than I could ever imagine. I was 28, living in a bachelor villa, work was easy, not a care in the world. Parties all the time, they were the good days.'

TOM

Was there an optimum income where you had enough not to worry but not so much that you had to work yourself into the ground to get there? As we sprawled on the deck of HMS Hubris *and listened to the clatter of the helicopters shuttling overhead, I wondered where Ben and I stood on the scales of success.*

Shoes, shirts and shorts. We had the basics covered, but beyond that it got a little sketchy. The property boom had passed us by; if it hadn't been for my flatmate Rupert's munificence, I would have been sofa-surfing my way round the extended Fordyce family's spare rooms. I had four bikes, which was almost certainly unnecessary, and Ben had a Pisaesque tower of Visa receipts that both baffled and depressed him. If there was one thing worse than spending too much cash in too many late-night bars, it was that the only memory you had of it was a small scrap of printed paper with your banjaxed signature scrawled on the bottom.

Our sole substantial investment? Our just-about mobile home during our world championship quest the previous year: the Champervan. A 1981 Bedford CF, as heavy as a house and only slightly faster. Just hearing its name made us feel nauseous. It took a special kind of fool to part with £2,000 for the world's worst campervan in the first place, but our luck with it had defied belief. Tyres had burst. Brakes had not just failed but fallen off. Batteries had gone flat and squirrels died in the open-roofed shower. Eventually we had forgotten to renew its road tax and woken up to find it being towed to a car-pound in Southend, but even then it had refused to go. Such was the weight of its twenty-eight-year-old chassis that it had snapped the crane of the removal truck. Faced with a £100-a-day fee for storage by the seaside, we had shelled out for the tax and had it brought back to the Dirs family front lawn in Brentwood, Essex, where Ben's mum could look at it with disgust from every room in the house. Still, our chequered financial records did at least allow us to view the monetary maelstrom that was Dubai with an element of impartiality.

'Registration plates are a big deal over here,' Stef told us. 'The lower the number, the more important you are. Cut up someone with three digits or less and you're in big trouble.' Cut them up in the Champervan and they'd probably die of embarrassment.

We climbed back into Stef's sleek Mercedes and cruised along the coast, cranes teetering on top of skyscrapers that other cranes were still constructing. Vast advertising hoardings loomed out of the dusty desert air. 'The path to happiness,' proclaimed one, 'is the new pay-as-you-go mobile package from Etisalat.' Across the eight-lane highway was an enormous portrait of a sheik, staring straight-faced into the distance. Did he use pay-as-you-go? Something about his gold tooth made me question it.

BEN

A couple of hours later and already a few beers in I was carving my way down the black slope at the indoor ski centre, an Arab in his traditional white kandura robe criss-crossing beside me, ghutra headwear fluttering in the wind behind him. When I reached the bottom, I put in a flashy stop, spraying the window of the bar with snow. But no one was impressed, no one was even watching, they'd seen it all before.

They say the facility consumes the equivalent of 3,000 gallons of oil a day in electricity, and the pistes are covered with 6,000 metric tonnes of manufactured snow – but you should see the one they wanted to build: the proposed Snowdome was going to cover 130,000 square metres, which would have made it more than 60 times as big as the existing ski centre, but was an early victim of the global financial crisis. The Snowdome was to be among 1,001 other Arabian nightmares, including a man-made archipelago in the form of a map of the world, which remains little more than hundreds of piles of sand offshore. In 2009, at the height of the financial crisis, the chairman of Dubai World, the state-owned real-estate giant that has driven much of the economic expansion in recent years, proclaimed: 'Dubai has a vision like no other place on earth.' Thank God for that, otherwise we'd all be living in mud huts and eating each other in fifty years' time.

Tom and Stef had eschewed the cold for the Après Bar overlooking the slope, where we were joined by Stef's girl-friend Libby, a man named 'Lush' and a couple of characters called Thomas and Thierry. Thomas who owns half the bars and clubs in Luxemburg and who once brought a girlfriend's lavish thirtieth birthday party juddering to a premature halt by dropping his trousers and making furious love to the cake ('I didn't believe it when my friend phoned to tell me the next morning – until I pulled the sheets back to find icing all over my dick'), and Thierry whose sister used to be Madonna's nanny and who once accidentally sucked the collagen out of a girlfriend's lips.

It quickly transpired that there had, indeed, been plenty of good times on Stef's boat, including the occasion he lost three people off the back and the coastguards had to call a halt to an F1 powerboat race while helicopters carried out a search overhead. 'They turned up in the end,' said Stef, 'which was lucky, as, unbeknown to me, I didn't have the proper insurance at the time.' Then there was the time Stef short-circuited the entire marina by setting sail while he was still plugged into the mains. 'He was always a bit of an immature twat anyway,' chimed in Lush, who once went missing for two days before being discovered arm-wrestling a German tourist on a ferry. 'But since he's had money he might have pushed the boat out more so, as if he's saying, "Hey, I've got a bit of money, but that doesn't mean I'm serious," so he ends up doing even more stupid things.'

There is a tendency, especially in modern Britain with its hoggish politicians and unethical bankers, to think of anyone who has made themselves plenty of money as a bit of a wrong'un, but I am glad to report that at no stage did Stef throw the table over and announce that lunch was for wimps, or that he wanted to tear my eyeballs out and suck my skull. In fact, Stef was more lounge lizard than Gordon Gekko, with a winning 'I'm not entirely sure how I got here' air about him.

'I've never had the classic comment, "You've changed,"' said Stef, 'but I've had "I'm surprised you haven't changed" and been complimented on not being a twat who talks about money all the time and gives it the big man. I don't know how people would become like that really, although I've seen it happen. But it would be horrible to become a twat over money and then lose it all, because then you're just a twat.'

If anything, Stef felt he'd been too giving when his fortunes began to soar, handing out roles to old mates without much thought of the consequences, some of whom would rather play golf all day than dirty themselves under the bonnet of his various businesses.

'I wanted to help people out and spread the wealth a bit, to me that's what making money was always about,' said Stef, 'but unfortunately a few people took the piss. I didn't necessarily sack them. I just cut them adrift so that it was them who had to deal with the mess they'd created.'

About five pints in and I was starting to feel events getting away from me somewhat, so there were mixed emotions when Stef announced, with a sly smile and a twinkle in his eye, that he knew a chap who was holding an event in a club that night, and that all the booze was free because he also knew the bloke who supplied it.

'Must . . . have . . . sleep,' slurred Tom, who looked like a man teetering on the verge of a Wetherspoons breakdown. So off we tottered back to the boat, with the intention of grabbing a couple of hour's kip before the evening's activities. Alas, I happened upon a skipper's hat, complete with golden brocaded anchor, and spent the first hour shouting, 'Ahoy there!' at any woman unfortunate enough to stroll past – looking for Aristotle Onassis, finding some bell-end from Essex instead. Whoever you were, I extend my greatest sympathy.

'Foxy' lived on the Palm Jumeirah, the world's largest manmade island rendered in the shape of a palm tree, consisting of a trunk stretching out from the mainland and sixteen fronds arching off it. It is four times the size of Hyde Park, has doubled Dubai's forty-two-mile natural coastline and when it was completed the sheikhs, not known for their humility, dubbed it the 'eighth wonder of the world'. But try telling that to one of the estimated 40,000 migrant workers involved in its construction, who are bussed in from labour camps in the desert each morning and earn about £25 a week; or many of its inhabitants, who were promised acres of paradise but have ended up living on top of each other like coconuts clustered on a palm tree.

Reaching Foxy's gaff meant uttering the never-to-be-repeated directive to the taxi driver, 'To the palm tree, guv, Frond D', and there in Villa 42 we found a smattering of ex-pats, all with personal tales to tell of the havoc the financial crisis had wreaked. James had spent five years trying to make it as a musician back in the UK before heading to Dubai and 'accidentally' becoming a property developer, along with thousands of other Brits. The name of the game was 'flipping', with people buying apartments off-plan and selling them on a couple of months later before ground had even been broken on the overall project. The second buyers in the chain were then re-flipping when the first phases of construction were over and the third buyers were flipping them on completion. For a few glorious years 'every businessman, every chancer and every gangster' was having it off, but when the crisis hit, explained James, 'everyone got burnt'.

'There were no checks and measures and no warnings,' said James. 'When things were going well, things seemed easy, but when it all went pear-shaped, I suddenly realized I hadn't really known what I was doing in the first place, I just didn't have any business nous.'

Property in Dubai plummeted 40 per cent in the first three months of 2009, and there were still hundreds of thousands of properties waiting to be completed. Plenty of westerners, on whom Dubai had come to rely for investment, were running for the hills.

'Everyone just went, "Hold on, what's going on, everyone stop buying!"' continued James. 'If you've got a property in London that goes down 40 per cent then you've lost 40 per cent, but if it's not finished and it's not going to be finished, you've lost all of it, which is what happened to a lot of people here. There were thousands of cars just dumped at the airport, people were pissing off without paying property debt or car loans. I had a lot of people investing in me, I felt terrible. And it was all based on one basic human trait: envy of what other people have got.'

'During the boom-time, we were consuming everything like locusts so that in the end there was nothing left,' said Stef, who lost £4–5 million in a fortnight after the crisis hit. 'I was just chasing numbers, gambling, but with poor judgement and at high risk. I'd look at the returns and think, "I'm getting 10 per cent, I'm losing out on 90 per cent I could be getting from elsewhere." When the crisis hit, it wasn't ideal by any stretch of the imagination, but it was a chance to say, "Hold on, I can stop now – maybe I don't need to do all those things I did last time, because they didn't make me happy anyway." I feel happier now and calmer, I don't feel the need to chase everything, I just want to have a stable business that works. There were the wrong kinds of people here before, the fly-by-nighters who were ruining the place a little bit. It was becoming not really a very pleasant place to live. But it's all slowed down now and people have got back to basics a lot more, asking themselves whether the direction they were going in was the right way, rather than just following everyone else like sheep.'

The rest of the evening was little more than a haze, so that when I hauled myself out of bed the following day it was like climbing from a mangled wreck, caused by a head-on collision between Grey Goose vodka and champagne. 'Champagne in Dubai,' I recall Foxy saying at one point, sweeping his arm across the dance floor, 'fandango dripping off you.' There may well have been, but it's impossible for me to say with any conviction. I'm told it was a fun night, I'm told it was a happy night. Just don't ask me how I got home, why I was wearing someone else's shoes when I got there and how it was I didn't drown.

TOM

I was there, and it was still something of a mystery. That night was a microcosm of everything Dubai stood for – opulence on fast-forward, excess chasing excess until eye-watering extravagance became normal and normal got laughed out of town. But was it happiness?

Palm trees with beads of muted light wrapped languorously round the trunks. Cream-coloured leather sofas arranged in circles on the sand. DJs who were also full-time models playing light Euro-trance as waiters slid noiselessly round our marble-topped table, depositing bottle after bottle of Dom Pérignon at our service, each one reclining in a silver ice bucket and draped in a white linen napkin. Around us was a velvet rope, keeping the hoi-polloi at a safe distance. The sand at our feet was so soft you suspected it had been carefully sifted and sorted to remove any irregular or uncomfortable grains.

Dreamlike though the surroundings were, there was no mistaking the manic mood filling the warm night air. 'Vodka!' bellowed one of the boys, glaring around with a wild look in his eye. 'Let's get some fucking vodka! Or more champagne?' He glanced at Ben, slumped on a sofa, and mistook his expression of befuddled disbelief for one of displeasure. 'What's the matter, Dirs? Not enough for you? Want me to put some fucking boot polish on my face and serve you? Eh? I'll get you some fucking Jacob's Creek, you cunts!'

I found myself in a half-cut conversation with an Australian girl. 'I've been having a baby-shower today,' she told me. 'I'm adopting next week. Little black girl. Got a deal from an orphanage in the Congo. They're only $7,000. I'm going over there with my bodyguard to pick her up.'

'What's her name?' I asked, as Ben toppled slowly backwards off the sofa. She made a face. 'One of those African ones,' she said, 'not that that matters. We're going to change it when we get her over here. I'm going to call her Sade.'

It was a night without end, one crystal-cut flute after another, a succession of shots and shouts and pratfalls and party-moves. I premiered a drunken dancefloor special, tailored for Dubai's unique specifications – 'The Crane', one arm out straight, swinging imaginary girders round the skyline, the other on hip as ballast. Ben preferred 'The Human Wrecking-Ball'. It was hard to say which looked worse.

Moods swung and slumped as the booze wreaked a fizzy havoc. 'The women out here', roared one of the gang, 'are sexual cougars. Sexual cougars!' A moment later he was down again. 'Look at this place,' he muttered, shaking his sozzled head in maudlin fashion. 'House of cards. Vacuous fools, everywhere you look.'

Ben had disappeared. I phoned him but got only a strange clattering and some screaming noises. I tried a text. 'Leaving now,' I wrote. 'Waiting by the limousines. Everyone's ready.' A moment later my mobile beeped. I looked at the message. 'Oh,' it said as if it had been sent from a chaise-longue, pinkie placed to the corner of the mouth. That was it.

'He's relapsed,' I muttered to Lush.

'To the boat,' he replied. 'Do you think he knows the way?'

BEN

On the Saturday Stef took us out on the catamaran so that we could better see Dubai in all its splendorous insanity: the Burj Al Arab hotel, mirroring the sails above us, a vast mast of steel and concrete seemingly billowed by the desert wind; the Gate, looking immovable on its two prop-forward's legs, an Arc de Triomphe for the cyber age; the Al Fattan Marine Towers, like two trees side by side in a rainforest competing for the sun; the $1.5 billion Atlantis hotel, with its fairytale central arch and shark-filled aquarium wall, the sort of novelty kitsch they used to build in Vegas; and in amongst these monuments to the sheikhs' rapacious ambitions those lifeless cranes, looking rather embarrassed next to their ostentatious neighbours, what with nothing to keep them occupied.

'You'll always take your money for granted,' said Stef, 'you can't help it when you have lots of it.' He was talking about himself, but he could easily have been talking about the madmen in charge of Dubai, creators of a Never Never Land bought on the never-never.

Even out at sea, with leagues of azure blue water between us and the hallucinogenic island-sized doodlings of the sheikhs (how many lashes, I wonder, for spunking hundreds of billions of dirhams that you haven't actually got?), Stef was unable to escape the curses of success. 'My mobile is almost constantly ringing,' he explained after terminating yet another business call. 'You can be sipping a piña colada under a palm tree, or driving around in your sports car or drinking beer on your yacht, but if your phone keeps ringing, you're thinking, "I can't enjoy my money anyway because I'm on my fucking mobile phone all the time."' So did Stef ever think about cashing it all in and swapping the stresses and strains of business and Dubai for a less complicated life?

'I do have moments of clarity,' chuckled Stef, 'usually at the end of every weekend when the fear and loathing kicks in. Seriously though, I could retire now, put my investments in something safe and have more money than I need. But what the fuck would I do? Go on the piss all day? I'd just fall apart. You've got to keep active. Before I wouldn't get out of bed for less than x amount, but now just getting x amount is great. Not because of the money, but because of the sense of achievement. But at the same time I do hanker after the simple life, because making a load of cash in an afternoon isn't that exciting any more, I've done it already and I know I'm just going to dump it all back on the table and spin the wheel again. So when I go back to London and I'm in some spit and sawdust, shitty pub, I love it, there are normal people and there's no marble anywhere. And you miss the countryside and cycling through the woods – little things that don't actually cost any money suddenly have a lot of value. Sometimes when I'm feeling a bit stressed out I'll text Lush and tell him I just want to pop round his house for a cup of tea and some toast.'

That night Stef took us to one of his old haunts, Ravi's Pakistani restaurant in downtown Satwa, about as far removed from the suffocating luxury of the marina's upmarket eateries as it was possible to get. Ravi's was furnished with plastic tables and wipe-clean tablecloths, and there wasn't a slab of marble in sight. We slid in beside a couple of cabbies and ordered up our food – butter chicken, smoky chicken tikka, karahi lamb, dahl, pillow-soft naans and mountains of rice, it topped anything we'd eaten all weekend, and at a fraction of the price.

'I remember being in a club in Ibiza,' said Stef, 'I was in the VIP area, looking over at everyone else and thinking, "This is rubbish, I want to be over there where everyone's enjoying themselves." Like this place, nothing fancy, no marble, just good down-to-earth food in the company of normal people.'

As a group we picked through the carcass of the previous night. 'Any sign of my trainers?' I asked.

'Oh yeah, I meant to tell you,' said James, 'the bloke you swapped them with so you could get into that club got banged up for punching a bouncer. He won't be out for days.' Oh well, I never liked those trainers anyway.

'People say money can't buy you happiness, but it's definitely better than being poor,' continued Stef, while picking at the leftovers from our neighbours' meal. 'But people shouldn't forget that money and success come at a price. You have to ask yourself, is it a worthwhile forfeit? I really started to think about happiness after I lost a lot of money, because I think you have to see both sides to realize. Everyone in life aspires to be rich, that's the dream, and they relate happiness to money, think that the more of it they have the happier they'll be. But when you don't have a lot of value for money, because you're earning so much you can pick up bills, buy sports cars and designer clothes and it doesn't touch the sides, you take it for granted and you don't appreciate it anyway. So you're working hard, squeezing out the happiness, ruining your life with all the stress and the risk to earn a lot of money to buy a lot of shit you don't actually need. That's the dilemma everyone here seems to find themselves in.'

Stef footed the bill and we left Ravi's fat and satisfied, as well as somewhat heartened to have discovered a more authentic side to Dubai.

'Cracking place,' said Tom as we made our way through Satwa's narrow streets, swirling with music, car horns and the fragrant smoke from a thousand hookah pipes, its inhabitants like mischievous mice scurrying at the feet of the skyscrapers looming contemptuously above.

'Yeah, it's great,' said James, 'only thing is they're supposed to be knocking all this area down, so Ravi's might not be here for much longer.'

'What are they knocking it down for?' replied Tom.

'Not sure to be honest,' said James, 'probably to build some megazone or something . . .'

*

BEN

While we were bobbing up and down in the Persian Gulf on a £400,000 boat, drinking beer and mentally congratulating ourselves on how good life can be, an Irishman called Mark Boyle would have been crouching outside his caravan on a farm just outside Bath, brushing his teeth with a mixture of cuttlefish bone and wild fennel seeds. He would have woken at 5 a.m., before preparing some porridge on his rocket stove, made from oats procured in exchange for helping out at a local co-operative, and brewing up a cup of pine-needle tea, blended with yeast and malt extract. Then, perhaps, he would have taken to his compost throne and pinched out some 'humanure', which he'd later spread on his crops as fertilizer, before wiping his arse with a discarded copy of the *Sun*. I'd wager there's only one thing you've ever considered doing from that list, although I should remind you that Richard Littlejohn now writes for the *Daily Mail* . . .

'How much money is enough?' the American industrialist and philanthropist John D. Rockefeller was once asked. 'Just a little bit more,' was his reply, a sentiment Stef admitted to sharing during the boom-time in Dubai. Mark sees things rather differently, believing that a world without money would be a far richer place. And he's put his lack of money where his mouth is, following his hero Gandhi's teaching to 'be the change you want to see in the world'. He lives entirely off-grid – his caravan has solar panels, from which he runs his mobile phone and laptop, and a wood pellet boiler for heating – and he earns his keep on the farm (organic, naturally) by volunteering his labour. For food he forages, grows his own, barters and lifts stuff from skips or bins, although he insists, in the face of charges of freeloading, that only 5 per cent of his diet is waste. He has a bike with a trailer instead of a car, and he washes his clothes using cold water and an improvised detergent cobbled together from boiled nuts. All in all, it sounds like the sort of hippy nightmare that would have Stef coming out in cold sweats and screaming into his Hungarian goose-down pillow.

Mark's original plan was to live moneyless for a year, but when I finally caught up with him – no mean feat when he can't make outgoing calls and his laptop runs off the sun – he'd existed without cash for sixteen months, and still seemed to be loving every minute of it.

'I've never been happier, never been fitter and never been healthier,' said Mark, 'so I thought, "Why go back to the way that was making me less happy, less healthy, less fit?" I can't foresee going back. I live next to a river under a tree in a beautiful valley. I get to eat my own food and grow my own food and I get to spend all my time doing all the things I love doing, and not just because I need to pay the bills. I've never felt more liberation and more freedom. That's one thing we all crave, but maybe we're not all aware of it, to be able to do what we want to do when we want to do it.'

While Mark has the support of many, some of the criticism has been fierce. As well as a freeloader, he has been called an idiot, a berk, a hypocrite, an egotistical maniac, a middle-class trustafarian, an arrogant Brit (even though he's Irish) who knows nothing about the poor brown people who need our charity, an imbecile, a scrounger, a jerk, a loser and a disgusting pathetic low-life who jumps in bins. There may be more, but Mark made it easy for me by listing all of the above on his very own blog. Mark has brought some of the criticism on himself – his attempt to walk 7,500 miles from Bristol to the birthplace of Gandhi was perhaps the most ill-conceived adventure since Jade Goody attempted to do the London Marathon after training on a diet of chow mein, bhunas and Stella. While the People's Princess came a cropper on the Isle of Dogs, Mark made it as far as Calais, where he was forced to abort his mission because of his lack of French.

'The problem was that I just couldn't explain to people in France what I was doing,' said Boyle at the time. 'People seemed to think I was a refugee looking for work. The idea was to ask people if I could help them and in exchange receive food and a place to stay. But they thought I was begging. In France clearly they are a bit more sophisticated and they weren't impressed.'

To be fair, Mark, I don't think it's got anything to do with sophistication: if you had tried to explain your mission to the good burghers of Romford, you quite likely would have been covered from head to toe in spittle.

The point of Mark's walk had been to let the world know about his 'freeconomy' philosophy (or 'philosofree', as he likes to call it). The freeconomy community's aim is to 'help reconnect people in their local communities through the simple act of sharing', which in practical terms means a website where people can list their skills and tools and donate them to others in exchange for other people's skills and tools. Mark's short-term goal is to start up a physical freeconomy community, and to that end he intends to buy a plot of land with proceeds raised from a self-penned book charting his moneyless existence. His dream is that so many people will be won over by his vision that one community will eventually become a network of communities and then, who knows?

TOM

On the way home from Dubai, I'd read about an equation that scientists claimed could explain happiness. It looked like something from an algebra exam, as complicated as Mark's formula was simple.

'Happiness = P + (5xE) + (3xH),' it said, 'where P stands for personal characteristics, including outlook on life, adaptability and resilience. E stands for existence and relates to health, financial stability and friendships. H represents higher order needs, and covers self-esteem, expectations, ambitions and sense of humour.'

I ran through the accompanying questions with Ben. 'Are you outgoing and energetic?' said one. 'Do you have a positive outlook and bounce back quickly from setbacks?' read another. 'Are your basic life needs met, in relation to personal health, finance, safety, freedom of choice and sense of community?'

Stef and Mark could barely have been more different, yet when you calculated their scores, something spooky emerged: they produced remarkably similar tallies. In some ways it didn't make any sense. Mark could no more have survived in the dusty decadence of Dubai than Stef could have lived off vegetables nurtured by his own faeces, but from divergent routes they had arrived at the same goal. 'Dirsy,' I said, 'there's a lesson for us there . . .'

BEN

'If we don't localize our economies and our means of production, we're going to find ourselves in a lot of trouble pretty soon,' explained Mark. 'I come from a business and economics background [he used to manage a couple of organic food companies before he started living his dream] and a few years ago I started looking at all the different issues in the world, like factory farming, sweatshops and our damage of the environment, which weren't separate issues, they were connected. It's because of the disconnection between us and the things we consume that the other symptoms occur. What allows this disconnection to exist is money, so I decided to give up cash. You don't actually need money to produce anything, everything comes from the earth.'

Critics have argued that Mark's freeconomy philosophy is hopelessly naive, in that economies lacking money, which are therefore reliant on barter or in-kind transactions, are hamstrung by something called the 'double coincidence of wants', in that both parties require what the other party has to offer at the same time and place. Which is precisely why money was invented in the first place, pretty much so that some poor fisherman back in the day didn't have to swap one of his daughters for a new net because his old one had a hole in it and he hadn't caught any fish. However, others would argue that to call money, as some do, the greatest invention ever, when it has led to the wholesale rape of our environment, the creation of a relatively small elite who hoard most of it while billions live in poverty and spiritual meltdown, is a little bit wonky.

'We're born with the idea we should make as much money as possible and that money equals happiness,' said Mark in his thick Donegal drawl. 'Most people's identity comes from how much they earn and what kind of job they have, and so when somebody comes along and says their relationship with money is destructive then it's not going to go down well. You're hitting at the core of some people's identity and it will trigger an angry response. Sometimes you've got to accept that if you're telling someone something quite uncomfortable, they're not going to like it and it may take years for that seed to germinate.'

To be fair to Mark, he isn't suggesting we withdraw all our cash tomorrow and use the notes as bog-roll substitute until they all run out before knocking down the banks and ploughing the dead bodies of the bankers back into the soil as fertilizer, he's merely suggesting another way to live our lives, a road less travelled.

'It would be a complete catastrophe if everyone did it overnight,' he conceded, 'but what I'm saying is that if you can see anything within what I'm doing that you feel is beneficial, then use it as a resource. Far be it for me to tell people what it is that makes them happy, I just want to show them another option, that another way is possible.'

While I could no more envisage myself eking out my days drinking pine-needle tea in the woods than I could see myself owning a £400,000 boat, it wasn't difficult to see that aspects of Mark's way of life made a lot sense. While I couldn't see his economic principles catching on in a million years – or until they're forced upon us by man's rampant disregard for the planet – I saw Mark's lifestyle as a challenge to the commonly held belief that everything outside of a money economy has no value, a concept he wholeheartedly agreed with.

'I'm not out to make my life unhappier,' he said, 'I like to be happy myself and I like to show other people there are happier ways of doing things. Happiness is waking up first thing in the morning, at 5 or 6 o'clock, and you can't wait to get out of bed – that's a pretty good sign that you're happy. I think when you wake up on Monday morning and you're already looking forward to Friday evening, that's a pretty good sign you're unhappy.'

But surely there are things about his old life he misses? Dixons? Jeremy Clarkson? That shower gel you can buy that looks and feels like melted marshmallow?

'I miss envelopes with clear plastic windows on the front, traffic jams, utility bills, bank statements – I used to love bank statements – spreadsheets, angry people in the city who get stressed out because you cycle an inch too far from the kerb . . . no, I'm being awkward. I miss going for the odd pint with my friends to be honest, and occasionally going to the cinema, but if you can't forgo the odd pint or the odd trip to the cinema when your ideals are at stake, then you've got a bit of a problem. I could probably go back to my old life, but it would kill me to be honest. It would grate against everything I hold dear.

'I'm living moment to moment, from day to day. I literally have no worries any more, and happiness is those moments when you realize you haven't got a care in the world. I'd define how happy I am by the amount I smile during the day, and I'm pretty much smiling the whole time. It's not very scientific, but then I'm a pretty basic guy!'

*

BEN

The plan was to pass on the findings from some of those fine academic institutions I mentioned earlier (yes, there was some proper research involved with this book, we haven't just been knobbing about on boats), but the truth is they could have saved stacks of taxpayers' money by just sticking Stef and Mark in a room together and listening to what they had to say.

Modern scientific thinking is that money matters less than most of us think, and that while a poverty of material resources certainly contributes to unhappiness, an increase over and above a certain amount – namely that which we need to clothe, house and feed ourselves – does not make us that much happier. The problem is, as both Stef and Mark pointed out, humans are hard-wired to relate money to happiness, and most of us don't take the time to stop and think, 'What is it that actually makes me happy?' Instead we hurtle blindly along assuming money does, trampling Walmart employees to death in our haste to snap up a Wank-pad or some such latest gadget, which some bloke wearing horn-rimmed glasses and standing in front of a giant screen in New York has promised you is the greatest thing in the world ever made, or stabbing rival bargain-hunters in Ikea over a floral-print pouffe.

There is a magnificent quote from American man of letters H.L. Mencken which hits on our complicated relationship with money: 'A wealthy man is one who earns $100 a year more than his wife's sister's husband.' In other words, it all comes down to comparison – it's not your fault you're unhappy, it's your neighbour's fault, him and his top-of-the-range Mercedes and his mobile phone that he probably also uses to wax his chest, and his blonde wife with her big plastic tits who's better-looking than your wife and has an AGA range. We crystallize happiness, value tangible things over experiences, and picture happiness in our mind as a 56-inch wall-mounted LCD TV, a home cinema system or an air-conditioned, glow-in-the-dark Japanese bog with posterior-wash setting. But as Stef will tell you, the memory of a cycle through the woods or tea and toast round a mate's house is more likely to provide a longer term pay-off. We think having what our neighbours have will make us happy, the irony being that by working so hard to get rich we might 'squeeze out the happiness', only to discover that when we get rich, we're no happier than we were before. As Stef said, 'You have to ask yourself, is it a worthwhile forfeit?' Or as Mark might say, 'The hippies are getting their revenge.'

And do you want to know two of lucre's filthiest tricks? There is a plethora of research that shows happy people do better in life than unhappy people, have better social relation-ships, better health and more money. So money might not make you happy, but being happy might make you money, although Morrissey might disagree. And while the rich aren't actually getting happier the richer they get, they are succeeding in making those left behind more miserable, because those left behind think rich people are that much happier than them. And where does that leave us? Well, it all depends if you've got money or not. Or does it?

2. NATURISM

'It's not easy the first time'

BEN

To get naked in one hit or to get naked in stages? That, when it's your first time at a naturist camp, is the burning question. 'What do we do, just start off with our old fellas hanging out of our flies and take it from there?' I asked Tom as we waited for the rather forbidding iron gates to open.

'If we want to look like a couple of flashers,' he replied. 'Let's just play it by ear. Or buttock.'

'Here, take one of my cards and ring me when you want a ride back,' shouted the cab driver who'd dropped us off. 'You can shove it down your arse-crack, just make sure you don't smudge the ink.' To be fair, he hadn't seemed at all bothered when we told him we wanted a ride to the local nuddy camp, although surrounded by his tattooed cabbie mates back at the train station, I'd had the sudden urge to blurt out, 'The working man's club please, guvnor.'

'Don't see nothin' wrong with it myself,' the cabbie had said as we weaved our way through the Kent countryside. 'If my missus was up for it, I'd be all over it. But the next time I see her naked, she'll probably be on a slab with a label on her big toe.'

TOM

There is one great advantage to going away to a nudist camp: packing your bag doesn't take very long.

No 'shall I take a smart shirt', no mental arithmetic involving pants-to-days-away ratio, no spare set of jeans in case the others get spoiled. Toothbrush, towel, factor 50 suncream. I could have stuck them in my pockets. Which made me think – where were we supposed to keep our small change when we got there?

BEN

After a twitchy couple of minutes, the automatic gates parted and what promised to be the first day of the rest of our lives, a naked Eden, opened up before us. The first thing I noticed was gnomes. Thousands of them. Little ones dotted round tree-stumps, child-size ones lurking in the doorways of tents, inflatable ones tethered to the tops of caravans.

'These are gnome people,' I whispered to Tom, but if they'd suddenly sprung to life and started whipping their togs off, he probably wouldn't have noticed. Something else had caught his eye, namely a seventy-year-old man wearing nothing but a pair of tennis shoes waving at us from a clearing up ahead. 'Fucking hell,' I whispered to Tom, 'that's shattered one or two illusions . . .'

Now, I'd done a fair bit of background reading before taking the naturist plunge and I should have been fully aware that naturist camps rarely resemble a Hugh Hefner pool party at the Playboy Mansion. This place had nothing to do with sex, its members were making a proclamation of freedom, their happiness derived from sharing the glory of being in complete harmony with nature and like-minded people. But, if I'm being totally honest, as I'd flicked through old copies of *British Naturism*, grimacing at the ancient, the crumbling and the misshapen, there had always been the nagging hope that our visit would coincide with a particularly raucous hen-do from Croydon.

So having Brian's rather pendulous appendage dangling three feet from my nose as he leant over to photocopy my passport was rather a shock to the system. Form-filling done, it was a blessed relief when he settled in behind his desk and Tom and I were forced to start taking things a little bit seriously: the previous five minutes, I'm a little bit ashamed to admit, we'd spent kicking each others' feet and grinning like a couple of naughty schoolboys about to receive a dressing down from the headmaster. No pun intended.

'There may be people with a more spiritualist reason for doing it, but it's just nice not to wear clothes,' explained Brian. 'It's freedom from the restriction of clothes, freedom from social convention. There are other people who like the "close to nature" aspect of it, but the bottom line is it's comfortable. When the weather is good, you don't need clothes. It's only society and our cultural conditioning, social taboos that arose from the Victorian era, that make us believe there's something wrong with the natural form.'

Brian, as if he could see right into my sordid little mind, smiled faintly before continuing. 'People immediately make the link with sex, because most people are only naked when someone else is in the room when something sexual is about to happen. They can't imagine both genders can mix while naked without that sexual charge. Some men can't imagine that a woman without her clothes on is anything but provocative.

And a lot of men imagine naturist places are full of beautiful women, but it's not like that, it's just ordinary people, all shapes and sizes, just like at a supermarket checkout. Naturists are no less sexually active than anyone else, but it's no more of a meeting place or dating agency than the local tennis club. It's just nice to eat naked together, listen to music together naked and play sport together naked. Oh, by the way, you must get involved in Saturday's table-tennis championships . . .'

Jesus wept, there I'd been envisaging a weekend spent reading a book with only my top half hanging out of my tent, and the next thing I know I'm signed up for a spot of naked whiff-whaff. Not that Tom seemed too bothered.

'I'm not bad at table-tennis,' he said as we made our way to our pitch. 'I used to play against my mum in the back garden. It used to get quite competitive – her sledging would make Dennis Lillee blush.'

'It's one thing hearing the c-word,' I replied, 'and quite another seeing it across the other side of the net. Let's see who's blushing then . . .'

We'd lucked in weather-wise, or lucked out, whichever way you wanted to look at it: incessant rain and we would have been sentenced to a weekend of solitaire in our tents, but the sun shining brightly overhead rather painted us into a corner. It was a case of either tackle out or look like a couple of perverts bowling about in full dress, which is a phrase you could probably only use in relation to a naturist camp.

'Right then, we may as well do this thing,' I said to Tom as he struggled with my ancient tent (age: 15 years, times used: one).

'What, now?' said Tom. 'Before we've even put the tents up?'

'Yeah, everyone's looking at us,' I replied in hushed tones, not wanting the denuded couple preparing lunch next door to hear.

'Can't we put the tents up first and then get undressed inside?' said Tom.

'What's the point in that?' I replied.

We surveyed the scene. All very *Carry on Camping*, but it could have done with a Babs Windsor or two to perk the place up. To our left, an undressed couple reading in front of their camper van; off in the distance, a family heading off on their bikes, not a stitch between them; to our right, an elderly lady scrabbling about on her hands and knees in the doorway of her tent. She had stitches, but it looked like they were holding her stomach together.

'Maybe you're right,' I said. 'All of a sudden the thought of watching you wrestling with a tent with your arse up in the air is making me feel a little bit queasy.'

Half an hour later and I was cowering in my tent like Captain Oates contemplating one final ambulation. Except I didn't fancy going outside, and certainly not for some time. Taking the naturist plunge was clearly like taking the plunge in anything, whether it be jumping off the high board at your local swimming pool or reaching for a copy of *Razzle* down Mr Patel's: if you bottle it first time, it just gets harder and harder. But then it occurred to me: while buying a copy of *Razzle* down Mr Patel's was one rung down on the fearometer from buying your first pack of dunkies from Boots, buying a copy of *Razzle* when you had a mate in tow was simply considered a jolly jape, the subtext being, 'I don't actually look at this stuff, I'm just buying it for a bit of a laugh'. So while mulling over whether *Razzle* was still rude, naughty and £1.40, I got naked and strolled outside, wearing nothing but a towel over my shoulder and a Mona Lisa smile.

Tom appeared to be taken by surprise. 'The full moon rises', he said in wonder, his bottom half defiantly concealed by board-shorts, 'while the sun is still in the sky.'

'Thought I'd go for a dip in the pool,' I said brusquely. 'Coming?'

TOM

I've never had a problem with being naked in changing-rooms. You do it all the time after football and at swimming pools. What you don't find there – unless you've played in very different football teams to me – are 60-year-old women soaping down their enormous, free-ranging bosoms.

'I'm terribly sorry,' I said, frantically covering myself with my towel. 'I thought this was the men's.'

One of them gave me a funny look. 'There is no men's,' she said. 'We've only got one changing-room here.'

It made sense. When you could stroll into the bar sans *stitches and were expected to play table-tennis with both your forehand and backhand on full display, there was little point in suddenly going shy before a swim.*

'Don't forget your mandatory shower,' said the woman, pointing to a sign on the wall. Of course. Basic rules of hygiene still applied. We tiptoed over the tiled floor and hit the dials. The water was freezing. Our first naked pool appearances, and we would be shrinking violets. Perfect.

The pool's temperature was comparatively pleasant. So too was the sluicing sensation you experienced through your exposed areas. I swam a length underwater and tried not to look too closely at the specks floating past me. A shadow passed over my shoulder. It was Dirsy, his pale belly hanging down, arms and legs thrashing about, his manhood drifting between his legs like an ineffectual rudder as he zigzagged through the water. There were others, floating about with gently ballooned stomachs, pink and rotund. I felt like a cameraman shooting an underwater wildlife documentary on hippos.

I stuck in a few lengths of energetic front crawl. The breathing pattern was a huge help – head to the side, big lungful of air, face into the water and three strokes of raucous secret laugher, the sound of it bubbling away before anyone could hear.

For some reason I was wearing my swim-cap. Old habits die hard. I flipped onto my back, threw in some energetic backstroke and then glanced down to see my old chap periscoped above the surface of the water. Surrounded by a floating mat of seaweed-like pubic hair, bobbing gently from side to side as I moved my arms, it looked like a sea anemone chasing me down the pool.

BEN

While Brian was clearly from the 'I just like sitting about with my lad out' school of nudity, he did also stress that naturism means many things to different people. And as I strolled back to my tent, the sun's rays lightly toasting my dough-white arse cheeks, grass scrunching under the soles of my feet, a soft breeze tickling the old jaffers, I understood what John Muir, the Scottish-born American naturalist and pioneering conservationist, had meant when he wrote: 'The body seems to feel beauty when exposed to it as it feels the campfire or sunshine, entering not by the eyes alone, but equally through all one's flesh like radiant heat, making a passionate ecstatic pleasure glow not explainable.' For a few seconds I felt, like Muir, liberated, in harmony with nature, and all because of the shedding of a few skinny pieces of cloth.

While I imagine Muir to have written those words while curled up under the stars by a waterfall in the Sierra Nevada, I was on a campsite with Tommy, trying desperately not to look at his cock, my romantic little tryst with nature well and truly busted.

'Jesus, an hour ago you were shitting it, now you're strolling around bold as brass. What happened?'

He stood with legs spread, hands on his hips. 'Nothing like a swim to calm the nerves. Now then, any chance you could rub some of this suncream on my lower back?'

I impolitely declined his offer, before disappearing into my tent: the middle of a field in Kent is no place to be rubbing suncream all over your mate's arse, naturist camp or not.

After ploughing through a raft of text messages, ranging from 'Any decent clunge?' to 'Have you had wood yet?', I left Tom to his book and went for a wander. And on my way down to the bar and cafe area, I stumbled across 20 or so men and women, all in the buff, rehearsing a play on the boules courts. I soon discovered the play in question was Noël Coward's *Blithe Spirit*, to be performed at some undecided point in the future.

'It's just a bit of fun really,' explained Pam, 'it may never even happen. You one of the first-timers?'

'Yeah, got here this afternoon.'

'Blimey, you're brave, it took me five or six weekends before I got my kit off.' And that was how it started, my first non-sexual naked conversation with a woman since I became an adult.

Pam discovered naturism when her then boyfriend, now

her husband revealed, a few months into their relationship, that he liked to go nude.

'It was a bit of a shock if I'm being honest,' explained Pam. 'By that time I didn't mind being naked in front of him, you know, but in front of other people, I didn't know what to think really. Like most women, there were loads of things about my body I didn't like, but I was very fond of him so I decided to give it a try. It took me a little while to get over the embarrassment, but I love it now, it just seems like the most natural thing in the world. I think women get a lot out of it because they realize there's no such thing as a perfect body, that what they look like doesn't matter. And, ironically, they're not being stared at and judged.'

'Me and the future wife were over in France on a caravanning holiday when we stumbled across a couple walking naked across a beach,' said a man called John, while I repeated the mantra 'look into his eyes, look into his eyes' in my head as he spoke. 'And just the whole moment of it, this naked couple walking together across this fabulous beach, got us thinking, maybe we should give it a go. So the next morning, we decided to head down there. To be honest, I was shitting myself, thinking stuff like, "Am I really in the right sort of shape to be doing this sort of thing?" Or "Will I get a stiffy?" All sorts of stupid stuff. So we get down there and reluctantly take our clothes off, and, just like that, it seemed so normal, I had this kind of calm come over me. Only a couple of days earlier the idea of walking around naked would have mortified me, but we didn't put our cozzies back on for the next two weeks.'

I shared John's sense of freedom as I strolled back up to the tents, and I also began to muse on one of the deeper philosophical planks of naturism: that the casting off of clothes is a great leveller, that it fosters a mutual respect within that society, regardless of age, sex, body shape, fitness or class. And it was true that even in my short time at the camp I had been struck by the sheer range of ages and body types on display, and the fact that the accents covered north and south and both working and middle class. Naturism appeared to celebrate difference, instead of difference being hidden away. So what if John's tadger reminded me of one of those huge, bell-like key rings you get at old-fashioned hotels in Devon, he probably wasn't that impressed by mine either (although, and I can't stress this enough, I've been told on several different occasions that it's magnificent).

While I was perfectly comfortable chatting away fully peeled to a man with a key-ring shaped schmackel, both Tom and I were a little bit more uncomfortable where kids were involved. Now, while that old quack Dr Benjamin Spock, and many other eminent paediatricians back in the day, decided that seeing adults naked could engender all sorts of problems in kids, ranging from hyperactivity to excessive masturbation, I can't help feeling that such opinions only succeed in scandalizing children. It seems only logical to me that a child who is exposed to nudity, or at least not consciously hidden away from it, is going to grow up pretty blasé about his or her own body, and everyone else's for that matter. However, growing up as I have in a society where the arrest of a paedophile can lead to all the pedalos in his local park being scuttled, I couldn't help but feel a little bit wrong as I strolled by the playground, even though I couldn't quite explain what I felt wrong about.

'Our general culture is rather buttoned-up,' Andrew Welch, a spokesman for British Naturism told me. 'They have a more liberal attitude towards nudity in Europe, including around children. It's a challenge, we have to overcome these misunderstandings. It doesn't help our cause that there are all these people out there with a lot of passion for naturism who, because of these cultural issues, think, "I'd better not, in case it's misunderstood." I know teachers who can't tell anyone that they're naturists, because they think, "What if the parents of the children I teach make a fuss and think there's something wrong with what I do? I may lose my job." But we always say to people, "Go on, try," because actually the teachers and high court judges and policemen who are known to be naturists have never experienced a problem. It causes an issue because it makes us seem like a secret society. Most people would be hard-pressed to name a naturist they know, but I bet they do.'

I found Tom in front of his tent doing naked press-ups, and from way off in the distance I thought I heard Sid James spluttering out a hacking yak-yak-yak, although it was probably one of the gardeners starting up his lawnmower. I had a plan.

'What's happening?' said Tom. I looked carefully into the middle distance.

'I thought we'd pop down to the bar for a few pints,' I said. He paused mid press-up.

'Naked, you mean?'

'Yeah, they won't let you in unless you're naked. I was just chatting to the barman.' Tom ceased his drills and stared apprehensively down the campsite, eyes narrowing, the corners of his mouth twitching wildly. This is going to be fucking dynamite, I thought to myself, and I struggled to suppress a grin. 'Tommy, there's no point coming all this way to just engage in a spot of foreplay. Now we're here we may as well plunge balls deep.'

Tom stroked his chin and then shrugged. 'Benjamin,

you're right. When in Rome, get your toga out like the Romans do. Let's get involved.'

An hour or so later and we were ready. Actually, in the time it took me to slip on my flip-flops I was ready, but Tom can't just do a few press-ups, he has to do a hundred press-ups. In every conceivable position. With stuff balanced on his back. My plan was simple yet devastating: stroll down towards the bar together, and just as we're within eyeshot and a few of the locals sprinkled out the front have noticed us coming, spark the ringtone up on my mobile and take the imaginary call. I'd sound a little bit concerned, chuck a u-ey and toes it back up to my tent before Tom knew what had hit him. And my, it worked like a treat . . .

I was already twenty metres up the hill, snickering into my phone, when I heard Brian hailing Tom and offering to buy him a drink. The next time I saw him, I was fully clothed and Tom was standing at the bar looking a little bit like a bald dog in a kennel full of Afghans.

'All right Tommy?' I chirped, struggling unsuccessfully to suppress a smirk. Tom ignored me and carried on chatting with the barman, who seemed completely unfazed that there was a man in his pub drinking Fosters with his spuds out. I had seen something similar in Brannigans on Romford high street once, but the elderly chap in question was simply so banjaxed he hadn't noticed his strides had fallen down. And at least Tom hadn't shit himself.

TOM

There were two things I noticed when I wandered into that bar: the chap pulling pints looked like Ron Pickering, and most other people had clothes on. Weren't we in a naturist camp? It was like walking into the MCC in blazer, neatly pressed slacks and egg-and-bacon tie, only to find everyone in Speedos. Except, that is, there were women, and everyone greeted me like an old friend.

'You tried the Bishop's Finger?' enquired an old soak on a stool at the bar, as I brushed my way somewhat awkwardly between two seated pensioners. 'Barbara, get this lad a taster of the Finger.'

I glugged down the proffered half pint and gave the thumbs-up. 'Very nice,' I said hurriedly. 'Two pints of that, please. I've got a friend with me. He'll be here any minute.'

I looked around the small room. It was a strange mixture of the mundane and the extraordinary: tired 1970s decor, lime-green paint on the walls and plastic-covered maroon sofas, plus two enormous men in the corner discussing Transit vans with their cocks out.

'The thing about the Transit, Ray,' said one, 'is that it's a great workhorse.' His mate leaned forward, the movement nudging a single testicle over the edge of his seat like an over-ripe fruit falling from a mighty bough.

'You don't need to tell me that, Keith,' he said. 'As you know, I've been using Transits for over twenty years. Superb vehicles.'

I found myself feeling a little more at ease. When I'd been walking round before with clothes on, I felt I was sticking out like a sore thumb. Now I actually was sticking out like a sore thumb, I felt less self-conscious. Maybe Ben had done me a favour. At the same time, it was hard to fully adjust to these unusual circumstances. With one of the major rules of society suddenly having gone out of the window, your brain is left confused – were other behavioural norms also suspended? You half-expected to see people shagging over the fruit machine in the corner, or urinating casually against the bar.

I let my thoughts drift as the old soak enjoying the Bishop's Finger rumbled away about the range of guest ales they had on. When Ben first suggested we try naturism, I'd pictured us enjoying a Mediterranean week of pétanque and pastis down at glamorous Cap d'Agde, breaking off from the sunbathing to play volleyball with a brace of doe-eyed sisters from Aix-en-Provence, sharing a four-person bouillabaisse in a candlelit bistro as a warm night breeze cooled our bronzed buttocks. Instead we were knocking about with a bunch of fifty-year-old plumbers in Kent, our arses sticking to the plastic seats, eating Hula Hoops and readying ourselves for a ping-pong battle with a perspiring Brian. Was this really the kind of happiness we were looking for?

Still, the night was young, and the ale was £1.60 a pint. So what if there were gangs of hungry Kentish mosquitoes looking for a bite to eat for dinner? So what if Ben was now walking in wearing jeans, a shirt and a smug grin?

'Oh hello,' grumbled the soak, tugging off his jumper to reveal a torso like a melted candle. 'Here comes another "textile". Still, better make him welcome.' He stood up, unleashing a spectacular series of downward ripples. 'Evening, young man! Have you tried the Golden Badger? Barbara! Give this lad a taster of Badger!'

BEN

I quickly caught on that the rest of the regulars had got wise to the little trick I'd played on Tom and were none too happy about it, contravening as it did some of the golden rules of naturism, namely that naturism is supposed to boost a person's confidence and self-esteem and foster respect for others, not make him or her feel like a proper tit. So while Tom nattered away to all and sundry, I skulked about outside, the harmonious relationship I'd felt with my surroundings just a couple of hours earlier now rather more discordant. Sure, there were the same lovely trees and grass and all the rest of that nature stuff, but Andrew Welch had been spot on when he'd described most naturist resorts as 'a little old-fashioned, just a pavilion in the woods', and I couldn't help wondering if this was a lifestyle choice that had had its day.

'Our organization has about 11,000 members, which has been dropping steadily over the last five or six years,' Andrew had told me. 'But the attitude towards organization has changed across the board. It's probably difficult to fill posts on a parish council these days, people don't want to go to meetings and be a treasurer of something and all that entails, life's too busy. At the same time it's become more acceptable, but people want to dip in and out of stuff these days and there are lots of people who are stopping being members of organizations and clubs who are continuing to be naturists.'

Andrew was instrumental in organizing the annual Nude-fest in Cornwall, which attracts in the region of 500 nude folk, 'with music sets and discos and that kind of thing'. 1970s chart-toppers Edison Lighthouse topped the bill in 2009, and while the thought of busting moves to 'Love Grows Where My Rosemary Goes' with a few thousand disrobed others sent a shiver down my spine, Andrew rightly pointed out that it trumped lying about outside your tent doing a crossword in a field in Kent.

'Most clubs are great for a sedentary afternoon,' said Andrew, 'but that doesn't suit a lot of young people, they want a bit of action, which is why we get many more of them down at Nudefest. Sitting down and doing nothing is what most naturists will be happy doing but that's not necessarily "cool". There are more youngsters involved than you'd think, but they are people of the twenty-first century and have grown up in an environment where you don't have to join anything, you can dip in and out.'

When I popped back into the bar I noticed (it was difficult not to) that a few others had gone *au naturel*, and I was treated to the bizarre sight of a table of naked blokes engaged in an earnest conversation about reorganizing their sheds. And believe me, the line 'gaffer tape is like the force, it's got a light side and a dark side and it holds the universe together' sounds even more surreal when delivered by a eighteen-stone naked man dropping dry-roasted peanuts all over his plonker. When I caught up with Tom at the bar, someone else was complaining about one of the women trimming her clock springs in the shower – 'bold as brass, one foot up on the soap dish' – and I decided to take that as my cue to leave. And as I trudged back to my tent, the thought occurred to me: if God had intended us to sit about with our bits and bobs out in the pub, there's no way he would have invented bar snacks.

That night I slept fitfully. The slight euphoria I'd felt padding through the campsite shortly after our arrival, naked as a new-born babber, had been replaced by the realization that in a few hours' time I might be scrabbling about under a chair looking for a stray ping-pong ball. My bare arse exposed, like a randy baboon. When I did sleep, I had strange and wild dreams. In one, Brian commented that my cock looked like Bruce Willis' cock, and someone else chimed in that it looked more like George Clooney's. And in my dream I wondered, maybe my cock does look like Bruce Willis' cock. And I remember thinking, people can say I look like Alan Sugar, or Mike Tyson, or Seth Rogan, or Goldie, or whoever I've happened to morph into that particular day, but what they don't know is that I've got Bruce Willis' cock, and although no one will ever know, they can never take that away from me. In another dream, I was sitting an exam, and my old history teacher Miss Mitchell was handing out the test papers naked, and I turned round to see that everyone was naked, and a mad panic overtook me, as I suddenly realized I was fully clothed and this was a naked exam. Miss Mitchell leant over in front of me to tell me off and, oh my brothers and sisters, it was a horrible sight. And then I heard the flap of my tent being unzipped and I'd never been so happy to see Tom's smiling mug.

'Rise and shine Dirsy, it's the big tournament today,' said Tom, who didn't sound as angry as a man should sound who'd been tricked into drinking naked in a pub the night before.

'Sorry about last night,' I said when I'd extricated myself from my sleeping bag. 'Bit out of order.'

'Not a problem,' said Tom. 'I met the tournament director for the table-tennis. He's promised to sort me out in the round-robin. I could win this thing.'

TOM

I'd found another good thing about naturism – when you wake up with a bladder full of Bishop's Finger at 5 a.m., there's no fumbling about in your tent trying to find your jeans and a top. Straight out into the moonlight, naked as Mowgli, a trot over to the nearest bushes and away you go. Lavatorial liberation. It almost made up for the problems I'd experienced applying sun-cream the day before. Not wanting to risk under-application on an area which had only ever seen the sun through a bedroom window, I had slathered myself in as much factor 50 as I could squeeze out. Only after five minutes of unsuccessfully trying to rub it all on in did I realize that I was standing naked in a field, energetically massaging my genitalia in full view of three old ladies eating their breakfast. The tender skin on my undercarriage reacting badly to the harsh chemicals in the suncream only made me more visible. I might as well have attached a flashing red light to my testicles and daubed a large white sign above them.

For his part, Ben seemed less relaxed that morning. Gone was the cocky chutzpah of the night before. Gone, to be frank, was the cocky full-stop. While his top half was out, his modesty was entirely covered by a pair of baggy shorts. At some point during the night his brain had obviously rebooted and reverted to its original settings. The onus, if not the pants, was on me.

At breakfast we watched car-loads of keen table-tennis players piling into the car-park. There was the South Downs lot, a glamorous posse from Studland Bay and some stragglers from somewhere near Colchester. Hugs were exchanged, hands shaken. It was touching to watch, a gathering of the tribes from far and wide, a coming together to be in the altogether.

There were also more than a few sports bags and bat cases in evidence. The 2009 British Naturism Table-Tennis Championships were clearly a big deal. What would my chances be? There weren't that many young bucks on display – the average age was at least fifty-five – but that was also the perfect demographic for ping-pong performers. My only regret was that we hadn't come two weeks ago, when they had been holding the 2009 British Naturism 5km Championships. I'd seen the full results sheet, and I'd have won it by a mile. I could have been Britain's fastest naked man. I was genuinely miffed.

BEN

Like most men I'm a fan of women wearing nothing but shoes. High heels, ankle boots, knee-length boots, wellies, novelty slippers, flippers, leather, patent, PVC, fluffy, rubber – big thumbs up. But I draw the line at eighty-year-old women. Wearing Reebok Classics. Playing table-tennis. In a shed. On a campsite. In Kent. At least, standing there with my paddle placed over my shorts as an additional fig leaf, I didn't have to worry about turning *al dente*. And then there were the old men, hair sprouting from nooks and folds like weeds on a badly tarmacked drive, skin melting off bones like candle wax, buttocks subsiding like cottages over the edge of a cliff. This was more Lucian Freud than Botticelli, and, like Freud, it was a little unsettling. You see, when you're thirty-three, you don't really see old people naked. Not unless you're an undertaker, or a nurse. Or into pensioner porn. It's not pretty, and as much as I tried to tell myself that that's not really the point, that naturism is all about equality and acceptance, that old, sagging bodies are every bit as good as young, nubile bodies, I couldn't help but feel repulsed.

A chap called Dennis was my first-round opponent, and as we knocked up I found myself wondering if it wasn't only noses and ears that continue to grow as you get older. As if it wasn't difficult enough playing table-tennis against a naked O.A.P., I was in danger of being hypnotized by Dennis's Herculean appendage swinging from side to side at the other end of the table like the pendulum on a grandfather clock. By the time we'd started the match, Dennis had me psyched out good and proper. They say Mike Tyson had most opponents beaten before he'd even entered the ring, but his ring walk had nothing on this.

Then, with the game locked at 5–5, Dennis delivered his equivalent of a Tyson uppercut. Having lured him in with a beautifully weighted sliced backhand, Dennis, sprightly for a man of his age, lunged towards the net and left me flat-footed with a clipped cross-court forehand. But that wasn't the uppercut, that was just the hook that set up the uppercut. The uppercut was a wet streak running across the table on Dennis's side of the net. Either Dennis didn't notice it, or he chose not to. What was he going to say? 'Sorry old chap, might need a quick wipe down this end, the old bellend's rendered the surface unplayable.' Boxers have many different ways to describe the effects of a mind-scrambling punch. Muhammad Ali once spoke of 'a little room where alligators roamed'. Roberto Duran said he was 'taken to dark places no one else inhabits'. I was in a shed being assailed by a giant cock and balls and a nasty streak. It was time to take a dive.

TOM

The tables were so tightly packed together, the genitalia so gregarious, that bending down to pick up a stray ping-pong ball became an act of great bravery, the chances of coming face-to-flaps with a female player stretching for a wide backhand too great to ignore.

As Ben chased Dennis' cunning shots all over the barn, I found myself in conversation with a bearded middle-aged man with more than a little of Jimmy Hill about him.

'It's not just table-tennis we have here,' he told me proudly. 'The badminton tournament is wonderful, although since we play

it outside, the weather can be a problem.' He took a sip from his beaker of orange squash. 'We find we're rather reliant on heavy shuttlecocks.' I dropped my bat with a loud clatter. 'Yes. The ordinary shuttlecocks don't fly straight,' he said matter-of-factly. I bent down to retrieve the bat, ducking as casually as I could under an accidental swinging blow from his untethered truncheon.

I felt something grab at my elbow and wheeled round, ready to strike it repeatedly with the bat until it let go. It was Brian, looking excited. 'I believe we're on,' he murmured, pointing to a table where Ben and Dennis were shaking hands. 'I imagine you'll be out for revenge – Dennis has just sent your friend packing. 21–7. Wiped the floor with him.'

As we warmed up, several things became apparent. The first was that different shots made your unencumbered cucumber move in varying ways. A forehand top-spin, for example, sent you bouncing violently from left to right; a backhand slice made the old chap nod like a nervous elephant.

Your tactics also had to be altered to take account of the unusual circumstances and circumcisions. No more was a top-spin smash a killer blow; with players standing a safe distance back from the blunt edges of the table, that was far too easy to read and then return. No, the most effective shot was the little drop-shot just over the net. Who in their right mind wanted to risk a dramatic and unprotected lunge forward?

At some points the very fact that you were concentrating on the table-tennis helped you feel less conscious of your denuded surroundings. At others the nakedness was, well, in your face. It's not easy focusing on your opponent's side-spin serve when his plums are bouncing around vigorously directly in your eye-line.

Still, standards were high. Despite his advanced years, Brian was a handful, and not only in the appendage sense. So too was *my next opponent, the Jimmy Hill lookalike, whose elongated chin did little to hide his excitement. Come on Fordyce, I thought, focus on the game, not the player. Would my mum have allowed this sausage-sledging to put her off her stroke? Of course not. Strong mind, relaxed limbs.*

Three matches played, three wins chalked up. If there were drops of sweat dribbling down the small of my back into the ravine between my buttocks, they were well-earned. I was into the semi-finals.

Ben was speed-smoking by the barn door as I dabbed my brow with a towel. 'Shocker,' he grumbled. 'Three straight defeats. I'm a goner. It's all down to you, Tommy . . .'

BEN

While Tom nattered away to the kindly old ladies on tea duty over a slice of Battenberg, I sat in the corner, a ploughman's covering my modesty, absent-mindedly pushing a couple of pickled onions around my plate.

'Enjoying yourself?' said Brian, his member hovering dangerously close to my celery.

'Yeah, t'rrific,' I said through gritted teeth, 'having a great time.'

'Seventies disco tonight if you boys fancy popping along,' said Brian. Seventies disco? Is he talking about the decade or the average age? I felt like sticking my fork in Brian's bratwurst.

Instead I found myself mumbling, 'Yeah, you just try and stop us. Has the DJ got any Edison Lighthouse?'

The table-tennis tournament had provided a sobering glimpse into the future, of the ravages of time on the human body. But it slowly dawned on me that it wasn't really the nudity that was making me uncomfortable. Certainly, doing battle with the monstrously endowed Dennis had taken me out of my comfort zone – so far out, I'd felt like I needed a sat-nav to find my way back – but it was more the fact I was playing table-tennis on a Saturday afternoon at all. With a bunch of old folk. In a shed. On a campsite. In Kent. There was nothing natural about that. Not as far as I was concerned. And the more I pondered the philosophical side of naturism, the more it seemed like hokum to me. How was this group of people any more equal or harmonious than, for example, your average bridge club? A naturist club, like any other club, has rules, namely in this case that you're encouraged (although not forced) to be naked. And if everyone was naked, then surely we'd still have wars? Didn't cavemen fight naked with sticks and stones? Or did that only start when cavemen started wearing animal skins? And we'd still have poor naked people and rich naked people, and offices where some naked people did the cleaning and others told them to do the cleaning. I could see how naturism could have a spiritual side, how it might strip away, as well as clothes, any fear associated with your body, or indeed with mortality. And I could see how being free to follow your own path within a group of like-minded people, and not be judged and disapproved of, might give you a real sense of happiness and contentment. But to most people on this campsite in Kent, it didn't seem to be as deep as all that. They just liked being naked, it was as simple as that. But they also liked table-tennis tournaments. And caravans. And gnomes. Nice people. Just not my kind of nice people.

TOM

They say, don't they, that if you're standing in front of an intimidating audience, the best way to calm your nerves is to imagine your interrogators are naked. Quite what you're supposed to do if they already are starkers has never been explained to me.

As my best-of-three semi began, the sixteen-year-old prodigy across the other side of the net bouncing about with youthful vigour, I was aware of the crowd watching around the barn, perched on old wooden chairs or standing with legs akimbo. If the breasts drooped sadly and the testicles hung low, the support elsewhere was exemplary. Each rally was cheered to its conclusion, the best shots applauded with generous appreciation, and for the first game I let the encouragement fill my sails.

My opponent was skilful but mentally flaky. Adapting the stonewalling tactics espoused so successfully down the years by Mama Fordyce, I blocked and blocked until frustration overtook him and a wild stroke sailed out. When he tried to play defensively himself, I stepped up the pace and went aggressive.

At 21–18 and 18–16 up in the second, I was on course for a glorious victory. That was when I made the fatal error of letting my gaze drop just a fraction.

It always comes as a surprise to women, but the average male has seen surprisingly few penises in his lifetime. In the same way that I've never read the motoring pages of a newspaper despite flicking through thousands of papers in my lifetime, I've never examined another man's old chap in any detail, despite being in close proximity in showers and changing-rooms for over thirty years. It makes sense – when you've got no interest in something, why would you bother studying it? You might be the world's leading expert in your own, but it's an idiosyncratic pursuit. The wider world of winkles remains a mystery.

Now, as I gazed at the exhibition on display around the room, I felt like an explorer stumbling into a jungle glade packed with exotic orchids. The range of flowers on display was extraordinary – long dangling stamens, strange purple buds, stunted pistils and weird distended petals. It was an overwhelming sight – a troupe of triffids, a monstrous gathering of the glands.

In the earlier rounds perhaps I could have survived. Here, facing an opponent of a far higher calibre, there was no room for error. The second game slipped away 24–22, the third 21–19. My dreams of being crowned the country's premier ping-pong free-dong practitioner were over.

'How idiotic civilization is! Why be given a body if you have to keep it shut up in a case like a rare, rare fiddle?' I pondered Katherine Mansfield's famous words as we sipped tea and nibbled on homemade apple pie in the warm sunshine outside the barn. If the bodies on display were more battered euphoniums than rare fiddles, maybe that was exactly the point. Standing here with everything on display, there really was nothing left to hide. How liberating it felt to be accepted exactly as you were, your folds and faults and physical foibles as unimportant as the bumpy bark on the trees all around. Outside the campsite walls, the prospect of a naked pensioner offering you a slice of her strudel was as unappetizing as Dirsy's fag butts. Inside, it became a gesture of friendship, innocent and convivial in equal measure. I was beginning to enjoy myself.

BEN

Six hours later and I was glued to the wall of the campsite refectory, terrified in case anyone would ask me to dance or even look in my general direction. I couldn't remember being this scared at a disco since Sister Rosario caught me fumbling with Julie Coombs in the graveyard of St Helen's Cathedral back in 1989. Formidable woman, Rosario, and let's just say I didn't demand that she smell my finger. So I felt bad when Pam skipped over for a chat, fully clothed, as most of the revellers were, and confirmed what I already knew: that 'these people' were just like any other people, only they liked to walk around naked, which didn't make them bad people, just people I didn't quite understand.

'Having a good time?' said Pam. I hesitated and smiled a watery smile, a smile that said 'not really', a smile that said 'I'd rather be somewhere else, anywhere but here'. 'It's not always easy first time,' said Pam, 'but I think you've both done pretty well. I hope you come back. We're all quite excited about having a couple of newbies. Where's your boyfriend?'

I started to protest, but tailed off, my words trampled all over by 'Tiger Feet'. I pointed limply towards the bar, where Tom – wearing a running vest, hair dyed white, why was I surprised? – was bobbing his head in time to the music. Pam gently squeezed my arm and left me with my thoughts, before a child pretending to be a deflating balloon raspberried towards me and buried his face in my crotch. Before you ask, I was wearing trousers.

TOM

I'd found our spell in Kent a congenial experience. Our fellow campers couldn't have been a less pretentious bunch, but in their own low-key way they appeared as contented as any lauded intellectual philosopher. At the same time there was an unmistakable air of melancholy about the place – the tired, shabby outbuildings, the 1950s pursuits, the army of peeling gnomes on manoeuvres in the undergrowth. This form of naturism seemed as stuck in the past as caravanning clubs and sidecar-racing. Keen though I was to see if I could harness more of that naked happiness, the prospect of spending every weekend in a damp field in Kent filled me with a low dread.

'Take it into your private life,' Brian had told us as we left. 'Be naked at home, with your family, with your friends.' It got me thinking. While being nude with my fellow Fordyces was a definite non-starter – younger brother fine, three sisters plus Mum and Dad dear God no – there had been huge interest among my friends about our exposed adventures. How best to preach the Bible of Bare?

'I've got it,' Ben said. 'A naked dinner-party. Sophisticated, sociable, saucy.'

'I like it,' I said. 'If it leaves a bad taste in anyone's mouth, we can always blame the food. Now, who do we invite?'

Certain names were out. There was no way either of us wanted a couple of the Romford posse along – their table manners were a disgrace, for starters – while Big Al, although impeccably behaved, would only intimidate his fellow guests. Naturism was all about being comfortable with every size and shape of body, but the presence of a man who had once had a poem written about him by a female admirer that rhymed the words 'every girl's dream' with 'huge trouser-docked submarine' would simply be too much for the other male egos.

Certain names were instantly in. Bettsy had a German lady-friend. Some national stereotypes are outdated, but not this one. She was up for it in a flash. So too was Bettsy himself, although his honesty was a little uncomfortable. 'You should know,' he said, 'that I'll look at your girlfriend's tits. I won't be staring all night, but I'll definitely take a peek, just out of interest. It's nothing personal – I've just never seen them before.'

I wasn't sure whether to tell the girlfriend in advance or just hope she didn't notice. Finding enough blokes to come along wasn't a problem – pretty much everyone I mentioned it to wanted to sign up on the spot – but willing females were in much shorter supply. 'Give me three months to get in shape down the gym and I'll think about it,' was the standard response, which seemed to miss the point entirely.

Some potential guests were troubled by the practicalities. 'What if we get cold?' asked one. 'What if I get a random boner, and everyone thinks it's because of them?' asked another. Others were suspicious of our motives. It was clear that the words 'naked dinner party' were interpreted by certain ears as 'free-for-all swingers night'; the more you protested, the more suspicious they became that it wasn't only the table we were intending to lay.

There were issues for us, too. Rupert insisted the sofas be covered with old sheets, the dining chairs replaced with plastic garden furniture. Were we allowed to wear an apron while cooking by the stove? When guests arrived and we asked politely if we could take their coats, should we ask for their trousers too?

For all the enthusiasm the idea itself generated, it became increasingly clear that its practical application was another thing entirely. People were fascinated by the concept but repelled by the reality, delighted to offer suggestions for the menu but reluctant to tuck in themselves.

'Too scared,' admitted one RSVP. 'I take it you'll be serving nibbles beforehand though – breadsticks with a yoghurt dip?'

'Would love to, but the missus is shitting herself,' said another. 'What about bearded clams to start?'

And so it went on – asparagus spears, smeared in melted butter; pork medallions and loin of beef; chipolatas and fish fingers, served with fried eggs; melons for pudding and stewed plums for dessert. We had a menu the length of Big Al's submarine, and a guest-list as empty as his torpedo tubes.

'This is no good,' Ben said, shaking his head. 'Confirmed diners: me, you, your bird, Bettsy and Fraulein Bettsy. It's barely worth setting the table.'

'It's worse than that,' I said sadly. 'I've just had a text from Bettsy. He's split up with the German.'

'There's something I've been meaning to tell you, too,' mumbled Ben. 'I don't really want to come myself. I hated it at that campsite. I never want to do it again.'

I pictured the dinner table as it now stood. Me, dishing out the melon balls, my girlfriend looking for somewhere to tuck her napkin in, Bettsy leering at her over the celery sticks. Happiness? It was a recipe for nothing but disaster.

'Don't worry about it,' said Ben, putting an arm around my shoulder. 'There's plenty of other lifestyles out there for us to explore. It wasn't our fault this one went tits up.'

'You're right,' I said determinedly. 'So what if we made arses of ourselves?'

Ben nodded. 'Their cock-up, not ours. Now – what's next?'

3. FATE AND FORTUNE-TELLING

'You've probably got very delicious thighs'

TOM

It's an age-old conundrum: if someone offered to reveal what was going to happen to you in the future, would it make you happier?

Astrologers, fortune-tellers, tarot-readers, psychics. There was a modern-day army of soothsayers sweeping across the land. Everywhere we looked, conscripts were on the march, from the woman in Wetherspoons engrossed in her horoscope to the middle-class mums with their Middle Eastern mystics. Rationality was on the retreat, the age of enlightenment under attack.

We weren't the most obvious of recruits. I like to pick my own path through life's battlefield. The idea of taking orders from fate and fortune, to let a supernatural sergeant tell me where to go, feels deeply unsettling. For Ben it's more practical; so patchy are the campaign details lodged in his brain that he'd happily settle for knowing what had happened in the recent past, let alone the future. Like a historian uncovering shards of bone and weaponry in the soil, he has to piece together what may or may not have taken place from tiny fragments scattered on the wind, and where corroborating tales from brothers in arms exist, they don't always bring the sort of news a man necessarily likes to hear. 'Honestly – no more,' he'd groaned midway through my recap of the big push in Dubai. 'It can't have happened – my arms aren't long enough. Or that – the photo must be upside down. Who would say something like that to her?'

That we decided to embrace it all came down to a combination of the symbolic and sensible. We'd vowed at the outset to put our preconceptions to one side; this was the first big test. More prosaically, we knew all too well that our own lifestyles had failed to produce sufficient happiness. Something had to change. This was it.

We drew up the plan. Each would pick a clairvoyant and then live exactly as they prescribed. It was both frightening and strangely liberating, and we reacted accordingly.

'I can see something in my crystal ball,' said Ben, rubbing his hands together. 'I see stars, I see the moon, I see Uranus.'

'It's these running shorts,' I said. 'The lining's perished.'

A few years before, while trekking in the remote mountain kingdom of Bhutan, I had been encouraged to request an audience with the country's top astrologer. The Bhutanese were world leaders on happiness – they'd even changed their main economic indicator from GDP to GDH, or gross domestic happiness – and horoscopes were at the heart of most things they did. In such high regard was this old monk held that the king refused to plan so much as a stroll round the garden without first picking his brains for the most auspicious route through the begonias.

I'd had to wait days for a slot while earnest locals negotiated on my behalf, and even then we had run out of time. Sitting in the stone courtyard of an ancient monastery, cross-legged under a prayer-wheel the size of an oil drum, I had half-expected the guru to float down from the heavens on the back of a Himalayan eagle, or appear from the unfolding petals of a lotus flower. That he rocked up on a motorbike and asked me if Britney Spears was on drugs somewhat took the edge off things.

While he had taken note of all personal details required for a reading, he had never actually revealed what my future held. It had taken a good hour to work through the complex story of Britney's last few years; somewhere along the line he had merged her in his head with Baby Spice and Lindsay Lohan. 'Forget Beckham,' I had said testily at one point. 'He's got nothing to do with it.'

We had parted with each other's email addresses and a promise to get back in touch should Britney's career trajectory take another turn for the worse. With more hope than expectation I fired off a missive requesting the overdue prescription.

BEN

I'm sat on a bench in the Tate Modern with 'intuitive' tarot-reader Cilla. 'Maybe you don't want to look back at something. Is there a blockage?' she says.

'We have been ignoring the smell coming out of the sink,' I reply. 'Maybe we should get a plumber in'. Come on Dirs, stop fucking about. Open up the mind. Cilla seems like a nice lady, she's been good enough to give you an hour of her time, the least you can do is throw her a bone or two.

'Maybe you're planning to change something in your life?' adds Cilla.

'Who isn't?' I think. I gaze across the vast Turbine Hall below, screwing up my face in mock anguish. 'I have been thinking about moving,' I offer weakly.

This reminds me of Confession. 'Have you anything to confess, my son?' the priest used to say, and I'd be forced to make some nonsense up about not tidying up my bedroom or unscrewing the lid on the salt cellar in the canteen at school. If God had even been thinking about punishing me for that, then he was one spiteful son of a gun.

Next Cilla turns over the King of Cups. 'Maybe you feel as though you should be more generous?' says Cilla. Yeah, maybe, but doesn't everybody? I'm seriously floundering now, not to mention starting to get a little bit embarrassed.

'One or two of my girlfriends have pointed out I might be a little bit emotionally retarded,' I say, not wanting to leave Cilla hanging.

Then Cilla hits me with a classic Tarot reader line: 'There's some sort of mourning or grief . . .' she says. 'It could be that that's blocking you from getting on with your life . . .'

'I've never lost anyone close to me,' I reply, tapping the wooden bench a couple of times.

'It could be a love affair,' fires back Cilla. Touché.

Next up is a rather downbeat-looking bloke sitting in an ice cave. 'You've been underground and you want to come out and start growing,' says Cilla.

'Maybe I'm channelling my housemate,' I say. 'He works down Piccadilly Circus.' Cilla laughs a hollow laugh and gets straight back down to business. Now it's time for the Queen of Cups, and for some reason, she's got her norks out. Cilla sounds excited.

'You're either going to meet somebody who's like her – "Can

you handle me?" – or you're going to find that part of yourself which is feminine . . . I think you will have a female muse, and the Queen of Cups could be your muse . . .'

Let's hope so. Judging by her picture on that card, she looks like she might go like the clappers.

Now Cilla turns over a card depicting a towering inferno, replete with people jumping from windows, presumably to their deaths. 'You're going to dismantle all the structures in your life to do something completely outrageous,' says Cilla. 'You might decide to go off to China or Japan or India and live like a hermit in a cave . . .'

Now this is uncanny: Tom and I had been thinking about living like hermits for a couple of weeks, not necessarily on the other side of the world, but still . . . hang on a minute, I told Cilla this about half an hour ago while we were having a cup of coffee upstairs . . . cheeky mare, I'm fast losing faith . . .

TOM

With remarkable speed, a reply came through. If I'd been wrong to use a subject-line of 'Britney and Becks to wed', karma had taken its revenge. There were none of the pointers I'd hoped for – the winner of the Golden Boot at the World Cup, or the name of any future wife. Instead, the monk informed me I was to be reincarnated as a mountain goat.

By Bhutanese standards this was an acceptable return, but to a resident of Hammersmith it seemed a little unfair. Had I been that badly behaved? At times, sure, but I'd already taken my punishment – smacks with slippers and clogs as a mischievous child, the terrifying silent sulks of girlfriends as an adult. I was also uncertain of the practical implications. If I were reborn as a goat, would my brain be in a goat's body, or would I be blissfully unaware of the whole demotion? If it was the latter, by definition I wouldn't really be that bothered – but the mismatch implied by the former would cause constant problems. My hoof control would be poor. Other goats would consider me supercilious and stuck-up. Even the most sympathetic of listeners would soon grow tired of my constant bleating.

More to the point, how would I be able to get myself promoted back to human form the next time around? The opportunities for good deeds as a goat seemed limited. Would I be allowed to enter a charity fun-run? The odds had to stacked against it.

BEN

'What about my job?' I ask Cilla. 'I've recently been offered another one. Should I take it?' She turns over the Nine of Cups.

'Follow the path that gives you that sense of speaking the truth and become that free guy that can travel into this golden landscape.' This sounds promising. Cilla pauses for a second. 'Neither the job you have now or the one you've been offered will give you that.' Cosmic. Embarrassment has now given way to mild irritation and a strong sense of wanting to be on the train back to Essex.

'What about my health?' Cilla turns over what she assures me is the highest card of the deck, presumably the same card Michael Phelps gets whenever he has his tarot read.

'You shouldn't have any problems,' says Cilla, sounding a little relieved.

'But I smoke. And I don't do any exercise. And I eat a load of old rubbish.'

'Yes,' says Cilla, 'but you're obviously young enough to get away with it.'

Next, another health card, and this time it's the Shadow. See, I told you, you silly woman, I've got a bastard shadow on my lung, or on my kidney, or wherever else you can have a shadow. Cilla, sensing my alarm, throws back her head and cackles. It's a funny way of putting someone's mind at rest.

'It's more a shadow inside you,' says Cilla. 'Fury, anger and fear. You need to explore ways of getting it out or it will affect your health.'

Cilla turns another health card. Oh, bollocks, that's all I need, she's only gone and flipped over the Devil. 'Is . . . this . . . good?' I ask, wincing.

'You can untrap yourself by looking at the shadow,' says Cilla. 'There's something you've been hiding, keeping down. Look at that, and it will transform your life.'

I'm surprised to find that this actually strikes a chord – I do rather let things fester inside of me, I am something of a brooder, prone to being a little bit dark . . . but then aren't most people? Get a grip, you mug, she's cold-reading you, making intelligent stabs in the dark, probably based on the fact you come across as a morose old sod. I've read about this, it's called the Forer effect – off-the-peg statements that could describe anyone but which are perceived to be tailor-made by the person being read. But I wasn't about to let Cilla tie me in knots.

We move on to relationships. Cilla turns over another card, and on this one there's a black devil crouched into a ball with his hands over his head. Oh yeah, and he's got a load of swords hanging out of his back.

'Oh dear,' says Cilla. 'The ten of Swords is the very bottom of the pit.'

Cilla, I didn't have to be Doris Stokes to work that one out.

First the Shadow, then the Devil, now we've got the Devil with ten swords in his back. I'm beginning to think Cilla's left her tarot cards at home and mistakenly brought along her Horror Top Trumps instead.

Ten swords . . . let me think . . . I probably have had about ten proper girlfriends . . . but surely they didn't all hate me this much? Plus, when Wendy got the hump, she always said she wanted to cut my balls off, never stab me in the back.

'It's a difficult time for you in terms of relationships and you're struggling,' adds Cilla. 'The good news is, it can't get any lower.' Give Cilla her due, she was right about that, I hadn't had as much as a sniff in weeks, let alone a full-blown romance. Cilla and I then have a bit of a chat about relationships, and it dawns on me that she isn't far off being a therapist or counsellor – I don't remember talking about this sort of stuff with anyone before.

All these devils are beginning to make me twitchy, so I'm a little bit relieved when Cilla flips over the Archangel next.

'Have you ever tried manifestation?' asks Cilla. 'For example, when I wanted a house I went off and bought a hob, and then when I found that house I walked in and thought, "This is it," and it needed a hob. Make yourself into an environment that will work, imagine how you would be in a good relationship and allow that to take seed and make you feel abundant and golden in love.'

The hob bit – no idea. The other stuff – that kind of makes sense. Next up, it's the Seven of Swords.

'You're going to have to use all your cunning and ingenuity to find your way through,' says Cilla. 'You wake up one morning and there's a green sun, and you think, "This is not the world I went to sleep in, I can't manage this."' A green sun? I thought the BBC was moving to Salford, not Sellafield. I really must start reading my emails. 'But your guidance will take you out of this

place and you'll meet somebody. You'll be provided with an opportunity, but you'll have to work hard to keep it . . .'

Right, let me get this straight: I'm at the very bottom of the pit relationship-wise, I'm going to have to use all my cunning and ingenuity to get out of it, and when I do find someone, I'll have to work like a navvy to keep them.

'*I don't necessarily tell people nice things,*' says Cilla.

TOM

I was keen on a second opinion, not only to get a more optimistic diagnosis but also to factor in a more British perspective, but who to choose? I needed a soothsayer who understood how we'd been brought up, as well as someone whose cosmic calculations had endured where others had come and gone – someone possessing such mighty influence that they might call themselves the Astrologer Royal, not to mention the strength of character to have worn yellow jump-suits on breakfast TV and still be working twenty years later.

I needed Russell Grant.

Then again, where was he? It had been a while since I'd seen him on British television. According to his Wikipedia entry, Russell had been busy. In addition to tireless charity work and learning to speak seven languages (including Gaelic and Afrikaans) he had been dubbed 'Mr Middlesex' and been made Lord of Ashford. At the time it seemed quite a revelation. Then again, at that point I didn't know what would follow over the next few weeks.

That trademark chubby-cheeky face beamed out impishly from his personal website's homepage. The site was a cornucopia of clairvoyance – dream-decoding, text-a-psychic, astro-dating, a phone-an-angel line.

And horoscopes. Sagittarius – there it was. I clicked through and read on. 'Sat 4th April. You might wonder whether you're doing the right thing in making some much-needed changes. But why should you let other people's doubts and reservations get to you?'

It was as if he'd been at my shoulder at the National Cross Country Championship and at Ben's in Vegas. Spooky. With some anticipation I returned the following day: 'You feel peeved that relationships could be improved if only other people would tell you what they are thinking. Since moping around watching each other's glum faces will only add to the tension, you're best off finding some other company, at least for today.'

'Darling, what are you thinking?' I asked the girlfriend that evening, smiling encouragingly. Thirty minutes later, with an interminable stream-of-consciousness tale about someone at her work I'd never met still in full swing, the smile had somewhat slipped. I held my hand up like a traffic policeman and stepped bravely into the flow of words. 'Listen,' I said hesitantly, glancing for reassurance at the words on my laptop screen. 'Maybe you're best off finding some other company.'

Ben was sympathetic when I knocked on his door. 'Women are always crying,' he said dismissively. 'Don't worry about it. Take her down Wagamama's for some vegetarian noodle shit. She'll be like putty.'

'Friends have wondered where you've been for the past few weeks,' was Russell's next daily tip. 'It's time to get back on the social scene. The warm reception you'll get will prove gratifying. Sometimes you wonder whether anyone loves you.'

This was more puzzling. I was seeing more of Dirsy than ever; he was due at Rupert's that evening to discuss how we might be able to dump the Champervan at sea. Rupert and his exotically named coterie of friends – Joffe, Quintin, Jose – had even offered to cook dinner. The social scene had seldom been warmer.

Then there was that somewhat ominous final sentence. I hadn't been at all concerned that no one might love me, but maybe I'd been naive. What had Russell spotted in the stars? I phoned the ladyfriend with a tightening feeling in my throat.

'I hope you're going to apologize,' she said. 'You've made me very unhappy in the past few days.'

'Look,' I said. 'This is important. Do you wonder if anyone loves you?'

She sniffed pensively. 'When you behave like you have recently, it worries me.' There was a pause. 'You could prove it to me, you know. That you love me. Move out of Rupert's, Fordyce. Move in with me.'

'I can't,' I said. 'Not now. Ben and me – we've got so much to do. This is big – we're only just starting, but it feels good already, and . . .'

Silence, followed by the unmistakable sound of a girl quietly sobbing. Dirsy, I thought – this might take more than a Wagamama's.

BEN

The thing about attempting to live your life by horoscopes is that it highlights just how tedious and humdrum your life is. 'Oh, one more thing before I let you go,' says Jonathan Cainer in the Daily Mail *on 10 April, 'it's a wild world out there.' Not for this Sagittarius, Jonathan. I spent all day sitting in an office in White City writing about netball and hockey before traipsing home at 10 p.m. and knocking up a Marks & Sparks meal for one. 'Single?' asks Mystic Meg in the* Sun *a few days later. 'You will be smart with your heart and choose to love someone who is sincere and sexy.' Seeing as the only woman I spoke to all day was Mad Flo in the BBC canteen, I didn't really have much of a chance to turn Meg's words into actions. Nice lady, Flo, but our relationship has never really recovered from the time she caught me trying to secrete a rogue sausage under some chips.*

To be fair to Cilla, she was quick to point out how insane it would be to plan your whole life by astrology, or indeed the flipping of some cards. 'If you don't know what you want, how can some cards tell you?' she admitted. 'But it's useful as feedback because the tarot can give you some really off-the-wall ideas and make you think more laterally.' And I had to admit, I could see how putting your life in the hands of an astrologer or tarot-reader might give you a sense of control by at least making you believe you can work out what's going to happen next. And if you've got someone telling you that tonight could be the night that you bump into the love of your life, you're more likely to go out and put it to the test than sitting at home on your sofa, stewing in your own fatalism and pulling yourself senseless to internet porn.

'Single?' asks Mystic Meg on 10 April. 'Real love links you to an Aries.' I get straight on Facebook and ask some mates if their wives or girlfriends have got any single friends I might hit it off with. Preferably a spunky lady like the Queen of Cups, and preferably someone born between 21 March and 20 April. 'Fuck off you weirdo,' fires back Perkins, quick as a flash. Two more mates send pictures of morbidly obese females in various states of undress, while most of them simply ignore me. But just when the fatalism is starting to kick in, someone comes up with the goods.

'Hard to handle? Get in touch with this bird Tina,' writes back Dicky. 'Built for fun, loves a booze, and she's an Aries. If you don't get a bunk-up, you may as well chop it off.'

A few days later and I'm sat across from Tina in a tapas bar near Liverpool Street and I can almost hear the knife being whetted.

'Why did you say that?' says Tina, tears beginning to form in pools on her lower lids. This is what happens when you talk about 'stuff'. I didn't want to talk about 'stuff', I hardly ever want to talk about 'stuff', I just wanted to get a bit drunk and talk a lot of nonsense. Sometimes, conceit gets the better of me and I convince myself I'm a little bit 'complicated', but ask my ex-girlfriends and they'll gladly tell you I'm quite a simple cove: a few bottles of wine, something nice to eat, perhaps a sideways look at current affairs, a couple of knob gags, and I'm a pig in shit. Just don't talk about 'stuff', I have a tendency to say the wrong things and make girls cry when I talk about 'stuff'.

Then again, I blame Tina. Within five minutes of meeting she'd told me all about her father's sordid affair, how he'd seemed like the perfect husband to her mum and how he'd been busted on Christmas Eve, a rogue text message pulling the rug from underneath him. I don't want to know this. Why does she think I want to know this? Somewhere in my subconscious I must be angry, because when she asks me if I've ever been unfaithful, I pop a couple of olives into my mouth and casually inform her that, yes, back at university I messed about a bit.

'BEN!' she shouts across the table, hands clasped over her ears. 'BEN! WHY, BEN, WHY?' This is a dramatic development, and one I'm not expecting.

'It was a long time ago, everyone made a few mistakes at university . . . didn't they?'

'No, Ben, not everyone made mistakes at university . . . why *did you say that, Ben, why did you say that . . . ?' I catch the waiter's eye and flare my nostrils as if to say, 'Sorry about all this, old chap, I don't really know her,' but the frown on his face suggests he's not convinced.*

Eventually she comes round, only to become even more upset because she realizes how unreasonable she's been. I find myself making wild promises about meeting up again in an attempt to placate her, we move on to a Chinese karaoke bar and we end up kissing by the fish tank — too old to be doing that sort of thing. An anaemic-looking specimen, far too big for its environs, stares forlornly at us from behind the glass as a blonde from Accounts savages Bonnie Tyler up on stage. It gets late and I suddenly realize I've missed the last train back to Romford.

'You can sleep on my sofa if you like,' says Tina.

'No, you're all right, a cab will only cost me eighty quid.'

On the long journey home I read my paper and there's a story about the death of the world's smallest man: 'Pingping, who at birth was no bigger than the palm of his father's hand, was a chain-smoker and a ladies' man despite his height.' Seventy-four centimetres tall and he was having more luck than me. Look on the bright side, at least it's one of my competitors out of the way.

TOM

If the week had been a testing one, true pilgrims persevered, even when their journey took them through dangerous waters. It was time to set our sights on the grand fromage: a personal audience with Big Russ himself.

Phone calls, emails and more phone calls. For a fortnight there was silence. So hard was it to make contact that I might have been chasing a one-on-one with Greta Garbo. Then, at last, my inbox pinged: 'Tom, it's Russell G here. Can I suggest we have a telecon before you make the journey up to my bolt-hole in Snowdonia, as you might have a completely wrong impression about how astrology SHOULD be used. It is a media myth that people should rule their lives by it.' No wonder we'd been so lost. 'Let me look at your proper chart, date/time/place of birth (within half-hour) so you can see difference between sun-signs and the real deal. Russ.'

Some of those details I knew – the day and year, the fact it took place in Princess Alexandria hospital in Harlow. Others were missing. 'Time? How should I know?' snorted Mama Fordyce down the phone. 'I've had five of you lot. You think I can remember that level of detail? I'll get your father.'

'Time,' mused the old man. 'I've got a feeling I was playing badminton, which would make it a weekday. Unless it was a tournament, in which case it would be a Saturday. There are more weekdays than Saturdays, though. Let's say I'd be at work from 9 a.m. to 6 p.m., over to the social club, get changed – 7 p.m.? 8 p.m.?'

I chewed my lip. 'Why weren't you there when I was born?'

'Between you and me,' he whispered, 'it was bad enough being there when you were conceived.'

I emailed Russell the information I'd gleaned. Three days later, his number was sent through. I got Dirsy over, stuck on the speakerphone and dialled.

For a man with the myriad demands on his time that Russell had, he was generous in the extreme. Of the forty-odd minutes he was on the line, I spoke for perhaps two of them. Pleasantries had only just been exchanged when he hit his straps.

'Astrology is forewarned, forearmed, Tom. It's very much a subject of personal understanding. I know myself well enough that if I walk into a Post Office and see the old girl in front empty out her piggy bank, take out 2,000 groats and florins and five farthings, and the Post Office have to count them all, I know I'd probably kill the old woman, and probably the Post Office assistant too. So I have to leave, and that's probably how it should best be used.'

Russell had achieved even more than his Wikipedia page had disclosed. Among his revelations were that he'd designed the Brentford FC club badge, bought Middlesex and England cricketer Owais Shah his first bat and been the first character seen on screen in the debut episode of *Spitting Image*. 'They needed me on the cover of *TV Times*,' he explained.

Barely pausing for breath, Russ segued into eloquent lament for his lost friend Princess Diana. He had been her confidante for many years, and the shock of her passing had upset him terribly. It was almost twenty minutes in, cramp spreading through my note-taking right hand, when he turned his attention to the future.

'I've drawn your chart up here in front of me. Your main sign is Sag, you're Leo rising and you've got three planets in Aries, and you've got a really rather beautiful grand triangle in fire, which makes you charming and sexy and gorgeous, and people will love you and you'll make them laugh. It's incredibly creative, and it's the sort of chart I would expect to see if you were going to be an Olympic sportsman, or what I would call a Hollywood-style chart. Barack Obama is the same – you've both got Jupiter in Aquarius.'

I waved a fist delightedly at Ben. 'Barack Obama!' I mouthed. He rolled his eyes and took a bite from one of the grissini Rupert had brought back from a recent trip to Siena.

'This is a pioneering chart of yours, Tom. If you were Victorian, it wouldn't have been "Dr Livingstone, I presume," it would have been "Dr Fordyce, I presume." The important thing is Jupiter returns – it's in the same position as when you were born, and that means this is a very important year of your life, a year to realize all the things you've ever wanted to do. You're going to be popular at work, you'll be popular with your colleagues, people are going to like you. And yet there will always be this quest for you to better yourself creatively, and explore your potential and do things no one else has ever done.' So true, I thought happily. This was perfect. 'And you've probably got very delicious thighs.'

I jerked upright. 'I'm sorry?'

'These are all the things I can tell without even knowing what it is that you do at the BBC,' breezed Russell. 'You're going to tell me now that it's all a load of crap, and if you do I'll have to kill you. And the old woman at the Post Office.'

Some sages seek refuge in silence and the occasional pithy pronouncement. Not Russell. Quite why he had the soubriquet Mr Middlesex rather than the Garrulous Guru or the Oral Oracle was something I would have pondered had there been a moment's pause.

'Can you identify with some of those things?' he asked me at one point. I looked down at my notes, which already ran to seven pages. 'Well,' I said, 'obviously it's all very flattering . . .'

'It's a very flattering chart,' interrupted Russ, 'but there is negative stuff. Tom, you're a psychological beast who will use psychology to get your own way. You will use your charm to cover your real intentions, and you will abuse people who get in your way and you will be utterly totally ruthless. Some people, when they're being manipulated by you and your psycho-therapeutic way of doing things, they don't know they're being moved by you – and woe betide them if they did know, because you'd have to blast them.'

I sat back. I'd wanted a more personal reading than I'd found on the website, but this was almost too much to take in. 'Could you send all this in an email?' I asked, somewhat dazed.

His tone became abrupt. 'No darling. I don't work like that. I work totally as I'm talking to you. I don't have the time – to be honest with you, I'm just on the verge of a massive breakthrough in America. My own show for Fox. It's old friends who've come through. I've got so much work to send them this week. But now we've done your chart, if you want to visit me to take the next step and go the Russell Grant way . . . I'm an individualist, you're an individualist . . .'

Dirsy gave me a thumbs-up and helped himself to some Piedmontese olives. 'That would be fantastic,' I said. 'I've been doing some reading on astrology, and I'm very keen to find out if . . .'

Russ jumped in again. 'Be careful. If you read other astrologers' books, you may find they interpret in a different way, which is why I'm still here after forty-five years and they've all buggered off. It's a bit like politics, if you're Labour or Conservative or Liberal, you'll write slanting towards your party, won't you? It's the same with astrology. For example, Johnny Cainer – a dear, dear friend of mine – tends to go much more for an astrological level, while I tend to come at it from the psychological point of what's behind the individual.'

After eight aborted attempts to say goodbye I succeeded on the ninth, just as my mobile phone ran out of battery. I felt like a man lost in a mist. On one hand I was the reincarnation of a Victorian explorer, on the other identical to America's first black president. My grand triangle was in fire and I hadn't even noticed, although that was probably about par for a psychological beast like me.

While Ben logged onto Facebook to see if Tina had posted any more accusatory status updates, I threw myself into further research. If I was going to truly live my life by horoscopes, I wanted to be convinced that I was taking the right path.

There were several questions that had been puzzling me. Why was the exact moment of birth so important, rather than the conception or the intervening nine months, and since labour often took hours, how did you decide what that exact moment was? Waters breaking, first dilation, head appearing, umbilical cord cut – which one mattered most? Let's say you did settle on a specific time. Why then was the position of the sun in a constellation likely to have more of an effect on you than the sanitary conditions in the delivery room, your mother's health or the level of medical treatment you received?

The pioneering studies had been done by a French psychologist named Michel Gauquelin, who claimed to have discovered that the birth of sporting champions was strongly correlated with Mars rising or culminating in the sky. On the surface of things Gauquelin was my kind of boffin. He preferred cycling to maths, and was so obsessed by sporting success that at one stage he was ranked among his country's top fifty tennis players. Unfortunately, he also had more critics than ranking points. Trying to follow the arcane arguments over his methodology involved diversions into the percentage increase in the use of forceps by midwives and from which Parisian arrondissements forty-two of his samples were drawn. My brain couldn't cope with it, and neither could the wider scientific community. Gauquelin committed suicide in 1991, his work unvalidated and his theory unproven.

I popped out to buy Ben and myself restoratives: a packet of Wheat Crunchies for him, a copy of Russell's book *You Can Change Your Life* for me. As he munched, I read from its pages.

'Are you looking for a greater sense of self-fulfilment and happiness, something to breathe new life into your day-to-day existence?' Ben nodded. So far, so good. 'Mars and Jupiter, Venus and Saturn are not remote objects, but a collection of tangible personalities that fill the inner space that is our selves. Think of them as a collection of friends or confidants, on hand at any time to help you deal with a problem, think something through or simply provide the kind of company you need at a particular moment in your life.'

Russell had described in detail the personality of each celestial body. I gave Ben a *Family Fortunes*-style quiz: how many of the characteristics mentioned could he guess?

'The sun,' I began. 'Four adjectives. One of Rupert's Amoretti di Saronno for each one you name correctly.'

Ben scratched his stomach. 'Hot. Fiery. Bright. Yellow.'

'You said hot; our audience said "creative". You said fiery, they said, "arrogant". And "true self". And "heart and soul".'

'Not hot? Or yellow?'

'Try again,' I suggested. 'Have a go at Uranus. The planet.'

Ben sniffed contemplatively. 'Cold. Distant. Name-wise, the Ben Dirs of the solar system.'

'Uranus represents the anarchist within us all,' I read. 'Masculine in nature, he is the fierce, rebellious spirit that helps you shake off your chains.'

'Uranus might do,' said Ben, 'but mine doesn't.'

A few days later I unearthed a research paper published in

2006 by Peter Hartmann, Martin Reuter and Helmut Nyborg. Their snappily entitled 'The relationship between date of birth and individual differences in personality and intelligence: A large-scale study' had gone down a treat in academic circles. The sample size was massive (15,000) and the conclusion unequivocal: no connection existed in either that relationship or between zodiacal signs and personality traits.

There was one massive weakness in Hartmann *et al.*'s case. None of them had ever been immortalized on *Spitting Image*. I owed Russell the chance to argue his case in the flesh. To Snowdonia and Grant Towers I must go.

*

TOM

Rain, grey buildings and sodden hills. The pilgrims of hundreds of years ago might have endured hardships on their way to Jerusalem, but at least the sun shone in the Holy Land. The seven-hour drive to Blaenau Ffestiniog felt like being stuck in an endless car-wash. What little of the landscape could be seen through the rain-sploshed windscreen appeared to have lost almost all light and colour, as if the contrast button had been turned right the way down when we'd left the motorway.

I glanced to the left. My ladyfriend, Sarah, was staring at an upside-down map with an angry expression on her face. Since the disastrous events of the last fortnight I had embarked on a sustained charm offensive, culminating in the offer of a trip to spend a weekend at her parents' place just outside

Runcorn. Only as we passed Birmingham on the M6 had I dropped in the fact that we might be taking a small detour en route, and only by promising that she too could share the audience with Russell had I got away with it.

After five or six missed turns and bouts of map-snatching, a set of iron gates loomed out of the dampness. They opened as we approached, silently revealing a long driveway curving up to a grand Victorian house. Through the dripping, over-hanging trees we drove, stones crunching under the tyres. I parked up by a small van, stepped out and knocked on the large wooden front door.

With a creaking noise it swung open. Russell stood there in a Cotton Traders polo shirt and baggy blue trousers, glasses perched on his nose and a rather uneasy look on his face.

'Tom darling,' he mumbled. 'Come on in.'

That Russ had opened his house to us at all was a gesture of considerable kindness. Not only was he incredibly busy filming the daily video stars for his website and updating all the written horoscopes, but he was also somewhat unwell. A leg injury had left him limping around with a stick, and a physique that had always been chubby had filled out even more since I'd last seen him on television.

Initially, too, there was little evidence of the zing he'd had on the phone. Two large, fluffy cats with malevolent looks on their faces padded around silently, licking their whiskers and staring unblinkingly up at us. Only when awkward small talk gave way to a discussion about Russell's royal coat of arms and how he'd come by the title Lord of Ashford did any animation return to his voice.

'The chap in charge told me that I'm allowed to shag a virgin from Staines. I said to him, "Don't worry about that – you can shag the virgin!"'

Russell had an idiosyncratic way of communicating. There were flamboyant hand gestures, cartoonish expressions of shock or displeasure and more diversions than a bagatelle board. Each sentence seemed to contain at least three repetitions of, 'and I said . . . so they said . . . so I said.' While it was entertaining, he didn't strike you as the sort of chap you'd want to get directions from. It was also difficult getting a word in edgeways. I'd been doing further research and was keen to get Russell's thoughts on a few more thorny issues I'd come across – but finding a safe point to wade into the torrent was almost impossible. On the upside, I did find out more about Russell's take on Quentin Crisp, the multistorey car park in Uxbridge, Tamla Motown and candlelit suppers in South Kensington.

He might yet still be talking, fingers tracing patterns on the glass coffee table, had it not been for a sudden crashing and a ghastly squealing noise coming from the room next door. There was the unmistakable sound of something biting something else and the something else not enjoying it all that much. Russ was on his feet and hobbling for the door in a flash.

'Aghhh!' he yelled. 'My boys! What have you done? Tom! Come here!'

I jumped from my seat. What in God's name—
'QUICKLY!'

I dashed over, a thousand dreadful scenarios playing in my brain. On the floor were Russell's two enormous cats, evil looks and wet blood on their paunchy faces. Between them on the carpets lay a large bird. A large dead bird.

'Oh my God I can't bear it!' howled Russ, bustling out of the room in a state of considerable alarm. 'It's just too awful!'

I could hear him banging around in the hall like an out-of-control wind-up toy. 'Tom! You'll have to get rid of it! Please!'

I looked down again at the bird. Was it really dead? It was certainly bloodied, but was that a tiny heart beating frantically in its chest? I bent down for a closer look. The cats reared up at me, teeth bared. I gave them the finger and backed off.

Russell had taken refuge in the kitchen, clearly distressed by the bloodshed. 'I've got a bag! Come here quickly!' I jogged through the corridors until I found him, holding a plastic bag out with his arm at full stretch, looking in the opposite direction with a hand thrown across his face. He shook it at me. 'Please!'

Back in the lounge the cats were bashing the bird around between themselves like enthusiastic tennis players. I waved a foot in their direction until they backed off snarling, and put the reversed bag over my hand like a man about to pick up a dog turd. Slowly I knelt down next to the corpse, moving my outstretched fingers ever closer. I'd never touched a bird before. What wonderful indigo-black feathers it had, its beak so yellow, its wings so—

WHUMP! Like Lazarus on a slingshot it exploded up from the carpet. Beak and claws were everywhere. Wings beat in my face. I fell backwards, just as the cats leapt up with flashing paws. 'Tom?' came Russell's muffled enquiry. 'I'm not coming out till it's gone. Is it gone?'

The bird was flying round like a demented stunt pilot – smashing into the walls, rebounding from the window, dropping a trail of exploding shit bombs in its wake. 'Nearly!' I shouted.

I ran back next door and grabbed Sarah. With a lion-tamer's skill she held the cats at bay while I tried to shepherd the reanimated avian towards the opened bay window. With a last clatter against the frame, it careered out and away into the sopping woods.

Russell remained in the kitchen. I went through and knocked on the closed door. It opened a fraction and his worried face poked through. 'Is it gone?'

Returning to serious debate about the accuracy of astrology after that proved difficult. Russ, I slowly realized, could talk for Middlesex, the south of England and Great Britain. In full flow he was an incredible sight, his grounding in repertory theatre clear – leaning forward conspiratorially, waving his arms around, his voice trilling high and then dropping down low. Opportunity, regret, career, love – all were examined and discussed in terms that had become familiar from his website writings.

When I drove back down to the main road, a good two hours after first pulling up, there was a long silence in the car. I wasn't quite sure what I'd learned. I'd seen a dead bird seemingly come back from beyond the grave, and Sarah had met her first celebrity since Seb Coe turned up to dish out the certificates at her school sports day, but beyond that, I feared my understanding and faith in astrology, and the happiness it might bring, had progressed no further.

I thought back over the month's experiment. Dirsy had been scared twice by two very different women. I'd made another one cry. We were neither happier nor more fulfilled than when we'd set out. On the evidence of those experiences, the predictive arts had not provided the answers we were looking for. Mars certainly had the power to influence Ben's life, but mainly because he insisted on eating so many of their confectionery products.

I glanced in the rear-view mirror at the disappearing outline of Grant Towers. While astrology and tarot had failed Ben and me, they had clearly worked for someone else. Russ was a multi-millionaire TV star with a gorgeous house and a long-term partner, on the brink of that new show in the US with Fox. Ben and I were in limbo, stumbling blindly from one sorry shambles to the next. Who was really right and who was wrong?

I turned the car north-eastwards. In the distance lay the delights of a weekend in Runcorn. Happiness might be on hold for a while yet.

4. HEDONISM

'Together we will experience some magical things'

TOM

Four months into our quest, increasingly spicy suggestions were being put to us by increasingly enthusiastic people. Word seemed to have spread of our malaise of misery and everyone who heard about it had their own course of treatment to suggest.

The most popular of these was that we embrace a lifestyle of pure hedonism. The exact recipe varied – for some it concentrated on bedroom gymnastics of the unfettered kind, for others a heady pharmaceutical adventure through uppers, downers and the lesser-sampled diagonals – but the philosophy remained the same: pleasure through massive illegality.

It had its attractions. Ben and I liked to consider ourselves men of the world, but the world in question consisted of Romford and Hammersmith. Even after a night of abandon at Abra-Kebabra or the Lillee Road swimming baths, we both suspected there might be finer, more toothsome delights out there that we were yet to sample.

I had a dream of a freer, more experimental time and place – the morals and creativity of Big Sur in 1968, transplanted to a state-of-the-art gymnasium complex run by the pick of

King Solomon's 300 concubines and soundtracked, somewhat bizarrely, by mid-period Mamas and Papas.

For Ben it was slightly simpler: a four-day stag-do in Tallinn. 'Thirty blokes drinking giant jugs of lager in the main square, blondes as far as the eye can see and some poor bastard tied to a lamppost with his old boy hanging out,' he said with satisfaction.

'No concubines?' I asked.

'It's a piss-up, Tommy, not a trip to the fucking zoo.'

Sadly, there were barriers in our way. Solomon's harem had been scattered to the winds, Tallinn taken over by a new hard-line mayor intent on halting his city's transformation into the Baltic Blackpool. Back home things weren't much better. Gone were the days when Queen Victoria would entertain guests at Windsor Castle with a post-lunch pipe of opium, or when the most popular fictional sleuth of the day could lean on high-grade cocaine cappuccinos to kick-start his investigations. If Sherlock had existed today, I mused, he would have been hounded from office after an undercover tabloid exposé and forced to eke out a meagre existence playing himself on murder mystery weekends.

Then there were our day jobs at the BBC to think about. The last thing the beleaguered corporation needed were tabloid accusations that its online text cricket commentators were a pair of acid-sozzled libertines who spent their time lying prone on velvet chaises-longues, dictating a series of nonsensical words through slurred lips while Danish depilatory-cream models blew powdered rhino horn into their darkest corners through foot-long golden bugles. As it was, a large proportion of *Daily Mail* readers already believed this to be the case.

It was a conundrum that would have tested Holmes himself. How could we push the boundaries of accepted human behaviour while at the same time keeping our noses clean and our arses out of the slammer? A sustained campaign of police bribery might have worked for some, but we had neither the cash nor contacts to pull it off. And while assuming new identities appealed to half the partnership ('Farewell Ben Dirs, hello Johnny Thunder!') only one of us had the ability to grow a decent distractor of a 'tache.

The answer, when it arrived, came in unexpected fashion. 'Fuck it!' yelled a travel journalist mate of mine over the phone. 'You're probably right,' I muttered. 'It was a stupid idea anyway.'

'The holiday, not the curse,' he replied. 'You, Dirs, a new-age retreat in Italy and 16 fellow Fuckiteers. Fill your flaming boots.'

A moment's frantic Googlage did the rest. 'We are The Hill That Breathes,' I read, 'a space with a difference. When you return home from a Fuck It Week, nothing will be the same.'

There were photos of lithe women lazing around by a pool, suntanned revellers glugging down buckets of booze and a young lady reclining in a hammock wearing nothing but the leanest of bikinis and cheekiest of looks. Dirsy, I thought, you're going to forget Tallinn ever existed.

'Plenty of people have come to The Hill and seen their lives transformed,' promised the blurb. 'When you say "Fuck It!" and take your hands off the steering wheel, you discover that life is the most amazing chauffeur. You can really start experiencing the new!'

I read on. Quotes in parenthesis swam onto the screen and then faded again – 'a magical space', 'the freedom, the beauty!', 'my favourite place in the world'. Specific details of what the week might actually entail were thin on the ground, but it seemed churlish to worry. What could possibly go wrong? We would be free at last, unshackled from guilt, knee-deep in leggy liberation and discarded bikini tops. If there was no mention of the Mamas and Papas, my iPod could sort that out.

'Fuck it,' agreed Ben with satisfaction when I phoned him shaky-handed a few minutes later. 'A holiday, an insult and a mandate all rolled into one. Stick our names down now before someone wakes me up.'

Not everyone was quite so enthused. It didn't take a degree in body language to deduce that my ladyfriend had issues with me heading off into the sunset with a Dirs in tow and a maxim that we fuck it. 'Will there be women there?' she had demanded, arms folded tight and an expression on her face that could have scared Rommell. I thought back to the beguiling bikinis.

'A couple,' I said breezily. 'I'll make sure Ben behaves.'

BEN

'Hedonism?' said Mrs Dirs, looking like I'd just walked a freshly coiled bull mastiff turd all over her newly vacuumed carpet. 'I've seen a documentary about that, it's that thing where desperate old women go abroad to have sex with black men? Where would you fit in?' As far as I knew, she might have been right and I had a week's 'fluffing' on an Italian beach to look forward to.

I've never been big on asking questions ahead of our big adventures. I find it spoils the surprise, and I deliberately asked Tom even less this time round. Instead, I let my imagination run wild: Fuck It? . . . Fuck It? . . . crumpet, there had to be crumpet . . . preferably hot buttered crumpet, browning by a secluded rock-pool . . . reclining on Roman infantrymen, on their hands and knees, *doubling as sun loungers. Inflatable champagne buckets ferrying Nebuchadnezzars of Cristal from shore to shore; dwarves dressed as bell boys with trays on their heads, the trays overflowing with chopped-up coconuts, Coca-Cola and Ferrero Rocher. A tiger cub to wrestle with; American frat boys body-slamming and shouting, 'WOOOO!' very loudly for no apparent reason; naked chocolate wrestling; dining tables made of Japanese women covered in live lobsters and whelks; some bird, dressed as Princess Leia, tied to a fat bloke being thrown live fish; Van Halen smashing out an ear-splitting version of 'Jump', up yonder in a treehouse; sparking up $1,000 cigars while wearing vintage smoking jackets, getting halfway through, lobbing them in the pool and saying to each other, 'You know what, I don't even like cigars.' Buglers and Bovril.*

Nah, I'm a simple man really, plenty of red wine and a drunken fumble in a tepee at the end of it all would do me just fine.

TOM

How do you spot a fellow Fuckiteer? As we stepped into the minibus that picked us up from Ancona airport, we found a red-haired Scotsman and world-weary middle-aged lady from Hastings, chatting animatedly to a curly-haired woman who bore a remarkable resemblance to 1980-era John McEnroe. There wasn't a wild-eyed look between them, let alone a foot-long golden bugle. 'They break you down completely,' we heard McEnroe say. 'You look down and you see all these pieces of you lying on the ground.'

One by one the empty seats were taken. There were two serious-faced girls in their mid twenties, a silent, glowering

Frenchman being towed around by his domineering South African girlfriend and a woman who looked a little like a spaced-out Juliette Lewis. 'It's amazing what can happen up there,' the South African was saying. 'The past-life regressions I was getting last time just blew me away.'

I began to feel a little apprehensive. I glanced across at Ben. He was nodding in an uneasy way as the McEnroe lookalike described the angel that had recently visited her. Where were we going?

The minibus wound its way along the coastal path and then up into the hills. I stared silently out of the windows, watching the folded fields and sleepy hilltop villages slip by and listening to snatches of conversation from other parts of the bus. There was talk of psychic gifts, paranormal powers and painful divorces. One woman had her nose buried in a book. 'Good read?' I enquired politely. She nodded and held it up so I could see.

'*The Wisdom Of Trees*,' she confirmed. 'Quite wonderful.'

Talk moved on to the meals we would be enjoying at The Hill. 'It's amazing,' stressed the Scotsman. 'All vegetarian, all organic.' There were murmurs of approval from around the group.

Ben crammed a fistful of Doritos into his mouth. 'I ate a horse once,' he informed McEnroe. There was a sudden stunned silence. Ben chuckled wistfully, spraying crisp crumbs into the wavy hair of the French chap in the seat in front. 'Raw horse, too. Bastard Japanese bloke told me it was carpaccio.'

With a bump and a brake, the minibus turned off the paved road and began to descend a long gravel track, past twisted olive trees and chocolate brown ploughed fields. Strange signs appeared on the dusty verge – 'You Can Slow

Down Now', 'Shhhh', 'Left, Right'. Down we went, further and further from the eyes of the world, bouncing and turning until a large stone farmhouse came into view, flanked by swaying, waving oaks and pines. A middle-aged man with a smiling woman by his side walked slowly out to greet us as we climbed out. 'Hi,' he said, blinking slowly. 'I'm John. This is my wife Gaia. Welcome to The Hill That Breathes.'

As gurus go, Father Fuck It's initial appearance was decidedly low-key. There were no flowing white robes, merely a navy-blue T-shirt and baggy cotton trousers, no staff in his hand or crown upon his head. His glasses were the sensible, sober-rimmed frames of an accountant, his beard the neatly trimmed variety rather than the waist-long unkemptness of a Maharishi or Manson.

'Thank you,' he smiled, 'for coming to share the week with us. You're in a wonderful place, and together we will experience some magical things.' Ben and I exchanged surreptitious winks against an eager chorus of yeses and mmms. 'Until then, look around, become at home. We'll meet inside the Dome in the morning.'

I looked past him to the scene behind. There were brightly dyed hammocks strung between the trees, a cluster of cream tepees next to an enormous bonfire and a sparkle of swimming-pool blue through the trees. Away to the right, wedged into the side of the hill and overlooking the valley down below, was what looked like a gigantic golf ball. The Dome.

Back inside the farmhouse were a series of austere bedrooms with polished flagstones underfoot and exposed brickwork walls. Small polished statues of a chubby Buddha were tucked into alcoves, old wooden chests of drawers wedged into the cool, dark corners. On the single beds lay small booklets. As

Ben searched for his flip-flops, I flicked one open at random and began to read out loud.

'When you walk, bring attention to what it's like to walk. When you eat, be present to each mouthful; notice the tastes, observe what's happening in your body. When you're mindful, everything can be a gift. Slowly breathe in every moment.'

Dirsy sparked up a cigarette and rapidly breathed in a lungful of smoke, and I continued. 'If you ever feel uncomfortable, frustrated, upset, just watch that feeling. No feeling is any better or worse than any other. Not when viewed impartially.'

Ben flopped down on his bed. 'Watch this feeling,' he said, and gave me a big thumbs-up. 'This place is a winner. Birds, sunshine and talking bollocks. Some woman's even promised to show me how to do Reiki.' He made a chopping motion with his hand and let out a shrill Bruce Lee cry.

I threw the book on the floor. 'Any chance of you playing mixed doubles with McEnroe?'

'Whatever,' he said dismissively. 'This is the new me. The old rules don't apply out here. Just wait till we all get naked and start smearing blood on our faces.'

I hadn't seen him look so pleased since the taxi had arrived to ferry us away from the naturist camp. All the same, I had my concerns. We'd known at the start of our quest that we would be forced from our comfort zones, but I was worried that the path to happiness at The Hill might take him to places he didn't want to visit. Of all the comments I'd overheard in the minibus, one in particular had stuck in my head: 'We will unleash our deepest feelings.'

How would Ben react to being laid emotionally bare in front of sixteen complete strangers? This was a man who was comfortable speaking in public only when he was so mangled words ceased to make any sense, a man whose father, when he left home for the first time, had sent him packing with the infamous instruction: 'Trust no one.'

We were hardly surrounded by the sort of people Donny Dirs would instinctively relate to. 'The internet is the physical manifestation of our collective subconscious,' proclaimed someone loudly in the room next door. 'I find that both fascinating and frightening. Would you agree?'

That night, as we tucked into freshly made aubergine ravioli with a salad of rocket leaves and pecorino, the horse-eating gaffe from earlier still hung in the air like the odour of decaying flesh. Attempting to establish a little group empathy, I brought Ben into an ongoing conversation about tarot cards. 'You've practised it too?' said an anxious woman with the look of Suzi Quatro. 'Maybe you can help me. Last time I did it, one of the cards I turned over was blank. What does that mean?' Ben took a gulp from his glass of red wine. 'Maybe the devil's stolen your soul,' he suggested, and shoved a forkful of pasta into his mouth.

BEN

John might not consider himself a religious man, a sage or a guru, but that hasn't stopped him writing his own little Bible, called 'Fuck It – The Ultimate Spiritual Way'. The phrase 'fuck it', in his words, 'packs an offensive punch', as well as 'tapping into the philosophy of pure anarchy'. Now, when I was ten, I witnessed my nan call my brother a cunt because he refused to believe she'd won the bingo in the Mirror. *The most anarchic thing about her was her purple hair. And if you've witnessed your nan call your* brother a cunt, the word 'fuck' rather loses its sting. Don't get me wrong, Nan Dirs was a good woman (and anyway, she always maintained she called him a 'Cunning Isaac', the daft anti-Semite), it's just that in her world, as in mine, as in just about everyone's world I know, uttering the phrase 'fuck it' is about as rebellious as, well, Mirror bingo . . .

Nestled under a couple of blankets, staring up at the ceiling of the Dome, the nerve-centre of John's operation – St Fuck It's Cathedral, if you will – I felt like I'd been incarcerated in some hippy prison. Like a giant, translucent golf ball, half-buried in steepling pine trees and waiting to be found, The Dome was to be our spiritual home for the next week, so I'd better get used to it. Two three-hour sessions a day, one in the morning, one in the afternoon, lunch in between, free time after. But getting used to it is easier said than done. One minute John's talking about releasing Buddhist monks onto the streets of Detroit to reduce the crime rate, the next one of the female guests is talking about divorcing her husband when she gets home because 'he's a workaholic': 'Darling, am I glad to see you, I've been slogging my guts out all week. How was Italy?' 'Shove it up your bollocks, you workaholic bastard, I'm out of here . . .'

Out come the Crayolas. Everyone is instructed to draw their 'enlightened bitches or bastards', whatever they are, with speech bubbles and everything. Weirdly, and ever so slightly homo-erotically, I pretty much draw Tom (athletic body, blond hair, lots of it) while Tom pretty much draws me (pot-bellied, reclining, receding). Neither of us look particularly happy about it. I become even less comfortable when called upon to explain my drawing to the group because, while not exactly an emotional cripple, I am missing an emotional limb or two. 'Hmmm . . . I just, kind of, erm, not sure really,' is my eloquent attempt to open up. I'd have felt more at ease if John and Gaia had asked me to drop my strides . . .

I feel relaxed though . . . until Gaia keeps on imploring me to relax. How could I not be? I'm curled up in the foetal position under a fleece blanket, the sound of the wind rushing through the pine trees, tumbling towards the abyss of sleep . . . and then I hear it: Relax . . . relax . . .' followed by exaggerated out-breaths, really exaggerated out-breaths, like a Harrier Jump Jet taking off at sea . . . 'Let go of your hold on whatever is causing you pain . . . listen to yourself, stop resisting, relax . . .' This is a nightmare, I'd get more peace laid up in my bed in Romford, a bit of Classic FM on the radio, the sound of meat wagons flying down the A118. 'Go with the flow, give into the flow of life, experience ultimate freedom . . .' I'm starting to zone out when I hear strange sounds emanating from over my left shoulder. It sounds like a top-loading washing machine that's broken free from its plumbing. I open my left eye and see McEnroe clattering towards me, eyes clamped shut, like a giant, hungry caterpillar. It's been a while, but I think I recognize the expression on her face. And those sounds, I definitely recognize those sounds . . . Run for the hills! McEnroe's coming! McEnroe's coming!

TOM

'What makes you happy?' John asked the next morning, cutting to the very heart of it with breakfast still to be digested. Sat around him in the dome, wrapped in blankets like refugees from a war zone, we took it in turns to give instinctive answers.

'Riding my bike,' I suggested. 'A night out with my mates,' offered Ben.

There was a pause from Scottish Mike. 'I've just realized', he said slowly, 'that I am utterly miserable.' He shook his head. 'And I don't know what to do about it.' The South African girl, Nina, looked out through the enormous window. 'I feel divided,' she said. 'There's my inner warrior, who's so strong and powerful, but also there's my inner child, so scared and full of doubt. I think they might be at war with each other.' The smart money, I reflected, would surely be on the warrior.

In the background, McEnroe started making strange grunting noises. Dear God, was she off again? 'Well,' said another woman, trying hard to concentrate, 'in the last few months I've . . . I've . . .' She collapsed into tears and shook her head. 'Sorry,' she sobbed. 'I'm sorry.'

There were sympathetic smiles from around the circle. Gaia crawled over and began stroking Siobhan's tear-streaked face while John blinked out at us like a sleepy owl. 'Find the space within yourself,' he advised. 'It is the safest place.'

He rose slowly to his feet. 'Chinese medicine has so much to teach us in the West,' he said. 'It's about energy, about love and joy, and the West is still catching up with it all.' He gestured for us all to stand up and began shaking his arms vigorously.

'When you allow the energy – the *qi* – to flow, amazing things can happen. It can be the most delicious feeling, so incredibly powerful. I want you to swing your arms like me. Breathe in deeply. Shut your eyes. Feel a looseness in your shoulders, in your elbows, in your hands. Let all that tension go.'

I squinted furtively through half-closed eyes. People were flicking their hands around as if trying to dislodge a stubborn piece of Sellotape. Mike had a look of fierce concentration on his face. Siobhan had stopped crying. McEnroe was smiling serenely. I tried not to speculate why.

'Let the energy flow,' intoned John in a calm, serious voice. 'Feel it coming through your belly-button and bouncing down to your feet. You know, more and more people over here are starting to understand about this power – you hear Madonna talking about looking out over a crowd at one of her concerts and feeling the energy coming back to her, and this is what she means. In ten years' time, everyone will be talking like this.'

His words echoed and ricocheted around the Dome. For ten minutes we shook, our shoulders slumped and our limbs flopped about. 'Now,' said John, opening his eyes. 'I want you all to try something. Put your hands out in front of you, fingers a few inches apart. When we form a circle with our arms, it allows the energy to really flow.' He looked around. 'What can you feel?'

There were gasps of excitement around the room. 'Wow! My fingers – they're tingling!' 'Oh my God! So are mine!'

John smiled drowsily. 'Great!'

I took a deep breath and focused on the feelings coming through my hands. Yup – a definite tingling sensation, like pins and needles in every finger. I glanced to my left at Ben. He had his hands out in front of him like a gunslinger in a Wild West shoot-out. 'Any good?' I whispered. He made a face.

'You know the shaking thing? Wouldn't that have messed about with the blood supply in our ha—'

The thought was interrupted by an exclamation of delight from the other side of the dome. Nina was making expansive hand gestures like a politician on a podium. 'Mine's like a warm ball!' she laughed. John chuckled indulgently.

'Play with that ball!' he said. 'Turn it over in your hands, let it expand, move it around!'

We split into pairs and stood opposite each other, taking it in turns to hold a palm out in front of us while the other person waved their hands around it. 'Let the healing energy flow,' droned John. 'What can you feel? Heat?'

Ben hovered his hands over mine. 'Anything?' I asked. He frowned.

'That is seriously weird. Your hands feel . . . cold. I can feel a definite coldness!'

'They are cold,' I said. 'I went for a swim before breakfast.'

'No, but I can feel this real coldness coming off them.'

'Yeah. I've got cold hands. The pool's not heated.'

'Just ordinary cold?'

'Yeah.'

'Oh.'

We changed partners, me to Nina, Ben to her boyfriend, Jean-Pierre. This time we were told to move our hands slowly up and down and around their entire bodies, sensing pain and injury, beaming healing energies into them.

If it looked a little like we were measuring each other up for invisible suits, it was tailor-made for some in the group. 'Uuuaaah,' sighed McEnroe, as Siobhan hesitatingly wafted a palm over her face. 'Ooofa-ooofa-oooh.'

I had my own hands poised over Nina's hips, my nose an inch away from her sturdy rear end. I glanced to my right, where Ben's hands were poised an inch above Jean-Pierre's burgeoning crotch.

'Still cold?' I mouthed silently. 'Or nice and warm?'

BEN

Everyone will be talking like Madonna in 10 years' time? Did someone just say that? That's all we need, the planet populated by eight billion bell-ends in leotards . . .

I'm crouched down now, bent at the knees, waving my hand over Jorge's old fella like a customs officer who suspects he's packing a piece. 'Oh,' I think to myself, 'so it's spiritual *hedonism . . .' I want to feel Jean-Pierre's* qi, *I really do, but I'm getting nothing. I'm far too rational for all this. I'll grant you, I'm relaxed, but then I'm going to be, I've got nothing more strenuous planned for the afternoon than a full body massage in the woods with an Italian lady called Sonia. I must remember to touch wood that I don't get wood in the woods . . .*

'I've learnt how to do nothing and not feel guilty about it,' announces Quatro to the group, to knowing smiles all round. I should be teaching this group, I've never felt guilty about doing nothing in my life . . . we're all lying down again, and I've only been up for an hour.

'Lying down is like plugging in your phone and recharging the batteries,' says John, 'sitting at a desk can slowly kill you'. Maybe John knows someone who can get me a job which involves lying down all day?

TOM

'So you see,' said John, 'the mind is a very powerful tool.' The sixteen of us were spread out against the Dome's walls like numbers on a clock face, listening to some astonishing tales. Buddhist monks had been wired to machines that showed the 'happiness centre' of their brains glowing more brightly than any other person's. During the Cold War, the Russians had developed a crack group of psychic spies who had become so highly skilled that they could see into military bunkers thousands of miles away, without ever leaving Moscow. Concrete walls, metal filing cabinets, sentries armed to the teeth – nothing could stop these supernatural secret agents from reading the West's confidential documents. 'When the CIA saw this, they were like, wow! We have to do this too!' recounted John. 'This was Harvard, Berkeley – mainstream science.'

McEnroe had set up an electronic keyboard by the window and was noodling away like Peter Gabriel *c*.1975. 'Imagine you are floating along in a beautiful boat,' whispered Gaia. We lay in our nests of blankets like incubating eggs. 'Floating, floating, floating. The current is taking you just where you want to go, and you feel a deep sense of contentment. Smell the sweetness on the breeze, feel the warmth of the sun on your face.'

As she spoke she was stepping gently around the room, kneeling by each prone figure to lay her hands on their shoulders or thighs. 'You feel the boat come to rest on a beach. You step slowly onto the soft sand. In the distance you can see a small cottage, and you walk towards it, feeling safe and secure. In the house there is someone you care very deeply about. You push open the door. They smile at you, and tell you something very special.' She paused. 'Now, slowly come back to the Dome, to us all here today. Who is that person, and what did they say?'

I could hear a strange snuffling noise. Lord alive – surely McEnroe hadn't reached another Grand Slam final? I turned around. Just visible under a huge pile of blankets was Ben's upturned face, his mouth wide open and his eyes firmly shut. He was fast asleep.

I tried not to make eye contact with Gaia. I had pictured Ray Stubbs, and he had told me the football scores. It was something I preferred to analyse in private.

*

TOM

That evening, five days in, the mood around the long dining table was as muted as the candlelight. Everyone, from Nina to Siobhan and Mike, looked like they'd been through the emotional wringer. For all the Fucking It that had been done, it didn't seem to have produced much obvious happiness.

For the past few days I'd found myself humming an old Sheryl Crow song. It had become a way of rationalizing everything that had gone on in the Dome: 'If it makes you happy, it can't be that bad.' Looking around the group now, I began to wonder if we'd been missing something. Maybe it was time to experiment a little, to alter the balance. As the old Essex proverb goes, it ain't easy smiling when your head's stuck up your own arse. Maybe it was time to crank up the old-fashioned fun.

John and Gaia were tucked up in bed at their house across the hill. Outside there was a perfect pyramid of a bonfire just waiting to be lit. Inside there was only the library, with its *Power Animal Meditations, Celtic Shamen* and *The Indian Tipi.* The moment was ripe for Ben and I to step in. 'Right!' shouted Dirsy, holding two bottles of red wine in one hand and a tray of glasses in the other. 'Who's up for a campfire hoe-down?' I grabbed a lighter and lantern and pushed open the door. 'Last one down there buys the next bottle!' I yelled, and legged it into the darkness. One by one, two by two, the ranks by the fire were swelled. By the time the flames were flickering high we had a full platoon of Fuckiteers out under the stars.

It worked. Whether it was the marshmallows we toasted ('Flump! Who needs a Flump?') or the extravagant use of brandy as a fire-booster ('Argh! My face is blistering!') there was an instant and obvious improvement in the general mood. Bongos were brought down from the farmhouse, a cobwebbed didgeridoo was dug out from somewhere. Bottles with various amounts of booze left in them were transformed into one-note flutes and used to form an impromptu octave. 'Tommy,' whispered Ben at one point, as strange honks and tootles filled the chilly night air, 'is this my beer or middle C?'

Stories started doing the rounds – the first single anyone bought, their first snog. 'Tell me one thing you've never told any other adult,' one woman murmured to Ben. He frowned.

'When I was six,' he said, 'I used to go foraging in the woods for Smurfs.'

People who hadn't smiled all week were laughing and joking like old friends. If no one was getting naked or dancing sensuously through the smoke, at least there was some high-fiving and hugging breaking out.

'It was incredible how I met Jean-Pierre,' Nina whined, looking proudly at her near-mute French beau, face glowing in the firelight. 'I saw him across a pub, and I just felt this connection. He started walking across the room, and I ran over to him, and I said to him, "Where are you going?" And do you know what he said?'

'For a slash?' Ben suggested jovially.

There was another trademark silence. 'Wine,' I said hurriedly. 'Who needs some more wine?'

BEN

Sitting around the fire, chatting about our most embarrassing moments and the first records we bought, I think to myself, 'I couldn't be hanging out with a sounder group of people – so what are they all doing here?' Sure, there's plenty of baggage on display, plenty of genuine sob stories, but I still feel like R.P. McMurphy in One Flew Over The Cuckoo's Nest *on discovering most of his fellow patients are voluntary: 'What do you think you are, for Christ sake, crazy or something? Well you're not!'*

After an hour or so the mood turns spooky, as inevitably happens at bonfire chats, before everyone runs out of ghost stories and things take a turn for the maudlin.

'What's your worst loss?' asks Siobhan, and I stare into the flames, turning over logs with a stick, anything to avoid catching her eye. As the sad stories are churned out, I shift uneasily, feeling slightly guilty. Nothing that bad's ever happened to me. Loving parents, good mates, no illnesses, easy life. Worst loss? England losing to West Germany in the semi-finals of Italia '90 stung a bit, but next to all the death and despair, it's pretty small fry . . .

There's a passage in John's book where he states: 'Me? I don't usually do any work. I just do things I like.' He doesn't mention his days as an advertising whizz, the hours of slog that entailed, the mental turmoil. One of the keys to happiness is, in John's words, 'taking your hands off the steering wheel'. Then again, it's easy to take your hands off the steering wheel when your car's a Roller, the handbrake's off and you're rolling towards your destination down a mile-long gravel drive . . .

TOM

With a mellow autumn sun warming our faces and crisping the windblown leaves, John led us solemnly up a winding path to a wooden platform jutting out from the top of the hill. We stood silently with hands clasped behind our backs, looking down at the dozing valley below like golfers on an elevated tee wondering whether to play safe with a three-iron or dig out the one-wood for a mighty swipe.

For a while, no one moved. John was lost in his own world, hands in the gunslinger pose in front of his hips, staring dreamily at a spot on the ground a few feet away. To his left, same faraway expression on her face, Gaia was gaping at her fingers and moving them slowly about with wonder. To his right, McEnroe was slumped forward from the waist, arms hanging over her toes like a broken doll.

I looked at Ben. With one hand meditatively scratching his chin, the other absentmindedly scratching his arse, he looked like a down-at-heel philosopher specializing in Epicureanism. A butterfly flapped towards him, circled his head twice and then landed on his chest. He regarded it seriously, its colourful wings opening and closing like delicate bellows, before it fluttered away on a wonky, drunken route through the trees.

John roused himself and smiled sleepily. For the next hour he took us through a series of *qi-gong* exercises, slowly punching an invisible opponent, miming an archer drawing a bow, unhurriedly raising and lowering his hands and arms while we followed suit like a slow-motion disco troupe.

At first it felt frustrating. I wanted to do it at normal speed, or have some music playing in the background, to make a competition out of it and see who could throw the best left jab. Wasn't there a way we could split into teams or get a ball involved?

The movements went on and on, eight of each, in the same order and fashion. Gradually my thoughts became less frenetic, the questions quieter. I listened to the wind shushing through the trees, focused on the ivy that was draped over branches and trunks like bucolic bunting. At the grass by my feet, a confused-looking hornet stumbled through the blades and bumbled onwards. The minutes went by, but I was barely aware of their passing. It was the calmest I'd felt in months.

'What I'd like you to do now,' John said eventually, his voice startling against the still silence, 'is to take a piece of paper and make a list – all your best qualities on one side, and all your worst on the other. We'll meet again in the Dome when you're ready.'

McEnroe was back on the keyboards when we reconvened, draped over the coffin-shaped instrument like a devastated mourner. For a moment I thought she was asleep, but then the noise of her sobbing became audible. I looked down at my lists. Maybe this hadn't been such a good idea. Could this constant self-obsession be part of the problem? As a pseudo-sage might put it, self-indulgence is only a few characters away from being self-ish.

Gaia gazed around at the unhappy faces and spread her arms. 'Devote yourself to the fact that you feel shit! Acceptance isn't trying to put it right – you are okay as you are. Say it with me, "I love myself for being stuck! I love myself for being unhappy every single day of my life! I embrace myself as a complete loser!"'

John turned his head towards her with warmth in his eyes. 'The key thing that keeps you imprisoned is "I am not okay",' he said. 'The liberation is, you are okay as you are!'

A golden light was filtering through the Dome, fractured and veined by the swaying pines outside. 'You are okay as you are,' repeated Gaia, 'and we will use some ancient shaman magic to really confirm that in our hearts and in our minds and in our souls.

'I want you to take your lists out to the woods and fields, and find something out there that represents each of the things you hate about yourself. Collect these things together, and then find a space here that is special to you. Dig a hole and bury these things, and as you bury them, know that they are gone forever. This is your shrine to you. Show your love and celebration of you!'

There was an excited rush for the door. I found Ben leaning against a tree, looking perplexed. 'Let's do this together,' I said. 'What's first on your list? – Laziness? Procrastination? Gluttony?'

'All right,' he said angrily. 'You're not my dad. Anyway, I think I might have got the wrong end of the stick.'

He showed me his piece of paper. In large letters at the top of the page it said, 'SMOKE TOO MUCH.'

'Okay,' I said briskly. 'That's fine. Just get a fag out of that packet in your shorts and bury it. Job done.'

He bristled. 'Bury a fag? Have you gone mad?' He paused, pulled out a cigarette, jammed it between his lips and grinned. 'I've got a better idea. I'm going to cremate it instead.'

I scanned my own list. 'Easily bored,' I'd written. 'Daydream too much. Do what I want.' I looked around our feet. There were twigs, leaves and Ben's battered flip-flops. Nothing that really seemed to sum up bored.

'Maybe we're looking at this the wrong way round,' said Ben thoughtfully. 'Maybe we should find the object first, and then find a fault that fits it.' We strolled towards the house.

'The bike's over there,' he pointed out. 'You're always pissing off on your bike, no matter what anyone else wants to do. That's one of your list covered.'

I spotted an empty beer bottle by one of the dustbins. 'I like it,' I said. 'There's your gluttony.'

'If I'd written gluttony.'

'If you'd written gluttony.'

So it was that we found ourselves atop the very toppermost of the hills as the sun went down, two small mounds of freshly turned-over soil between our ankles, the dustbins emptier by one beer bottle, a bike missing an inner tube, a fag packet short of a butt and a small chopping board liberated from the kitchens, chanting lines from the Oompa-Loompa song, holding our arms aloft and urinating unsteadily on the makeshift shrines at our feet.

'Dirsy,' I mumbled, 'do you worry we might be going insane?'

'Tommy,' he replied, 'as they say in these parts: Fuck It.'

BEN

Some might choose to call it spiritual hedonism, others might call it lying about in a hammock. It's not rocket science, it's not even science: if you put your feet up for a week in an Italian bolthole, you're going to discover peace. The balls of energy, the qi-gong, that's not really doing much for me. My dad likes to relax by doing the gardening and he occasionally closes his eyes for half-an-hour on the settee, but no one's ever referred to him as the Sage of Stepney . . .

Parts of John's book puzzle me. 'Imagine someone meaning a tad less to you,' is his advice on relationships, with an eyebrow-

*raising disregard for the all-consuming power of love and the grip
it can have on people. 'Money doesn't matter that much, really,'
is his financial advice. 'The more the world values what you do
and what you are giving, the more it will give back.' Any nurses
reading this? Forget all that arse-wiping and wrestling with
drunks in A&E – apparently the world would value you far
more if you were playing top-level golf for a living. 'If you have
[no money] enjoy life as it is . . . if you have oodles, say fuck
it and start basking in the fruits of the world thinking you're such
an amazing person that it throws so much at you . . .'*

TOM

There were no two ways about it – cracks were starting to
appear in the facade of Fuck. 'John thinks because he had a
bad time and came to a hill, that will work for everyone,' said
a pale girl who'd been there for two weeks already. 'It won't.'
'I used to tell people that he wasn't like other gurus,' said
another. 'Now I think about it, he stands up talking, uninterrupted and unquestioned by any of us, while we all lie at his
feet. In a really weird dome.'

One morning, Gaia enthusiastically extolled the virtues of
doing exactly what your instincts told you, regardless of the
consequences. 'This is how you find true freedom,' she eulo-
gized. 'You might worry what other people might think of
you, but you shouldn't. The freedom you express will spread
to them too in the end. They too will benefit.

'Think about what you were like as a child. You didn't
worry about tomorrow, or whether something was right or
wrong. You just acted as you felt you should – you laughed
when you felt like laughing, you were angry when you felt

anger. We lose that as we become adults. That is a tragedy. When you follow your inner instincts, you will be amazed at the positivity that comes back at you.'

It was an attractive idea, the notion that we could all wander round doing and saying exactly what we wanted. It also looked like a social car-crash waiting to happen. 'I want you to complete these sentences,' said Gaia. 'If I followed my inner instinct in my job, I would . . . If I followed my inner instinct with the opposite sex, I would . . .'

My answers on the work one were easy: I would tell two people in my office they were complete twats. Sadly I couldn't see there being much positivity coming back to me; I'd merely be offending two people who were already social outcasts and probably no more twattish than I was to others. Wouldn't it be better to just try to get along with them instead?

I looked at my second answer as the group took it in turns to read out theirs. 'I would listen to my own music and dance to its rhythm,' said the Quatro lookalike, opaquely. 'I want a baby,' said the woman seated between us, and burst into tears. I cleared my throat. Either I'd misunderstood the question, or my instincts were rather more primitive than anyone else was admitting to. 'I would . . . I would . . .' I looked up at Ben. He was staring vacantly at Siobhan's magnificent bosom. At least one man understood.

*

TOM

The eighteen of us were back on the platform, sitting cross-legged in the lunchtime sun. A ginger cat was parading round the circle of seated Fuckiteers like a visiting dignitary, accepting tickles and scratches with a regal haughtiness before padding on to the next subservient subject.

'What is it we want from life?' John asked, half-rhetorically. 'We want love, we want to feel happy, but what specifics do we want?'

The endless hours of lying around, barely having to lift a finger, dissecting and discussing, had seeped into all our bones. Some slowly inclined their heads in thought, others simply gazed at the clouds tip-toeing apologetically by up above. All of us were moving at the reduced speed of action figures whose batteries were running very, very low.

'I read a very interesting thing about Posh Spice,' he said. 'When she was young, she had one very clear ambition: she wanted to be more famous than Persil. That was her motivation.'

Some kids dream of becoming doctors. Others want to be film stars. 'Toilet Duck,' I pictured the fifteen-year-old Posh thinking to herself as she cast her eyes along a supermarket shelf in Cheshunt. 'Not enough. Kellogg's Cornflakes? Just a touch too much.'

'Of course,' said John, 'she achieved what she wanted. She's a great role model for many of us in that respect.' I thought about the silicone-enhanced frontage, the swingeing diets, the single with Dane Bowers. If memory served, that duet had been called 'Out Of Your Mind'.

'You know what? You too can have it all,' declared John. 'You can have whatever you want. If you want £5 million in your bank account, you can have it. If you want a new job, you can have it.

'I'm talking about manifestation, and it's an incredibly powerful tool. The cosmos has a way of rewarding those who really focus on something. Just throw it out there into the energy field, and it's amazing what gets thrown back. Maybe you want a new sports car, a Ferrari. Imagine how it feels to sit in those leather seats, what that steering-wheel feels like under your hands. Picture yourself driving along in it, the noise the engine is making.

'Sometimes we get stuck on the how. Forget the how. Remember the what.

'Ask. Believe. Receive.'

Nina was nodding furiously. 'That's right,' she chirped. 'It happened for Seal. He manifested that he wanted a super-model girlfriend, and three months later he started going out with Heidi Klum!'

I put my hand up. 'World-famous rock star Seal – multi-millionaire, world-famous rock star Seal – managed to go out with a supermodel?' I scratched my cheek. 'How the hell did he pull that one off?'

BEN

Manifestation? You might as well do a Jiminy Cricket and wish upon a star. Sit back, expect positive change and it will happen. Just like that. I've never met a rich man yet who got where he was by day-dreaming, but I know a few dreamers who haven't got a pot to piss in. If Alan Sugar had relied on manifestation, he'd still be in Hackney knocking out car aerials he got from a mush in Shepherd's Bush. Instead, he's parading around in a Rolls Royce Phantom and shacked up in a mansion in Essex. Unlike Jiminy Cricket, who uses an umbrella to get round, has got holes in his socks and sleeps in a matchbox . . .

I'm starting to think McEnroe might be a stooge, it's the only way to explain some of the stuff she's coming out with at Gaia's tea ceremony. 'This one's like swallowing a sword,' says McEnroe as she necks another thimbleful, and I'm not sure if she thought that was a good or bad thing. 'This one's like being stroked . . . this one's like being punched . . .' Much more of this, and I'll be serving up a definitive comparison . . .

Don't get me wrong, this definitely isn't your average builder's splosh, and I'm definitely getting a bit of a buzz out of it. But essentially it is what it is, eight people sat round in the sun drinking tea. 'This one's sex tea,' coos McEnroe, and all of a sudden the rest of the girls are agreeing. If you suggest to someone that they might feel like sex, then the chances are they'll probably shrug and say, 'Yeah, come to think of it, I wouldn't mind a bunk up.' But at that moment, with McEnroe bearing down on me, I know what Boy George was getting at when he said he'd rather just have a cup of tea . . .

'I want the freedom . . . to wear a hat,' drawls Mike over in the Dome. He sounds like Marlon Brando free-forming in Apocalypse Now. 'You can tell everything about someone's life from their breathing,' says Gaia, 'you will get to a door . . . be open to it and walk through to the next level . . .' Come on, baby, take a chance with us . . .

We're scattered round the Dome now, some standing, others lying down, everyone gulping down great big slugs of air, like a school of fish washed up on a beach. After ten minutes, my head feels like it's been scooped out, my arms have fallen dead and I'm hearing strange noises all around me. I open my left eye and see McEnroe on her back, legs pedalling in the air, while Gaia is on her knees, shushing into her ear. John sticks on 'Stairway To Heaven', but the Gypsy Kings version, and I pull my duvet over my face . . .

I open my eyes again, and in my absence, the place has

degenerated into an apocalyptic rave. Quatro's throwing shapes like a woman half her age, while Jean-Pierre looks like he's either been struck down with some kind of palsy or he's overdone it on the mushroom shakes. On the other side of the Dome, Dave's ripped his top off and is going ruddy berserk. He's smashed through the doors of perception with an axe and God alone knows what he's seeing on the other side. There's a fair bit of crying . . . it looks like an explosion in a meow meow factory . . .

After an hour, the Dome resembles the last dregs of a full moon party on Koh Phangan. Bodies scattered everywhere, people rocking back and forth under blankets, only a man called Matthew is still standing, and it turns out he's just got back from a trip to the jungle where he's been visiting his ancestors. I find Tom leaning up against a tree outside, looking ever so slightly confused. 'What particular Chinese-made medicine did they put in that tea?' he asks.

TOM

I looked around at our compadres. We were on a meditation walk, following John and Gaia around the estate at an incredibly slow pace, told we should take in every smell, every noise and every tiny detail we saw. Like a lot of what we'd done it was better in theory than action. Creeping around at a lame snail's pace, staring slack-jawed at the back of each other's heads, we looked like a zombies' day outing. No one spoke, no one laughed, no one questioned anything.

I was filled with a sudden desire to run around whooping, to do something active, to lose myself in everything that was out there rather than just lying around endlessly thinking about myself. For the first time since that dreadful muddy afternoon at the National Cross Country Championships, my life-long love affair with exercise felt like it might be back on.

I turned away from the silent statues and crept down the hill, filled with the liberation of the truant schoolboy. I'd have a swim, that's what I'd do – dive into that freezing water, see how far I could swim underwater, ride a lovely wave of adrenaline and endorphins. With a spring in my step and a whistle on my lips, I grabbed my trunks and goggles from the farmhouse and trotted through the trees towards the pool.

I had been beaten to it. The first thing I saw was John, his eyes shut, standing with his arms outstretched like a man about to dive off the high board, but they were all there – McEnroe, lying face down by the pool, trailing her limp fingers through the water, Siobhan's waving healing hands over Mike, Nina measuring Jean-Pierre up for another invisible suit.

Never had there been a scenario less suited to energetic front crawl. For a moment I considered taking a running jump and doing an old-fashioned bomb. It would be in the spirit of Fuck It, after all.

I sighed. It was impossible. There was doing what you wanted and there was becoming a figure of hate. With a heavy heart I edged over to one of the sun-loungers, lay down and shut my eyes.

In the distance came a faint droning sound, like a fight between two angry wasps. There had been no state-of-the-art gymnasium and no Mamas and Papas, but I'd learnt a few things: that I didn't have the faith for faith healing, that Ben and I weren't the only ones wanting big answers to big questions.

The sun seemed to go behind a cloud. I opened my eyes to see Georgie straddling my sun-lounger, shaking Reiki fingers at my under-utilized Speedos. The droning sound had got louder. With a clatter like a machine-gun, two enormous camouflage-painted Army helicopters reared up over the hill and swept past with an ear-splitting howl. Another appeared from the other direction.

They hovered over us, rotor-blades battering the air, the pilot's faces visible as they stared blankly down. I glanced at John. He was staring back at them, arms aloft like an ancient wizard, the down-draft blowing the grass and leaves into frantic panics.

Waco, I thought. It's going to be Waco all over again. Ropes would appear from the helicopters' bellies, disgorging paratroopers, tanks smashing through the perimeter fence. No – John would reach out like Sauron or Darth Vader, plucking the choppers from the sky, smashing them into the hillside as blue streaks of electricity ripped from his fingertips.

Tallinn. Why hadn't we just gone to Tallinn?

5. MONKS

'Every day is like Sunday'

BEN

When I was six months old, I was baptized. Aged eight I made my First Communion. Aged eleven I made my first Confession. By the time I was fourteen, me and my mates had lapsed so far that our sole reason for attending Mass was to stare at the angelic-looking blonde who sat, looking chaste, on the opposite side of the cathedral. Her mother may well have thought how sweet it was that five adolescent boys be venerating God on a Sunday rather than venerating cider in the graveyard. What she wasn't to know was that we were actually paying weekly homage to her daughter's quite spectacular breasts.

By the age of fifteen we had discovered that spectacular breasts weren't confined to cathedrals and were in fact roaming free in the pubs, clubs and multi-storey car parks of Essex. So we stopped going to the cathedral. My attendance of an all-boys Jesuit comprehensive in Romford necessitated a few more years of enforced worship, but my faith dwindled to such an extent that by the Upper Sixth I was cheering every time Father McNamara raised the monstrance above his head at Benediction, as if he were Bobby Moore and the sacred vessel in his hands the Jules Rimet Trophy. But the nadir came when a friend's brother burst into Midnight Mass, high as a kite on Lowenbrau, and hollered his conviction that 'Morrissey is the only King'. We guffawed, saucer-eyed, as he wrestled with a game deacon before the altar, kicking and a' gouging in the bread and the wine and the beer. And I decided there and then that, except for weddings, funerals and Christenings, I'd never go back.

That I attended a Catholic school at all was down to some creativity on the part of my mum who, years ahead of her time, convinced a string of nuns, priests and headmasters that she and her offspring were suitably wholesome and devout. The truth was rather different, with Mum always adamant she be buried in the woods in a biodegradable cardboard box, not a holy man in sight. My dad is possibly the most religiously indifferent person I've ever met, although he and his mates have a lot of fun at funerals, including the time one pal was disappearing into the flames and a wag shouted to the old boy down the front, 'You might as well jump on Fred, we'll stick you on a low light.' My mother's mother was a believer, of that there is no doubt. But then she was perhaps the most miserable person I've ever met, a cheerleader for God minus the smile (or indeed the teeth) and the pom-poms. Administered the last rites more times than Evel Knievel, for her last fifty years on this planet Nan Langfield was genuinely irritated to discover she was still alive on opening her eyes each morning. So desperate to get to heaven, she forgot to enjoy life on earth.

Coincidentally, Tom also attended a Jesuit school, but while I look back on those days through a sweet, incense-infused fog of nostalgia (despite, or more probably because of, my lack of faith) he sees things rather differently. Some people draw strength from a religious education, some hilarity. Others let it grind them down. Tom let it grind him down, although it's not difficult to see why. 'Give me a child and I will give you the man' goes the old Jesuit maxim, but Francis Xavier probably didn't have in mind running round fields in his pants or playing rugby in three feet of snow when he coined the phrase back in the 1500s. While this cruel streak meant my school produced lots of very good rugby players, it also ensured many of its alumni view Catholicism with more than a hint of suspicion. My P.E. teacher, subsequently unmasked as a sex case, didn't exactly help. 'I've never been so embarrassed in my life,' he once said after watching my cricket team get bowled out for 13. I wonder does he feel the same way now.

How, then, did we find ourselves in a medieval monastery in the Scottish Highlands? That's a long way for two Essex boys to drag all that religious baggage. For a while I thought we'd been blackballed. The official reply to my letter (no emails or phone calls accepted) had been a long time coming, so long that I'd started to imagine one of the monks, surrounded by ancient pigments and quills, painstakingly illuminating an invitation in his cell. When it did arrive, it was disappointingly humdrum, just a photocopied note of acceptance. These monks had clearly let their calligraphy skills slip since the Renaissance. But to answer my earlier question, the way I saw it, where once we were boys, now we were men, although what part the Jesuits played in that transformation is open to debate. Perhaps through the eyes of adults we'd see things differently. This was our chance to contemplate Catholicism on our own terms, rather than through the prism of chain-smoking priests, sadistic swimming teachers and 1,001 detentions. I wondered if the monastic lifestyle –

the peace, the order, the self-discipline, the self-examination – just might have something to offer as I blundered towards middle-age.

TOM

I know some very nice priests. I know some very nice nuns. I also know that going into a church still conjures up in me the same intense feelings of doom and boredom that it did when I was six years old.

An hour every Sunday and an hour every Wednesday, plus countless hours on my knees in the days in between, from before I could talk to an age when I was finally allowed to speak out. Some tips for all religious leaders out there: if you want to get children into your belief system, don't make them sit still in a gloomy hall full of stern old matrons on their precious days off school, don't insist that they wear uncomfortable neat clothes at an age when a collar is a yoke and don't smack them with clogs even if they wilfully and repeatedly refuse to do what they're told.

On the way home from Italy, feeling tanned and relaxed, I had been filled with a sunny optimism. Maybe things have moved on, I thought. Maybe it won't be like it was in the old days. By definition there couldn't be any stern old matrons in a monastery. Why, monks don't even wear clogs!

Still, Ben's claim that he was looking forward to the 'self-discipline and self-examination' brought a smile to my face. The only self-examination I had ever seen him undertake involved a finger and his nose. As for self-discipline, this was a man who thought that abstinence was a green alcoholic beverage favoured by the nineteenth-century French.

'Mark my words,' he said cheerfully as we drove past Inverness,

'these monks might be able to teach me a thing or two about happiness and contentment, but religion-wise, I'll never let the bastards get me . . .'

BEN

Pluscarden Abbey is situated in a secluded glen six miles south-west of Elgin in Morayshire, a grey, imposing edifice that appears to have erupted, fully formed, from the soil beneath it. The monastery buildings date from the thirteenth century, but the Reformation meant that by the end of the 1600s, Pluscarden was already a ruin. The present community was founded in 1948 from Prinknash Abbey in Gloucestershire, and, while twenty Benedictine monks are currently in residence, restoration continues to this day. As we wound our way towards it, separating confused fawns from their mothers and dodging pheasants along the way, I began to wonder if we'd made a mistake coming almost directly from the sun-drenched Italian Marche. Trees swaying violently overhead, rain thrashing against the windscreen, it felt as if we'd swapped The Hill That Breathes for the Valley of the Dead.

Mercifully, when the doors of the abbey creaked open, we weren't greeted by Peter Cushing, but rather by Brother Gabriel, whose bald head attached to a pipe-cleaner of a neck poking out of a white habit gave him the look of a bespectacled tortoise trying to escape his shell.

'I swear I know you from somewhere,' said Brother Gabriel, at least half a dozen times, as he showed us to our rooms. Where did he think he knew me from? Ibiza 2003? Last year's world darts final in Frimley? His conviction that this wasn't the first time we'd met became even more mysterious when he revealed he'd been holed up in Pluscarden for the last twenty-one years. 'Up every morning at 4 a.m. for Vigils and Lauds for 365 days a year since 1988,' said Brother Gabriel with a disbelieving shake of the head, while Tom shifted uncomfortably, looking like a man who doesn't normally start prayers until five. Otherwise, Tom looked to be coping admirably, and had soon dropped the 'Brother' altogether and begun calling our guide simply Gabriel. Not up to speed with monkish etiquette, I couldn't help thinking this was a little bit previous. What next? Gabby? Bro? G-Dog?

Our rooms were, as expected, basic. No pink stucco walls, no distressed bedside cabinets and not a bronze Buddha in sight; just a child's bed, a crucifix hovering above it and a Formica desk groaning under a raft of Christian literature.

'The day starts at 4.45 a.m., with Vigils and Lauds for an hour and three-quarters,' explained G-Dog, as Tom and I exchanged pained expressions, as if we were cell-mates contemplating a five-stretch and G-Dog was our key-jangling jailer.

'Vigils usually takes place during the hours of darkness, while most people in the outside world are asleep, so it expresses our particular longing for God. We chant psalms and listen to Scripture and writings of the Saints. Lauds is the monks celebrating the coming of the new day, and the psalms and texts tend to be of a joyful mood.' I'll believe that when I see it, I thought. What did they have in store for us in the morning? A rousing rendition of 'Sit Down, You're Rockin' the Boat', with heel kicks and jazz hands? 'Between Lauds and the evening service at 6 p.m., called Vespers, there are four short prayer services called the "little hours",' continued G-Dog. 'Prime is at 7 a.m., Terce at 8.45 a.m., Sext at 12.35 p.m., None at 2.15 p.m. These last about ten minutes each and help keep us monks with our praying throughout the day.

Actual Mass, the Holy Eucharist, is at 9 a.m., while there's also Compline at 8.05 p.m., the last office of the day.' And after that? Buttered crumpets? A pillow fight in Brother Martin's cell? A couple of hours kicking back with the DVD box-set of *The Wire*? 'After that we retire to bed.'

No pumpkin risotto at Pluscarden. No sweet, plump Italian tomatoes still attached to the vine. No delicate ricotta-stuffed ravioli. No blood-red Chianti for quaffing. No mighty slabs of gorgonzola. No blondes with spectacular tits. Only bald men and omelette pie. Or was it eggy bread and butter pudding? In all honesty, Tom and I couldn't agree on what our first meal was. What we did agree on was that on a monk's dinner table, the pepper pot is king. Not that I could register my displeasure, for meals in the refectory are taken in silence, except for a lone monk reading solemnly from a pulpit on high. Perhaps it was this enforced muteness that had held monastic cooking back through the ages. Someone occasionally kicking up a fuss about the state of the menu might not do much for a restaurant's ambience, but it's quite likely to concentrate the chef's mind on turning out some platters that matter.

Taking meals in silence is as alien to most people as playing table-tennis while naked. It contradicts what we are taught from an early age, namely that meals are social occasions, when friends and family gather round a table in mutual respect and co-operation, discuss the day's events, banter and generally be merry. Staring straight down the refectory at Abbot Hugh, silhouetted against the background of a stained-glass window like a giant bat, grim-faced monks arrayed down either flank, I couldn't help thinking a steak dinner with Jeffrey Dahmer would have been less tense. Still, being mute has its advantages: no having to explain yourself if you don't fancy a second helping of omelette pie (just a polite raise of the hand and a smile as if to say, 'mmm, delicious, but I'm quite full thank you'), no spirit-crushing small talk with the other guests. Just the scraping of knives and forks on plates and G-Dog reading book reviews from the *Tablet*, a Catholic newspaper. An occasional belch from one of the old guys. The comings and goings of the black-habited novices, fetching syrupy fruit juices, apples and homemade cheese from the kitchen. The faint whistle of what I took to be Tom's will to live expiring.

As I nibbled on my cheddar with mouse-sized bites, mindful there would be no more food that evening, I noticed one of the elderly monks staring across at Tom intensely. And then I realized, he wasn't staring at Tom as such, but rather his platinum blonde hair. How old was this monk? Eighty? Eighty-five? When he came up to Pluscarden back in the 1950s, the only people who dyed their hair platinum blonde were sweater girls and deviants. The expression on his face said it all: 'What in God's name has been going on out there?'

G-Dog later told us silent eating serves a practical purpose, as with all things in the monastery, in that it enables the monks to concentrate on his (and His) words from the pulpit rather than the food they're consuming. Except for one monk, who spent most of dinner ignoring G-Dog altogether and reading the words on his tub of Flora over and over again instead. If I'd known they were that desperate for new literature, I'd have brought along a job lot of buttery spreads. When Abbot Hugh had heard enough of G-Dog's tales of saintly death, he tinkled a small bell to signal that munch was over, hoods went on and off again in unison, and we were finally shepherded out through the library, our ordeal over. When I finally made eye-contact with Tom, something I'd deliberately avoided doing throughout dinner for fear of dissolving into helpless and highly inappropriate laughter, he looked bent and crooked, as if someone had slit him from shoulder to waist and ripped out his spine.

'I'm not sure I'm gonna make it,' said Tom, 'it feels like someone's burgled my *qi*.'

'You've got to be kidding me Tommy,' I replied, 'we haven't even been to church yet . . .'

Our first experience of monastic prayer in all its glory was Compline, when the monks get together for a bedtime sing-song to invoke God's protection during the hours of darkness. And even Tom had to admit, it was pretty impressive theatre: twenty monks joined in Gregorian chant, illuminated only by candlelight. If I hadn't spent Latin lessons at school drawing rude parts on classmates' exercise books, I might have had some idea what the monks were trying to impart, but unless someone's trying to tell me '*Caecilius est in horto*', I haven't got a bloody clue. But while I was impressed by the ritual, the theatre and the religious majesty, and while I felt very much at peace, it was a sombre peace, a melancholy peace, like coming in from the icy cold and being swaddled in a slightly damp blanket.

Half-an-hour later I was in bed. I hadn't been to bed at nine since I was about nine. Even back then I'd be allowed to watch *Hart To Hart* on a Sunday night, usually while my mum fashioned me a rather monkish haircut with a pair of butcher's scissors. They even let me stay up to watch Spurs beat Anderlecht when I was eight, and that must have finished at about eleven, what with extra-time and penalties. When I was told to go to bed, I didn't usually put up much of a fuss because I'd have my brother to muck about with, or even Nan Dirs if she was stopping over. Her in one bed, my brother in another, me in a sleeping bag on the floor. She'd keep us entertained for hours with tails of Alsatian-sized rats in the coal shed, bombing raids and the rising price of haemorrhoid cream. In fact, sometimes we wouldn't sleep at all, for when Nan Dirs went under, she could snore like a bloody threshing machine.

No one gets tired at nine, whether you're up at four or not. What on earth did these monks get up to in their cells? Did the Flora-loving brother secrete tubs in his cell for a spot of illicit secular reading? Posted on a door in the church I'd seen a notice informing visitors of the death of a Father Camillus. Aged eighty-seven, he'd been in the abbey community for fifty-seven years. All those years of tireless devotion to God and all I could think as I stared at the ceiling was, 'I wonder if he ever knocked one out?' Dave Nash at school reckoned they had to, otherwise their balls would explode. I'm not sure there are any hard facts to back that up, but if not your balls exploding, then surely your mind instead. An old priest once told me that he didn't have time for sex because he was married to the Church. But I've always found all this talk of priests and monks being beacons of hope in a world enslaved by sensuality more than a little bit arrogant. Isn't a man, after all, just another animal, with the same innate urges and desires as your average chimpanzee?

TOM

Pluscarden was unlike anywhere else I'd ever been. So authenti-cally medieval was it that I expected us to be served goblets of mead and vast salvers of roasted swan at dinner, and then be burned as witches for arriving in a car with an automatic transmission. Was the omelette pie supposed to bring us closer to God, or closer to rifling through the pantry in the middle of the night? This was no wedding feast at Cana. The omelette was chewy; the plum juice stubbornly refused to turn into wine.

On the window of my room I spotted a scratched old sticker. 'A life without Whitesnake is not a life for me!' Hair Metal, in a place where everyone's head is shaved and there wasn't so much as a lute in sight? There must have been some ghastly mis-understanding, similar to a tale I remembered hearing from an Ursuline acquaintance of my mum's named Sister Joan. Another nun in her convent, having thoroughly enjoyed the 1986 Jeremy-Irons-as-a-Jesuit film The Mission, *requested an LP of the soundtrack as her sole Christmas present. Only when putting needle to vinyl did she discover that there was another version of the Mission out there, this one featuring the doomy Goth wailings of Wayne Hussey rather than the dishy adventures of Iron and chums in the South American jungle.*

Out in the expansive grounds after dinner, we wandered through rowan trees hung with red berries like Christmas baubles while Ben sneaked in an illicit fag. The brothers came across as a perplexing bunch. Gabriel, for one, was extraordinarily camp, combining the body language of Larry Grayson with the delivery of Pete Burns. Abbot Hugh, far from the authoritative figure I'd expected, appeared a sensitive, diffident chap who struggled to maintain eye-contact, the John Le Mesurier of the Pluscarden platoon.

Would we be able to fit in? Ben seemed twitchy. Post-fag he had pulled a bag of jelly babies out of his coat pocket and stuffed three in his mouth, muttering something about not wanting to be 'rumbled by Cadfael'. A few moments later, as we strolled round the orchard, he snagged his jumper on a stray bramble and called it a cunt. I couldn't imagine Gabriel doing either.

Our rooms were silent, lonely places. There was nothing electronically entertaining for miles around, nothing to read except a thick tome on the life of St Benedict: 1,000 days and nights alone in a cave, every one of them a page-turner. I sighed heavily, glanced up at the enormous crucifix hanging over the bed and tried to fall asleep.

That night I had nightmares about vampires. By 3.37 a.m. I was wide awake, the anguished wooden Jesus on his cross lit by the monochrome moonlight creeping through the tired old curtains. I glanced outside and saw a stag standing motionless on the driveway like a supernatural sentry. Where was Ben? Where the hell was I?

BEN

I tapped on Tom's door at 4.40 the next morning and found him pumping out some high energy Tai Chi. This brother was in the *qi-gong* zone, until I clicked my fingers in his face and reminded him that in five minutes' time we were going Gregorian. Big time. Just shy of two hours of praying, and we weren't even allowed to join in.

Two by two the monks swept in, before bowing to the altar, bowing to one another and sweeping out of sight again. At 4.45 a.m., this is pretty spooky stuff. Then they started, all twenty of them in unison, wafting ancient psalms our way, wave after wave of them, filling every cobwebbed corner of the church, creeping up stained-glass windows, curling round pillars and wrapping us both up in a dream-like stupor. After about ten minutes, Tom nodded off, before waking fifteen minutes later, mumbling something under his breath and staggering towards the exit. Somehow I lasted the distance, but the respite was brief. As I was pulling off my jeans and about to topple into bed, I looked up at the clock and remembered I had to be back in church for Prime in half an hour. If anyone reading this ever wants to get their kids into Catholicism, don't take them to stay at a monastery: it would be like trying to get your kids into cricket by dragging them along to a timeless Test.

In the breakfast room, we bumped into a few more guests, including Trevor, who delivered the stunning news that he was celebrating his tenth wedding anniversary at Pluscarden. A tenth wedding anniversary at a medieval monastery in the Highlands? However that conversation went, I can pretty much guarantee it didn't end in a blowjob:

TREVOR: 'Right love, pack your bags, I'm taking you away for the weekend.'

TREVOR'S WIFE (beams, embraces Trevor and showers him with kisses): 'Ooh, thank you darling. How exciting! Will I be needing my bikini?'

TREVOR: 'That's probably not necessary. Just make sure you bring some gloves, a fleece and plenty of Alpen.'

TREVOR'S WIFE (smiles wider): 'Ooh la la! Val d'Isère? Courchevel? Verbier? (She hugs Trevor close and whispers in his ear) Cancel ze chalet maid, I'll pack ze outfit. Ze frilly knickers, ze stockings and suspenders, ze tickling stick . . .'

TREVOR: 'If you like love, just make sure you leave space in your case for thermals. Oh, and bring some socks and sandals, we want to make sure we fit in.'

While Trevor was tucking into some cornflakes and a mug of steaming tea in the breakfast room with me, Tom and a couple of middle-aged bods from Glasgow, his wife was in the women's quarters about a quarter-of-a-mile down the road, presumably prostrate, boohooing into her French maid's outfit and periodically shouting, 'WHYYYYYYY?' very loudly at the crucifix hanging above her bed.

'Where did you go for your ninth wedding anniversary?' asked one of the Glaswegians slyly, 'Broadmoor?' I thought this was a bit rich coming from a bloke who had chosen to spend a week of annual leave praying with a mate for four hours a day, but then I suppose he could have said the same about me.

'I thought I'd be crawling up walls by day three,' said the other Glaswegian, 'but I haven't missed the Guinness at all.' He looked across at Trevor suspiciously before adding, 'I have missed the Missus though. Which is strange, as she's only in the lady's guesthouse down the road . . .'

Mass was at least easy to follow, even if it was almost exclusively in Latin. Years of indoctrination meant I could pick off the various proclamations and refrains, hanging like withered fruit from a hoary old branch in my memory. While I attempted to take some part in proceedings, Tom, like some rebellious novice, surreptitiously skimmed through a pamphlet on celibacy under the hood of his tracksuit. I, on the other hand, found myself being sucked further in, to the extent that on hearing the monks recite the *Agnus Dei* I felt a sudden compulsion to receive Holy Communion. I got halfway to rising, before what felt like two hands took me gently by the shoulders and pushed me back down again. 'Jesus, I must be incubating some seriously grave sins,' I muttered to Tom. Tom looked up from his pamphlet and pointed at the Abbot's feet.

'Socks with sandals, Dirsy,' said Tom, 'now that's what I call a sin.'

After Mass it was time for me and Tom to get down to

Dubai — it's as if God dropped his Meccano set in the middle of the desert. Tom and Ben, giddy with disbelief, hang on for dear life.

Every yacht owner's worst nightmare: Ben relaxes into the millionaire lifestyle in Dubai's exclusive marina. Shortly afterwards, the exclusivity rules were tightened still further.

Road directions, Fuck It style. We knew the path to happiness wouldn't be an easy one, but we didn't realize it would be quite this confusing.

It might look like Tom is measuring Ben up for an invisible suit, but this is actually *qi-gong*, a key part of spiritual hedonism. The temptation to flick his nose was almost overwhelming.

Every day is like Sunday – the fun of living as silent monks is clear for all to see.

Tom practises his Maori stick-fighting skills. Similar facial expressions were seen after Ben's startling emergence at the British Naturism Table-Tennis championships.

They say that laughter is the best medicine. Harish and the
Rayners Lane Laughter Club hand out an overdose.

Deep in a Provençal wine cellar, Ben samples *le plaisir des petites choses*. It disagrees with him, and he is forced to spit it out.

Quite why Michel the Butcher is smiling is a mystery. He's just handed a loaded shotgun to a man who has never touched one before; and who is drunk.

Not a scene from the Napoleonic Wars, but the aftermath of the extraordinary pheasant hunt. Note pale vegetarian on left and butcher with bloodlust on right.

The international language of cheese in full effect. Divided initially by nationality and outlook, by the end Ben and his peasant chum were considering getting matching tattoos.

some work in the monastery gardens. As we made our way through the orchard, a monk scooted past on a miniature tractor, so old and so small that I found myself checking to see if it was being propelled by the monks own legs, like some ancient velocipede. Brother Martin, dressed in denim smock and jeans and a yellow beanie, put us to work sorting potatoes in the greenhouse, protected from the rain that swept down from the moors at least. The spuds were so small you'd have needed a pair of nail clippers to peel them. Verily, it would be easier for a camel to pass through an eye of a needle than for a monk to have made chips from those spuds.

TOM

Sitting in the greenhouse, waves of rain breaking against the panes all around us, I thought of St Benedict in his cave at Sacro Speco. According to the biography in my room, the old boy had been tormented by two things: the dreadful weather and 'the memory of a girl whose haunting attractions tempted him to return to the world'. Years later, having founded his first monastery, a jealous local priest had attempted to besmirch his reputation by secretly smuggling in saucy dancing-girls. Maybe we had more in common with Benedict than we realized.

The latter-day St Ben rooted around in the mud at the bottom of an old sack and stood up angrily. He flicked away a potato the size of a rabbit dropping and shook his head. 'Fuck this,' he grunted, and stalked off for a fag.

On reflection, it was probably a good thing he hadn't been there at Sacro Speco. I imagined how St Benedict's diary might have read – 'DAY ONE, 8 a.m.: arrive at cave that is to be home

for next three years. 9 a.m.: begin to forage for food. 9.30 a.m.:
Brother Dirs declares 'fuck this' and returns to city. Alas. I am
alone.'

BEN

When we'd sifted through four barrels' worth, playing a game
of 'which potato looks most like Wayne Rooney' to make the
time go quicker, we made our way back to the orchard, where
Brother Cyprian was picking apples and showing them off to
a novice with a great deal of pride. '120 different varieties,'
beamed Brother Cyprian as we approached, 'you don't get
that in Sainsbury's.' No, I thought to myself, but you do
get potato-sized potatoes.

While the house rules were clear – 'It is never permitted for
guests to speak to the monks at any time,' read a large notice
in the guest wing – we'd received special dispensation from
Abbot Hugh to chat to a couple of the monks, should they
wish, while they worked in the gardens. And while G-Dog
had been reluctant to open up, Brother Cyprian was only too
happy to have a natter, so that once he got started, there was
no stopping him.

Brother Cyprian explained that manual work, while serving
to exercise the body, provides the monks with a means of
support and provides outlets for creativity (some of the monks
produce religious art, others tend bees) and also ensures that
none of them lost their marbles. 'The whole idea of the
Benedictine Rule is to develop the whole person, so the day is
broken up into bits, with worship, study, work and nothing
predominating,' he explained. 'If all we did was pray all day
in church, no one would be able to stick it.'

Brother Cyprian, an Essex boy like me and Tom, had been at Pluscarden since 1989, and his story was a remarkable and rather unsettling one. 'There was no "moment",' said Brother Cyprian as we strolled among the apple trees. 'It was a complete muddle. I was baptized, but was brought up with no Christian faith at all. My mother was a Hindu and I was brought up in eastern religion. I did the Buddhist thing, hanging round monasteries and stuff, and eventually came to Catholicism through Protestant sects. I became a Catholic when I was twenty-two and at the time I was a medical laboratory officer in Colchester General Hospital. It wasn't a terribly well-paid job and I got a bit fed up with it. So when I bumped into a chap who wanted to set up a community in Norway, I thought, "I've got nothing to lose, I'll join him." He turned out to be a bit of a nutcase. But the bishop there said I'd quite like you for the diocese as a priest. I hadn't really thought about becoming a priest, but I'd thought about the contemplative life. So I'd been five months a Catholic and I was up here. It was much too fast and I had a heck of a lot of catching up to do.'

Brother Cyprian's revelation that he'd been a Catholic for less than half a year when he arrived at Pluscarden was truly jaw-dropping. Catching up?! A monastic life is to a Catholic what an Ashes tour of Australia is to an English cricketer, an ascent of Everest is to a climber, a polar expedition is to an explorer. What Brother Cyprian did was the equivalent of someone ferreting about for some oven chips at the bottom of their freezer and suddenly thinking to themselves, 'You know what, I've got a bit of a taste for this,' before setting off for Antarctica a few days later.

'Yes, I agree,' said Brother Cyprian. 'I thought, "This is completely bonkers, it's driving me nuts, I want to get out." But then I kept thinking, "What to?" Whether it's your calling or not, at the beginning God takes you apart, everything gets blown up, like a depth charge dropping into a submarine. But a crisis in the beginning can be a pretty good thing in terms of working on yourself, looking objectively at what you're doing and working through it. If it's plain-sailing and smooth, something's not happening. As one of the older monks used to say to me: "Novice having a crisis, normal. Novice not having a crisis, worried."'

We were glad to have grabbed a chat with Brother Cyprian, because it helped make him and the other monks human, just like us, rather than spectral figures floating above the flotsam and jetsam of everyday life. Still, I had decided to hold the bigger questions back for a later date, including the million dollar one: what have monks ever done for us? Hidden away from the outside world like hermits in a glorified cave, it struck me as a selfish existence and contrary to what I'd been taught about Christianity from an early age. Jesus didn't sit about painting pictures of saints, sorting potatoes and making those little things with a sort of raffia-work base. He put himself about spreading what he reckoned was his Old Man's word, healing lepers and blind men, saving his mates a few quid on wine, dissing recalcitrant fig trees and generally being a bloody good bloke. And the monks should know, because it was their predecessors who wrote most of it down and bound it up in a big book called the Bible.

TOM

Three days in, still feeling a little divorced from our brothers in beige, it felt as if a grand gesture was required. Up to now we'd done no more than dip our toes in the Pluscarden pool, squealing feebly at the shock and refusing to abandon the safety of the shallow end for the icy depths inhabited by the true devotees. It was time for total immersion. It was time for silence.

In a strange way I was almost looking forward to it. What would be my final words before going under? Something suitably wise, I mused – the sort of sage remark that could hang in the empty air for hours and survive repeated inspection. Alternatively I could just say something really irritating to Ben and watch him squirm in mute frustration for the next forty-eight hours. Sadly, when the time came that night I had completely forgotten what was to follow at dawn. As a result, my famous last words were somewhat prosaic. 'Laters, Dirs.' The Algonquin set could rest easy.

'Silence is one of our most precious possessions – it is also one of the most difficult to preserve,' the notice had read. 'In a world of constant noise, spiritual silence may be a dimension as unfamiliar to you as the fourth. It may even be frightening at first. It is, however, an indisputable factor for the development of the spiritual life, for it is vital to the spirit of prayer. You have come to make contact with Reality, and so you are respectfully asked to do all you can to assist the monks to preserve their silence.'

When I woke that morning I lay under the thin, worn blankets for a while and tuned my ears to the background hum. The radiators dinked and popped. Noisy Highland birds shouted greetings at each other. Somewhere in the distance, a toilet flushed. Apart from that, there was stillness.

I slipped on my clothes and padded along the hushed corridors. Having packed an old Quiksilver hooded top before leaving home, I had taken to wearing it with the hood up in a subconscious attempt to fit in, and now, as I passed one of the brothers in a *doorway, I nodded with the austere, stern-faced calm of a fellow traveller. He nodded back. No words, no need for them. So far, so good.*

Ben's door. I paused with knuckles raised. I couldn't knock — it would make too much noise. At the same time I couldn't shout. So how was he supposed to know I was outside? I stood there, shifting awkwardly from one foot to another as unobtrusively as I could. Telepathy? I squeezed my eyes shut and tried to send an invisible greeting through the oak panels. Nothing.

I glanced both ways down the corridor and tried a surreptitious cough, and then a clearing of the throat. This was ridiculous. With an apologetic grimace I grabbed the door handle, gave it a brisk turn and marched in.

Ben was lying in bed, reading The Confederacy of Dunces. *He looked up at me in surprise. I stuck a finger over my lips and made a shhhing shape with my lips.*

'What?' he mouthed silently, and then raised a hand in contrition. I pointed exaggeratedly at him, mimed a monk praying, tapped my watch and raised palms and eyebrows skyward. He shook his head and made a gesture like a man asking a waiter for the menu. I tried again. He scratched his chin, made a 'sounds like' gesture by his ear and waved his arms around like a partying chimpanzee.

It was pathetic, charades played by two idiots without a language in common. 'Vespers,' I whispered furiously. 'Are you coming?'

'Silence naturally leads to a meditative "chewing over",' the notice had claimed. 'Such a way is alien to the information-saturated, results-orientated busyness of the modern world, but is in perfect accord with the heart of Christian religion.'

It might well be. It is also extremely impractical. No wonder the food was so bad at Pluscarden. No one could complain. No one could offer to help. No one could pass on any easy-to-follow recipes they might have found on the side of a tub of Flora.

BEN

When you're staying in a monastery, every situation is a potential Dave Allen sketch, so that as I tucked into my lunch of reheated omelette pie, I found myself staring down at Abbot Hugh and imagining him making his napkin into a bra and wiggling it about on his chest. And when you're used to chin-wagging through your meals, rowing about the day's big match, whether Gary Glitter should still be played on the radio or whether Bruce Forsyth has got long left, eating in silence becomes decidedly taut. So when the monks suddenly broke into peels of collective laughter, and I looked up to see two rows of smiling faces, it felt like a bomb had been defused, so much so that I'll never forget the line that triggered it: 'Britain had become a banana republic with a shortage of bananas'. Good old Andrew Marr and his *History of Modern Britain*: not exactly P.G. Wodehouse, but when your other book's the Bible, virtually every line's a side-splitter.

Later that same day we found Brother Cyprian tending to his beloved apple trees and it seemed like a good time to ask him, in light of the minor miracle we'd witnessed at lunch-time, whether he and the other monks were happy.

'There's a lot of humour in community,' said Brother Cyprian. 'If twenty blokes have got to live together without humour, it wouldn't bear thinking about. There's certainly far more humour in a monastery than there is in a convent!' But to Brother Cyprian and the other monks, being happy is more than about just having a giggle with your mates, or many of the other things the secular world identifies with happiness: getting hammered or high, having sex, making lots of money, the accumulation of 'things', letting rip under the duvet and wafting it in your girlfriend's face.

'There are lots of things I miss, but you get it back in other ways. There are times when you're working hard in the garden and you think, "I wouldn't mind going down the pub with my mates." But then there are other times, at Christmas for example, when drinks are available, and you appreciate it more, because you know this is it, this is my one can and I can enjoy it in a responsible way. There's no peer pressure to go out and get drunk, and you wonder, is that "being happy", or are we driven by other pressures? Ours is a long-term view of happiness, not a short path.'

In other words, while most of western society has a very self-indulgent concept of 'feeling good' and associates this 'feeling good' with happiness, the monks try to transcend superficial pleasures and achieve happiness through their relationship with God, through self-examination, through being virtuous and good.

'It's about going a bit deeper,' explained Brother Cyprian. 'It's not about feelings or even feeling good.' This line of thinking is totally at odds with the way of Fuck It, with its flinching and rather selfish entreaties to 'just be who you are' or 'do what the hell you like'. Brother Cyprian would argue that the keys to liberation, and therefore happiness, are not, as Fuck It would have it, 'essentially simple', but rather involve rummaging inside ourselves, wrestling with our failings and scrubbing up our souls, whether doing so causes us pain or not. In addition, while most of the tenets of Fuck It have an ulterior motive and are a means to an end – for example, it tells us that if we loosen our hold on things and stop wanting things so much, then we'll naturally start getting the things we want – the Benedictine way is to loosen your hold on things, full stop. No prizes at the end of it, just the inner happiness that comes with self-control.

'I think in the end that a lot of what you might call New Age spiritualism is dissatisfying, not sustaining,' was Brother Cyprian's take on the Fuck It philosophy. 'They offer all sorts of silly courses, talk about the spirituality of money or standing around and feeling the "vibes", but techniques on their own aren't enough, they can give you a false picture. There's a whole set of spiritualities in Christianity, with all sorts of help and techniques and they can be helpful for a time, a crutch to lean on, but it's about going deeper, and you can't put that down to technique. If Christ is a model, he went through suffering and crucifixion, and the Christian way is to go right through the middle of the suffering and find there's meaning in it, rather than a technique to get round it or a palliative to make it less.'

Later that day Tom and I went for a wander through the forest and it suddenly hit me: the reason so many people are unhappy in this world is because most of us have no real concept of what happiness is. We think happiness is lobbing ten sambucas down our neck on a Saturday night, shelling out 600 quid on a flatscreen TV or eating an entire Marks & Spencer cheese board at Christmas. But how often do we stop and gauge our happiness? Do I ever ask myself, sitting there watching *Danny Dyer's Deadliest Men* on the telly with a dirty great pizza on my lap, might I be happier if I was just sitting? No shite on the telly, no dirty great pizza. Just sitting. Or maybe going for a walk. Or looking out the window at the stars. Instead of asking whether monks dig living in a world without happy hour down Brannigans, giant electrical equipment and massive slabs of cheese, perhaps a more pertinent question is, are monks *unhappy* being free of such 'feel-good' things? Brother Cyprian doesn't think so.

'We have a long time to discern, and it's a bit like making a marriage commitment. There should be a long period of discernment, then you should stick with your choice. They say that often your reasons for joining are not your reasons for staying. Taking the marriage parallel, the things that attracted you to your partner might be pretty ephemeral, but the things that make you stick with the same person and grow to love them are deeper. One takes you to the other.'

Still, this realization that perhaps the monks are happier than most of us in the outside world didn't make us feel any less melancholy, and Tom in particular was beginning to fall into a listless state of befuddlement. That night, we ignored our bedtime curfew and headed for the breakfast room, where we read to each other from a week-old copy of the local rag, played guess the attendance at the Alloa Athletic v Arbroath match (469) and attempted to raise the spirits by seeing who could muster the loudest blow-off. In our search for happiness, we'd taken a wrong turn and ended up the headline act in a festival of anal acoustics.

When it was time for bed, Tom turned to me, with a hint of alarm, and whispered with a grimace, 'It's all a bit "samey", isn't it?' before disappearing down the dimly lit corridor and belting out a spot of Morrissey in the Gregorian style: 'Every day is like Sunday, every day is silent and grey . . .' Father Camillus had lasted fifty-seven years, Tom was shot to pieces after two days.

That night, I wandered the monastery gardens, smoking cigarette after cigarette, and drank in the stars, which came down almost as far as the tops of the pine trees. A million

million stars in our galaxy, so they reckon, and a million million galaxies. That's a fuck of a lot for one God to take on, and let's face it, He had trouble designing Croydon. How long has modern man been on earth? 200,000 years? And only for a tiny pin-prick of time has he shared it with clunking, clanking, whizzing, whirring machines. Then why is it that so many of us find peace and silence so oppressive?

Sunday at Pluscarden is indeed like every other day, except with Benediction thrown in and a spot of meat, which was like a double stake to the Fordyce heart. Now, normally I wouldn't like to see my vegetarian friend suffer, but having been reduced to passing wind for entertainment the night before, the sight of him tucking into a plate of spaghetti at lunch – without any bolognese sauce – was manna from heaven for me, and I struggled to contain my delight. Then, just as I'd recovered myself, a postman burst into the refectory with a fist full of letters and blurted out, 'Who's gonna sign for these?' only to be accosted by a burly monk with a bent nose like a boxer and bundled into the library.

By the time Benediction swung round, Tom didn't even have the energy to join me in a muffled cheer as the monstrance was raised above the Abbot's head, while the normally sweet, uplifting scent of incense, which is wafted around liberally at this particular ceremony, suddenly smelt like an eau-de-Cologne for the emo set: 'Maudlin – because you're probably not worth it.' Dinner that night wasn't, as I'd hoped, roast lamb, but a boiled egg, although there was Carte D'Or ice cream, which was like a ray of modernity piercing the stained-glass window, scattering light all about us and momentarily dispersing the medieval fug. But still the monk up on the lectern plodded away, ploughing through a *Tablet* book review of *Christianity: The First 3000 Years*, a tome weighing in at 1,180 pages, which the *Tablet* reviewer felt, in his wisdom, wasn't anywhere near weighty enough.

That night I considered trying to make naked ladies appear on my mobile phone. I'm not proud of it, but coming straight from Italy and a gaggle of women talking constantly about sex to a gang of monks talking constantly about God does that to a man. It was only the sight of the crucifix hanging over my bed that stopped me from going through with it. That and the fact there was no reception. Truthfully, I would have walked a couple of miles through the howling wind and rain for a copy of *Razzle* that night. *Razzle*, and a packet of crumpets. Mmm, hot, buttered crumpets . . .

TOM

Truly, that evening's dinner was one of the most depressing of my life – a solitary boiled egg, gone hard because the monk in charge of the stopwatch hadn't been able to shout to the one by the saucepan that the three-and-a-half minutes might be up; a beaker of undiluted orange juice, acidic enough to dissolve teeth on impact; rain, beating against the cold stone walls; a shaven-headed monk, reading in gloomy tones of death and decay and the ephemeral nature of each of our lives.

It wasn't as bad as church had been when I was a kid. It was worse. Even on Good Friday, that marathon of Mass, that joyless trudge through the thickest gospel and homily Rome could conjure up, you could escape by 5 p.m., run free up the street to home and a television and a nice tea and a dive about in the garden. Here there was no escape, just service after service – no noise, no life, no expression that I could find of happiness and joy and excitement.

Compline, the final prayer service of the day. Hunger and the melancholic chanting only adding to the sense of doom. What had briefly sounded, a few days ago, like a Latin version of Fleet Foxes, a timeless evocation of deep spiritual significance, now felt like the most painfully tedious exhibition I had witnessed since the qualifying rounds for the World Snooker Championships.

These men were here until the bitter end. Nothing new and different could come into their lives, nothing would take them away from Pluscarden until death itself intervened. Surrounded with such doctrinal doggedness, something clicked in my head. Month after month the ladyfriend had been badgering me to move things on – leave that rented room at Rupert's, get a place with her, make a long-time promise. I'd carried on resisting, reluctant to nail my colours to the mast. Here, surrounded by men who had locked themselves up in dogma, cut themselves off in the past, the future suddenly seemed a far more attractive place.

Stimulation and procreation. It wasn't quite what St Benedict intended, but it was a revelation just the same.

I was up early the next day, filled with an overwhelming desire for life and vibrancy, into the car and away. In Elgin nothing was open but a 24-hour garage, so I drank machine-coffee and read the papers until the swimming pool opened. I was the first one in, so happy to see lights and a smiling face that I almost kissed the woman behind the till. As the sky gradually lit up over the town, a faint light coming through the glass roof, I ploughed up and down the 25-metre lanes, Jefferson Airplane blasting through the public address system, adrenaline finally flowing and a sense of happy liberation fizzing round my brain. In the sauna I sat and chatted to a wrinkly old boy about front crawl; in the showers a bunch of lads in early for ice hockey practice told dirty jokes that had us all cackling like crones.

Freedom. Freedom to shout, to splash about, to meet new people and see new places. Even if they were all fitness fanatics and municipal leisure centres. Sorry, St Benedict, I thought. You've lost me. You might still get Dirsy, though . . .

BEN

There was no waking Tom for Vigils the next day, while I only managed to last half-an-hour, wondering the whole time why the Benedictines hadn't managed to come up with some new tunes in the last 1,500 years and how anyone could possibly have the discipline to put themselves through this day after day, year after year, decade after decade, whether they're crazy about God or not. And I had to keep reminding myself they were happy living this way, or so Brother Cyprian assured me, and that rather than being worthy of my pity, they had greater cause to pity me, scrabbling about in my bedroom at night, holding my mobile phone out of the window at strange angles, while they slept soundly in their cells, probably dreaming of angels.

After lunch, we tracked down Brother Cyprian in the orchard, and I felt the time was right to drop a couple of big bombs: What's the point of monks? And what if they're all wrong?

'One of the Desert Fathers [the first Christian hermits, who lived in solitude in Egypt from the third century] said, "The monk is separated from all in order to be joined to all,"' explained Brother Cyprian, who didn't seem to mind that I'd ambushed him and effectively questioned his whole reason for being. 'We've just moved to a slightly different vantage point. The monastery being slightly apart allows us an objective distance, the ability to look at things at a slightly deeper level. What we're trying to do, in our own weak and pathetic way, is live those right, ordered relations with creation, with each other and with God: what we are meant to be and what society is meant to be. And that's a bit more difficult today, because in years gone by a monastery would have been a part of the ordinary fabric of society, so the separation wouldn't have been dramatic as it is now. It's amazing to think that in late medieval times about 20 per cent of the male population would have been clerics.'

That may well be the case, but then life in a monastery in medieval times, which presumably meant bread on the table every day and a warmish bed to lay your head, was no doubt an improvement on being a peasant, toiling in the fields all day for the benefit of some feudal master and warming your hands at night on the belly of a pig.

So if being a monk in medieval times was in some part down to expediency, in modern Britain it is in large part down to absolute religious conviction. 'Monastic life is not higher than any other vocation, a good marriage is just as good,' said Brother Cyprian. 'The little old lady who prays in the pew with the daughter dying of cancer is objectively more holy than I am and on a more profound level. But St Paul has an analogy that the Church is like a body with different parts and you need all the bits with their own specific functions. My path is to be a Benedictine monk, and our job is liturgical and contemplative prayer.'

I liked Brother Cyprian's humility, his admission that the little old lady praying for her daughter was perhaps more holy than him. And my question suddenly felt impertinent: 'What use are sports journalists and authors of little-read "toilet" books?' Brother Cyprian might have retorted, and he would have been well within his rights. In fact, the more I thought about it, the more perverse my question seemed. If I didn't believe in what they believed in, then why was I slightly irritated that they spent their time hidden away instead of spreading the word of what I didn't believe in anyway? Their God, their rules, with thousands of years of thinking and philosophy behind them. Similarly, who was I to question their happiness?

'What a vocation is, is the paths that have been discerned through time and history in the Church that give people the graces they need to attain their happiness and their sanctity,' said Brother Cyprian. I admired his conviction, his absolute conviction, that his was the true road to happiness. And I admired the discipline it took to stay on that road, the patience, the self-sacrifice, the hard slog that is contemplation and self-examination. Not fannying about on the peripheries, picking and choosing from a smorgasbord of philosophies like some fussy eater – in the manner of Fuck It – but guzzling down what you're given. Because if you're allowed to pick and choose, you're likely to pick and choose what you like, and what you like might not necessarily be what's good for you.

TOM

'We are living in a world of intense selfishness. There has been a lowering of standards beyond belief. At the same time there are innumerable souls just longing for peace, and it may be that the hidden life of the monk in his monastery may obtain for these souls that comfort and support they so need, amidst all the difficulties and temptations of modern-day life.'

Not the words of Abbot Hugh when he finally granted us an

audience, but of his predecessor at Pluscarden in September 1948. If he thought standards had been low back then, it was probably a good thing he hadn't lived to see Whitesnake.

'These are the days of the specialist. Doctors, scientists and students of all kinds retire to their laboratories and studies, they get away from the distractions of the world to specialise on their particular work. The monk? He specialises in spirituality, in prayer, in providing an oasis of peace and spirituality in this world of materialism and unrest, and to pray, by night and by day, for the peace of the world, for the needs of mankind in general and for individual souls.'

I had found the peace and spirituality less of an oasis and more of a prison. Maybe that reflected badly on me; all these years of running and cricket, of swimming and cycling, seemed to have left me tuned in predominantly to the visceral and corporeal. Ask me how I was feeling and I was more likely to say 'sleepy' or 'tight in the hamstrings' than depressed or troubled. Then again, maybe that was exactly it. I was slowly realizing that physical exertion was where I felt most peaceful. Spirituality for Brother Gabriel might have been 8 hours of Latin chanting, 365 days a year, but for me it was whacking down a hill on a bike with my nostrils full of fresh air and my eyeballs full of onrushing countryside.

BEN

Admire Brother Cyprian I did, but did he ever wonder if he was wrong? That instead of St Peter at the Pearly Gates leading him to an eternal life in Christ, his death might involve nothing more glamorous than being buried in a wooden box and being slowly eaten by worms.

'Why is there anything rather than nothing?' argued

Brother Cyprian. 'The fact is that even if I'm not really seeing you and seeing a phenomenon instead, it exists, it must have a cause, and then there must be a God. And if God can create, it's not an unreasonable proposition that, if he's any kind of God, he can communicate who he is and how he is to us.'

It is this Grand Canyon-esque leap of faith that I've never been able to accept, the idea that because we exist, then there must be a 'Creator'. 'Being terribly bright doesn't mean you're particularly spiritually mature,' was Brother Cyprian's summation of atheists such as Richard Dawkins, who has spent much of his life trying to disprove the existence of God, which is rather like tilting at windmills.

But then accusing Dawkins of spiritual immaturity is rather big talk coming from someone who believes that a couple of thousand years ago some chap calling himself Jesus walked on water, could seemingly pull loaves and fishes out of his arse, and survived for forty days and nights without food or water in the desert before being delivered a takeout by a flock of angels; and who also believes that this chap's mum was a virgin and that his dad was God. Even Muslims have a beef with that last bit, and some of them think that when you die you'll hang out for all time with seventy-two virgins, presumably round the pool with buckets of Cristal, like some religious rap video. Seventy-two virgins? All those martyrs want to hope their mums have either got their feet up in an alternative heaven next door or that they never made it and are burning down in hell.

If Brother Cyprian, G-Dog and the rest of the Brothers had chosen to opt out of a life of sex, cheese-crust pizzas and flatscreen TVs that was their prerogative, it just isn't a gamble most people are prepared to take. But whether he ends up with

St Peter high-fiving him outside the Pearly Gates or Mike
Tyson biting his nose off outside the Hades branch of Brannigans, Brother Cyprian would argue that, hey ho, I lived a
happier life than the rest of you anyway. I certainly had more
respect for his position than I did for John and Gaia on The
Hill That Breathes. More respect because, although I no more
believe in God than I believe in New Age spies who are able
to rifle through enemy files from 5,000 miles away, the Pluscarden monks were unswerving, they got their heads down and
grafted, took their medicine and kept their eyes on the prize.

'People keep on coming back who aren't Christians who
find peace in this place,' said Brother Cyprian as we loaded up
the car. 'Perhaps it's the symbolic value, the buildings and the
monks, the idea of the spiritual continuity, that there are still
places where the main purpose is divorced from the rat race.'
I don't disagree with Brother Cyprian, I think the monastic
urge is in everyone, the urge to step back from the clutter of
everyday life, be still and look inwards. What I didn't tell
Brother Cyprian is that it was exactly this symbolism, the
buildings and the monks, the prayers and the rituals, all of
which amounted to unremitting gloom, which made it impossible for Tom and me to find peace in this place.

'There's one person, a former Channel 4 presenter, who
comes up here once a year and does weeding in the garden,'
said Brother Cyprian as Tom revved the engine, just a tad too
aggressively. 'It's his secret hideout. He loves it.'

'Former Channel 4 presenter?' said Tom as we swept
through the front gates, 'Do you reckon he's talking about
Normski?'

*

BEN

On my return to Romford, I had the sudden urge to do something altruistic. As much as I respected Brother Cyprian and his mates, I couldn't shake the conviction that they could have been putting their undoubted holiness to better use. At the same time it was a bit rich of me to be questioning their worth when I spent most of my spare time playing golf. Rather badly. And so remembering what Brother Cyprian had said about monastic life not being higher than any other vocation, I set off for the American Church in London.

'Is he a helper or one of the guests?' asked someone as I was shown round the church's soup kitchen by Jake, a student from Imperial College who was in charge of food that day. I thought I took it rather well, bearing in mind many of the guests are homeless.

The church, situated on Tottenham Court Road in the West End, has been providing hot meals, clothes and toiletries since 1986 and serves up to sixty people a day, five days a week. It also offers help in the form of letter-writing, art classes and first aid courses, as well as acting as a link between guests and social services. And it offers spiritual guidance, but on a take it or leave it basis. All this is possible because of the kindness of volunteers, without whom some of the guests I met that day would be going hungry on the street.

'Voluntary work may not make the pocket richer, but it makes the mind richer,' explained Mick, who gambled all his money away many years ago and who's been coming to the kitchen for ten years. Sharon used to be homeless but now works as a security guard at the kitchen to support her two kids. 'You come to a place like this and think, "Wow," there's plenty of people worse off than you,' she explained. 'They're not necessarily homeless, but people who have lost their jobs, or just their way in life. It's pretty horrifying really.'

But it was Wayne who had the greatest effect on me. Wayne used to work in the music business and own a house in Hampstead before he became one of those who lost his way in life, and would remain 'lost and confused for a hell of a long time'. 'It's a lonely place being homeless, you've got so much to say but you can't say fuck all,' explained Wayne, who now has a flat of his own not far from the church, where he carries out his own voluntary work, 'taking old mates from the streets back for a bacon sandwich and a coffee, reminding them that things can change'.

'This place kept me alive. Before, I would have woken up, gone to the public bog, strip-washed, changed my clothes, put them in hiding and then gone out thieving and selling drugs. But those days are gone. I've got a lot to be grateful for. I was a drug addict, sick as a pig. But I was shown some warmth, some compassion, I was listened to, and it seemed like they cared. People say these people are in it for themselves, that they get this and that out of it, but the volunteers here are incredible human beings, it beggars belief that they devote so much of their life. There was a time when I would have looked at someone like Jake differently, looked at him as an arsehole: what's he doing wasting his time, mixing with scum. But that's so negative and obnoxious. When I'm fully compos mentis, I'd like to come here and give something back. I was so self-absorbed and I harmed a lot of people. I owe the world something, life ain't all about take, take, take.'

Wayne's anger suddenly subsided, his face took on a wistful

look and then he added: 'A man's true wealth is the good he does in this world to his fellows.' He broke into a sheepish smile and raised a single eyebrow. 'Mate, don't look so surprised – you spend a hell of a lot of time in libraries when you're homeless . . .'

6. PAGANISM

'We only eat children once a month'

TOM

I've never been scared of spiders. Heights aren't a problem, and I've always enjoyed flying. Needles? Not bothered. Big spaces, small spaces, being alone, in the middle of a huge crowd – it's all the same to me. But the supernatural? Warty-nosed witches tapping on your window at midnight, long bony fingers beckoning you into the darkness beyond . . . bare-chested men with goats' heads and cloven feet, smeared in blood, dancing round a flaming pyre . . . blue-black crows, plucking at your clothes with razor-sharp talons, pecking and cawing and scratching and clawing, the beaks stabbing, stabbing, stabbing . . .

At the age of four I was sent home from school for crying hysterically whenever Danny Sutton-Long's mum arrived to drop him off. She had a hooked nose and long curly hair. That was enough to convince me she was a witch who wanted to eat me for her tea. At sixteen I tried watching *The Wicker Man* and was sobbing behind the sofa less than half-an-hour in. By the time I was twenty-five I was capable of having two nightmares about *The Blair Witch Project* on the basis of the trailer alone.

Perhaps it's a little clearer now why I was so reticent when Ben suggested we throw ourselves into the world of paganism. 'It's the obvious next step,' he enthused. 'We've done the Christian monk thing. Now it's time to try the alternative.'

'Gluttony,' I said brightly. 'What about gluttony? Complete opposite of the monastic life, gluttony. Or slothfulness. You'd be up for that, wouldn't you? Nice bit of slothfulness? If you can be arsed?'

'There are fewer than 100 silent monks in Britain,' said Dirs firmly. 'And there are 40,000 pagans. Those are big numbers. That's a lot of happiness. We owe it to them. And ourselves.'

For the first time in our quest I was genuinely apprehensive. Naturism had felt like a stroll in the park compared to this, albeit a rather well-ventilated one, while the hedonism of Italy had promised to fulfil several lifetime ambitions. But what happiness could possibly come of becoming pagans? By refusing to watch any horror films and by sticking my fingers in my ears while shouting 'LA LA LA LA LA' whenever *Buffy The Vampire Slayer* came on telly, I had just about kept my paranoia of the paranormal under wraps. To actively seek contact with the forces of the night seemed wilfully masochistic, an impression only strengthened when I did a little timorous internet research the next morning.

Within a couple of minutes I had found the site of the Pagan Federation, and under the 'London/South-east' section a group called Roharn's Grove. This sounds pleasant enough, I thought, clicking on the link, picturing a leafy clearing in the woods where a chap named Roharn – possibly Danish or Norwegian, a forestry expert, perhaps a woodcutter – would sit around with a few friends, whittling small figurines from broken branches and fashioning paperweights from old mossy stones while enjoying the birdsong, the fresh air and a few glasses of real ale.

'A little about Roharn,' read the first page. 'The crow feather, beech leaves and sickle carry and hold the magic essence of this spirit. Roharn first appeared to me many moons ago: he is the Raven-Crow guide who continues to wreak havoc along my journey, he is the initiator of great change, he brings the void of nothingness, the dark night of the soul, the womb-tomb where we sing to the bones of the ancestors.'

Void of nothingness? It didn't instantly suggest happiness. At best it sounded like Ely train station on a Sunday in November, or what went on in Ben's head after five hours of dedicated face-time with a wine-box and three-pack of blue WKD.

'Roharn guides us through the caverns of our soul, land and pagan heritage, the radiance of his presence, the moonlight reflecting off his iridescent wings. For many years he has been a guide that held me, pushed me, loved me; I know him as Crow-Man.'

For some reason I was picturing Roharn as looking rather like Ronnie Wood. The image provided a small measure of reassurance as I fired off an uneasy email, enquiring if there might be a gap in his punishing schedule to wreak a little havoc through our own journeys. While I waited for a response, half-expecting a crow to land on the kitchen windowsill and start pecking out a message in Morse code upon the pane, I dug deeper into our dark new doctrine.

Witches. No matter how fearful I felt about it, we would need to commune with the big hitters of the pagan world. Two hours of labyrinthine link-following brought repeated references to someone called Jeanette Ellis, and a coven based somewhere in east London. Could this be real? There was no contact number, although that might be because witches struggled to secure monthly mobile contracts. Walthamstow seemed a little prosaic a location for a witch's base. Then again, what were Hackney Marshes if not the archetypal blasted heath? Picking up the phone directory, I began a series of calls that followed a strikingly similar pattern.

(TF drumming fingers anxiously while dialling-tone sounds)

WOMAN: 'Hello?'

TF: 'Hi. Is that Jeanette Ellis?'

WOMAN: 'Speaking.'

TF: 'Jeanette Ellis the, ah, witch?'

(Short silence, longer period of swearing, phone goes dead)

After six fruitless calls I was considering sacking it off in favour of some arse-out table-tennis when suddenly the routine changed.

TF (resignedly): 'Hello. Is that Jeanette Ellis?'

WOMAN: 'Speaking.'

TF (flatly): 'You're not a witch, are you.'

WOMAN: 'Yes. Who's calling, please?'

Jeanette sounded astonishingly normal. There was no audible cackling, no incendiary incantations. My mobile failed to mutate into an adder. 'Send me an email,' was all she said. 'Put all your details in it, and I'll have a think.'

Part relieved, ever so slightly disillusioned, I read everything on paganism that I could find. There were get-togethers in places you wouldn't expect – in a pub in Holborn midweek, at the Dog and Bull in Croydon on the third Thursday of every month, at the Golden Lion in Romford (hadn't Dirsy celebrated his eighteenth there?) – as well as a bewildering range of groups and beliefs. Some of them sounded like soft-metal bands (Hunters Moon, Wolf's Head, Odinshof) while others had decorous, dignified names like the Loyal Arthurian Warband and the Order of Bards, Druids and Ovates. Impressively for something that sounded like it had counted Merlin and Getafix among its members, the latter also had a Facebook page and a leader, Philip Carr-Gomm, who not only posted regular status updates but also had a profile picture that depicted him less as a bearded high priest and more as a slightly spaced-out Leo Sayer.

Philip turned out to be a charming conversationalist. 'My own journey began when I read the *Life of Buddha* at the age of eleven,' he told me over the phone, his calm voice pleasantly soothing. 'As a teenager I became fascinated with the pagan ceremonies they held up on Parliament Hill. I used to go up there to photograph them, and that got me talking to a druid called Nuuin – or Ross Nicholls, as he was more commonly known. Ross had studied with a Bulgarian guru, and I began going round to his house more and more – the photography just became an excuse – and I asked him to teach me in turn. Then I read a book by John Michell called *A View Over Atlantis*, which depicted Britain as a magical land, full of ancient paths and sacred sites, and it all came together for me. I was initiated into the Order in 1970, aged eighteen, on top of Glastonbury Tor.'

'Is there any way', I asked carefully, 'that me and my mate Benjamin could join the Order in action?' I tried to shut out thoughts of screaming people tied to stone altars. 'Doesn't need to be anything, ah, spectacular. Just something to help us get a handle on it all.'

'Well,' said Philip, 'there is our winter solstice celebration coming up, down in Glastonbury. You'll see a lot of happiness there. Why don't I get you invites?'

'Fantastic,' I said, trying to keep the misgivings out of my voice. 'Winter solstice, you say – so that's, what, December 21st?'

'Ah,' said Philip regretfully. 'Unfortunately there were issues getting the town hall for that date. Problem with a double booking. So we're holding it on the 13th.' Even druids, I reflected, clicking on two new emails in my inbox, were not immune to the mundane frustrations of modern life. 'R.E. Roharn,' read the first subject-line. Crow-Man had spoken. 'Unfortunately it would not be appropriate for you to come along to our grove meeting, not that we have anything to hide. It is not an open group but a space for its members to have a deeply religious experience.' So. The womb-tomb would have to go unopened. It was a shame, but the next email made up for it. 'I've decided it would be okay to have a chat,' Jeanette had written. 'For safety reasons, can we meet in the Waltham Oak pub. Also for safety reasons, I will bring a male friend with me.' '*You* want to bring a friend?' I thought, slightly uncharitably. 'How do you think I feel? Which one of us here is the witch?'

BEN

I'm going to level with you here, I just didn't fancy it. Not because I was a bit scared like Tom, but because meeting up with a witch called Jeanette in a boozer in Walthamstow would have killed the romance before my relationship with all things pagan had even begun. I mean, you wouldn't arrange to meet a silent monk outside Niketown on Oxford Circus, just as you wouldn't arrange to meet a phenomenally rich bloke down the British Legion.

You've got to see these people in their natural environment to really get a handle on them, which is why I was a bit disappointed things hadn't worked out with Crow-Man and his little outfit: I can picture Tom now, cowering in the corner of some dank cave and being pecked to within an inch of his life by a Ronnie Wood lookalike while me and his mates caw maniacally and flap our wings behind him. Yeah, Crow-Man and his mob sounded proper satanic.

That said, I did have some misgivings about letting Tom go alone. Not because I thought he might come into work the next day with a pair of cloven hooves wedged into his Asics trainers, but because Jeanette and this 'mate' of hers sounded like sex people. What was it Philip had told Tom? 'There's no division between the spiritual and the sensual – we enjoy sex and food, in a responsible way...' 'BBC JOURNALIST KILLED IN SATANIC SEX RITUAL, CHOKES ON WICKER FIGURINE, DISCOVERED DEAD IN MOTORCYCLE SIDECAR'. The Romford Recorder *would have lapped it up...*

TOM

How to recognize a witch at rest? As I strode through the frosty air towards the Waltham Oak, burping away the double whisky stiffener I'd taken on board a few minutes earlier, I tried to ignore the inauspicious portent of a full moon overhead. Would I walk in to see a crabby old woman in a black cape and pointy hat perched by the open fire, lobbing bat entrails into the flames while absentmindedly munching dry roasted peanuts? Typical of Dirs to leave me to do this on my own, I thought, pushing open the door and almost tripping over a silver-topped cane held by a shaven-headed gentleman with a pentagram pendant round his neck, sitting alongside a statuesque middle-aged woman with dark Goth eye-shadow, extravagant silver rings on her fin—

'Hello Tom,' said Jeanette. 'Would you like a drink?'

As we shook hands, I took in their appearance. Even in civvies, Jeanette cut an imposing figure for a woman in her late forties – long wavy blonde hair, purpley-black lip-gloss and a magnificent shelf of a bosom. Her companion, Steve, was dressed in a crisp black shirt and black jacket and sporting a beautifully sculpted white goatee below his polished pate. 'I'll get these,' I said quickly, keen on another drink. 'Gin and tonic for me, please,' said Jeanette pleasantly. 'And I'll have a fruit juice,' smiled Steve.

The unmistakable sound of Betty Boo's 'Where Are You Baby?' was blaring from the jukebox in the corner as I returned to the table. At the adjoining table, two blokes in polo shirts were arguing over Harry Redknapp's decision to pair Peter Crouch with Roman Pavlyuchenko. 'Blessed be!' said Jeanette. 'Thanks for coming all this way. People tend to have a lot of daft preconceptions about us – they can sometimes be very frightened, you know. My house certainly has a tendency to scare some people.'

Steve chuckled. 'We only eat children once a month,' he said, and winked conspiratorially as I coughed Guinness halfway across the pub. Jeanette gave him a dig in the ribs.

'That's the first one,' she said. 'We don't actually do sacrifices. One of the coven is a vegan. She wouldn't even sacrifice a tofu burger.' She sipped her G&T. 'What else do you think us lot get up to?'

I puffed out my cheeks. 'Spells?' I mumbled. 'In grave-yards?'

'Never go to them,' shrugged Jeanette. 'I do all my work at

home.' She looked briefly upset. 'I used to have my own wood, and we'd do all our stuff there. Then I split up with my ex, and he got the wood in the settlement. Like an idiot I'd put him on the deeds.'

'The devil worship,' I said cautiously, 'would that be something we'd have to do regularly, or . . . ?'

She laughed. 'You can't,' she said. 'We don't have a Satan. That's all Christian propaganda. The closest we've got is Pan, but he's more cheeky really – mischievous, you know. There's an evil presence out there, but you won't attract it unless you're doing evil. It's not interested.'

'We don't have many rules,' said Steve, 'but if you have to sum it up, it would probably be "harm no one". We do a lot of work in the community. I drive disabled kids about – that's my job. Take 'em to swimming pools, activity centres, that sort of thing.'

'It's the law of threefold return,' explained Jeanette. 'If you do any evil spells, they'll be revisited on you three times.'

In the background, Dido had replaced Boo on the jukebox. I felt rather confused. Had I stumbled into some sort of breakaway Good Samaritan branch of the witchcraft world? Jeanette reminded me of a schoolfriend's mum, albeit one with a preference for racy make-up and uplifting bustiers, while Steve had the genial East End accent of Dirsy's old man. I'd felt more threatened walking up the escalators at Walthamstow Central tube station.

'Initiations,' I said. 'Would we have to go through some sort of, ah, ritual?'

Jeanette threw her hands up. 'Oh yes! The dying of the old person and a rebirth of the new – it's a very special occasion. Although I'm afraid I can't tell you what the ceremony involves.'

I nodded thoughtfully. 'Has to be kept top secret, I imagine.'

She looked askance. 'Not really. It's just we're initiating Steve next week, and I don't want to spoil the surprise.'

I looked across at Steve, who was sipping his orange juice with a contented smile on his face. 'Wish I'd got round to it earlier, really,' he said reflectively. 'But you know how it is. It's like fixing the patio doors: you keep forgetting, and then putting it off because you're too busy doing other things.'

'So we'd become wizards? Or warlocks?'

The pair of them roared with laughter. 'Warlock!' chortled Jeanette. 'You'd be witches, just like the rest us. You'd have to be pretty thick to call yourself a warlock – it's a Scottish swearword! It means oath-breaker!'

Steve wandered off to get more drinks, and Jeanette leaned in closer. 'I can tell you about the initiation if you like,' she whispered. 'It's an all-day thing. We'll start at mine, do some chanting work, maybe have a walk in the woods and contact nature, and then have lunch in the pub. Then it's back to mine – some work around the candle, and we'll have cooked something earlier, so we'll warm that up, have something to eat. And then afterwards a bottle or two of wine is emptied.'

I struggled to hide my disappointment. She seemed to have described the sort of pleasant Saturday my mum might enjoy with her friends from the St Joseph's church.

'You don't even get naked?'

She gave me a funny look. 'There's no sexual content in our coven. Some of the others do it in the nude, but we save that for afterwards, at home with our partners, particularly at Samhain – that's Halloween, the start of the new year, the start of life.'

Steve clunked the drinks down on the table. 'It's a very

sociable thing, paganism,' he sniffed. 'You make friends with all sorts of groups at the big processions. The Viking boys from up north are good lads – they even made us honorary Vikings, just like them. You should pop over and see 'em.'

'Sounds good,' I said. 'Where are they based – Norway?'

'High Wycombe.' He stroked his pointed beard. 'Super people. Dragon's a good lad. So's Zin. When I first saw him, he scared the life out of me – he looks like he'd slit your throat. But he's a lovely fella. Makes his own bows and arrows.'

Three-and-a-half drinks in on an empty stomach, I could feel a fuzzy warmth replacing my earlier misgivings.

'One policeman told me, down at the station they fight to come on our parades,' said Jeanette.

'We don't get spat at, we don't get cans chucked at us – everyone's having a laugh,' said Steve.

She shrugged. 'Our whole thing is to get as much happiness and enjoyment out of life as possible.'

If only Dirsy was here, I thought, as another mouthful of Guinness slipped down. This sort of boozy conviviality was right up his street. 'You don't get lonely as a pagan,' said Steve, with endearing openness. 'People are very eager to help you.' I burped contentedly. My earlier witch-wariness seemed increasingly absurd.

Jeanette glanced at Steve, looked down at her watch and then smiled up at me. 'I didn't want to do this before I'd met you, but you seem very nice, so I'm sure it'll be fine – shall we talk more back at my house?' She started zipping up her coat. 'It's quite something,' Steve remarked casually, and picked up his cane.

I looked at my phone. It was coming up to 11 o'clock. I should really be thinking about getting home – I was half-cut as it was, and it probably wasn't that sensible heading off with two people I'd only just met, especially witch— ah, why not. The two of them were as affable as old aunts. Who knew what pearls-of-happiness wisdom they were about to dispense?

We stepped out into the frozen night. 'You should come along to the Pagan Pride march,' Steve was saying. 'Lots of happy campers there. I'll have two hollowed-out horns on me waistband, one for beer and one for mead, three pints in each, and then someone shouts, "In one" . . .' He smiled fondly at the memory. 'Plus, we're all dressed up as ravens, crows' skulls round our hats, waving our daggers . . .' The moon eased out from behind a thin, scraggy cloud. 'Ravens?' I asked, noticing the bite of the frost on my ears and neck for the first time. 'Daggers?'

'Oh yeah. The raven's the bird that goes with the Morrigan, our goddess. So I wear a long sword, the skulls, a cape with strips of black material on it to give the impression of a raven's wings . . .' He stopped on the corner of a quiet street. 'You seen them new type of leggings with a satin finish that have come out for women?' I nodded, shivering. 'Brilliant for the legs.'

We turned into a road of sober-looking terraced houses. Iced-up cars were parked along the verges, but there was no one else in sight.

'The crows are road-kill, mind,' said Steve. 'You don't kill anything unless you're going to eat it. I did have a fox in me freezer, but I've got round to eating it now.' He sniffed. 'Trouble was, I prepared the meat without cleaning me hands from skinning it, and it's got quite a gamey tang to it, fox. Ended up frying it up with a bit of garlic.'

We had come to a halt outside a dark, unlit house. There were thick black drapes visible across the entire front window.

On the doorstep was a stone effigy of a snarling dragon. I suddenly realized that no one else had the slightest idea where I was. Come to that, I didn't have the slightest idea where I was. What street were we on? How far had we come from the main road? Where was everyone?

'In you come,' said Jeanette, pushing open the door, and I followed her into the darkness.

The first thing I saw were the skulls. They were everywhere – human ones, gleaming pale and cold in the flickering light of the candles Jeanette was lighting; the yellowed jaws of black bears, snarling and scowling from beyond the grave; a triptych of stags, jagged antlers jabbing into the room, empty eye-sockets winking as the candlelight spluttered and shook.

I stared around. Crows – stuffed crows, hanging from the ceiling, mounted on dead branches, bluey-black feathers glimmering and glistening, tiny eyes glinting, wings spread wide, beaks and claws open for attack; a carved ebony figure of an Indonesian god, tongue lolling, supporting six or seven ancient curved knives; the elongated, cutting proboscis of a long-dead sawfish, hooked up high on the dark panelled walls.

I took a pace sideways and almost put my hand through the pristine skeleton of a large animal crouched to attack. Jeanette was standing by the door, looking at me expectantly. I was going to be sacrificed, wasn't I, sliced up with those long knives and stuck on display with all the other dead beasts, skin fashioned into a hideous rug and my kidneys eaten on toast . . . Steve, where was Steve? There he was – slipping away into a back room, probably peeling off his clothes and—

'Tea,' said Jeanette. 'Can I get you a cup of tea?'

So English a remark was it, so domestic and so familiar, that I slipped into a sort of autopilot. 'White no sugar,' I said, and leant forward to stare intently at a stuffed fox's head wedged through the wall with teeth bared. 'W-w-what a wonderful collection! Where on earth did you get it all?'

We could have been talking about Dinky toys or decorative plates depicting scenes from wartime Britain. 'This piece here – I picked this up on holiday in France,' she said proudly, lifting up a man's skull and then pointing to a larger one alongside it. 'And this one here I got when I was in North America. Grizzly bear.'

I made what I hoped was an appreciative sound and pointed at the sparkling skeleton. 'And what's this?' Jeanette looked proudly at its bare bones.

'That, Tom, is a male badger.' She wagged a finger. 'Can you see what's so special about him?' I gaped at the sharp incisors, the trap-like ribcage and the thick, milky-white vertebrae.

'He's . . . he's very angry-looking, isn't he?' I mumbled.

Jeanette shook her head. 'Look closer. Look at his penis.'

The room began to swim. Where was Ben when I needed him most? I felt for my mobile phone in my pocket, but realized that I'd left it in my bag. Come on, Fordyce, I thought – you've come this far . . . I forced my eyes open and leaned in closer. The penis – yup, there it was, long and bony . . . hold on – a bone?

'The badger,' whispered Jeanette conspiratorially, 'is one of only five mammals to have a bone in his penis.'

I swallowed hard. Pub quiz, I thought, remember that for a pub quiz, as Jeanette picked up what looked like a child's snooker cue. It was an unusual ashy brown, as if charred, and had a red ribbon tied round the narrowest end. 'Any ideas?' she said, handing it over. I let it roll about in my hands and shook my head. 'That,' she announced with pride, 'is the penis bone of a male hippo.' I nodded feebly.

'And the ribbon, Jeanette?' She smiled.

'That, Tom, is a spell for sexual enchantment.'

With immense care, I placed the mottled todger down onto the table and stared intently at the floor. There was a shout from the back room. 'Here we go!' yelled Steve, bowling back into the room. He was fully clothed. In his hands were three mugs of tea. 'Be very careful,' he said, raising an eyebrow. 'The mug's very hot. You don't want to get burned.'

*

TOM

A few days later, when Ben and I drove down on a dark, stormy Friday night towards Glastonbury for our date with the druids, I tried to get the encounter into some sort of perspective. Without doubt it had been one of the most fantastical nights of my life, yet with each mile we put between ourselves and Walthamstow, the more preposterous my paranoia seemed, and the more I found myself warming to my new witch acquaintances.

'As a pagan I'll help anyone,' Steve had said. 'If someone comes up to me with a drink problem, I'll talk to them. To me I'm on the same level as them. It don't matter if you're a millionaire or sleeping in the gutter – I'll talk to you, whoever you are.'

There was a lot to like about that outlook. Sure, the

cadaverous crows and badger boner were a little outré, but I was learning fast that happiness could take many forms. Would I be trawling eBay for a second-hand hippo rod? Probably not quite yet, but at least the horny old boy had been dead when I'd cupped his cock. If the memory of those silent skulls would ruin my nights for months to come, it would add variety to the usual nightmare script; if a fox or two had been fried with garlic – well, on the up side, it had been organic and locally sourced.

I remembered something Jeanette had said as we'd sat there sipping our teas. 'In the coven they're your best mates. If you break down in Outer Mongolia, they'll come out to pick you up.' I glanced at Ben as he sat alongside me, singing along to Heart FM's disco hour in his trademark Curtis Mayfield falsetto, blowing smoke happily up through the sun-roof. Maybe we had more in common with the Walthamstow witches than we thought.

Then again, Steve would never listen to Heart. The station playing on his car stereo as we'd driven back into town? Magic. It had made me like him all the more.

BEN

'It's not my fault they keep calling me a fucking Satanist,' shouted a woman wearing a halo of mistletoe and a leather bodice as she was bundled through the door of the King Arthur. Moments earlier she'd been scrapping with a couple of tracksuited teenagers by the pool table, and I was a little disappointed when the barman intervened – it had been like watching a clash of civilizations, one old and decrepit, the other decrepit and new.

Every second person in the King Arthur looked like an elf or a wizard: velvet tunics, suede jerkins, one chap was even waving a staff about. However, the Adidas element rather spoilt the aesthetics, so that it looked like Tolkien's Prancing Pony had been infiltrated by chavs, perhaps out for a rumble with a couple of hobbits. For reasons unknown, Tom had chosen this weekend to unveil his Tony Mortimer from East 17 look – the 'Stay Another Day' period in particular. Ice-white bomber jacket with fur-rimmed hood, it looked liked one of the locals had put a spell on him and crossed him with an arctic fox.

I slurped on a pint of nut-brown ale in front of the crackling fire, wondering what the following day would bring. I didn't have to wonder long. The door was flung open and a wild-haired chap wearing a red fox-hunter's coat came prancing in, followed by a terrifying-looking manufactured beast, consisting of a horse's skull protruding from a flowing white sheet beneath. The beast zigzagged across the saloon bar, thrusting its skull in punters' faces, its jaws clattering open and shut. 'In comes Dick and all his men,' roared the chap in the red coat. 'We've come to see you once again. Once he was alive but now he's dead, and all that's left's this poor old head. Poor old head!'

Poor old Tom, I thought he was actually going to soil himself.

TOM

Slightly foggy-headed from the rustic ale, we stumbled out into the frosty pre-dawn morning and headed towards the rendezvous at Chalice Well. Ahead of us, a battered old Vauxhall Vectra rattled to a halt and parked haphazardly across the pavement. A hassled-looking man with a wild beard stepped out, dressed, with an impressive eye for detail, as a medieval peasant – baggy woven shirt, leather jerkin, soft deerskin boots. There was a loud buzzing noise. He groped inside his tunic and pulled out a mobile. 'On my way,' he said hurriedly. 'Sorry. Left the sickle at home. Had to dash back.'

We followed him round a bend in the road. By an old wooden gate was what looked like a wrap party for *The Lord Of The Rings*: white-haired men in long flowing robes, buxom ladies in shimmering velvet cloaks with hoods pulled over their tumbling, curly hair; stumpy, gimlet-eyed chaps in suede smocks, leaning on wooden staves; girls in white dresses with garlands of flowers around their temples. Some clutched ancient-looking lanterns, others bundles of mistletoe. As one they turned to stare at us. I nudged Ben in the ribs as he sparked up his first gasper of the day. 'Try to blend in,' I whispered. He shot me a look and snorted. 'Rich from you, Tommy. East 17 popular at King Arthur's court, were they?'

The first faint hints of pink were visible above the dark smudge of surrounding hills as the hundred-strong group moved silently through the gate and into the garden beyond. Running through the grass was a small sparkling stream. This was the source of the well, the sacred heart of pagan Avalon, the ground under which the Holy Grail was reputed to be buried.

Ben stubbed out his fag on the sole of his trainers and we formed an extended circle in the frost, holding hands with the awkward self-consciousness of true British males. 'If it comes to wearing cloaks,' he murmured, 'I'll go for a pastel yellow one. With a nice fur lining. You?' I nodded civilly at a long-lashed lady on my right, who appeared to have come as the star of the Scottish Widows adverts.

'Brown,' I whispered back. 'Fewer worries about it getting dirty in the woods.'

There was a reproachful squeeze on my fingers from the right, and we fell quiet.

'BREATHE. IN. THE SILENCE!' roared an old chap with a strong resemblance to peak-era Rick Wakeman as two articulated lorries thundered past on the road outside. 'By the power of star and stone, by the power of the land, within and without, by all that is fair and free, I welcome you to this rite of Arthur Alban!'

A middle-aged man in grey robes stepped forward on the far side of the circle. 'Let us take three breaths. Together with the earth beneath us! Together with the sea around us! Together with the sky above us!'

'May there be peace in the north,' echoed a woman to our left. 'May there be peace in the south. May there be peace in the west. May there be peace in the east.' She paused dramatically and looked around the ring of expectant faces. 'Let the circle now be cast!'

I glanced around. Some of the druids had their eyes shut, peaceful smiles on their faces, others their faces upturned to the brightening patches of maroon and mauve in the sky above. Some speakers were evidently more comfortable in their roles than others; while the best had the convincing, charismatic air of natural-born performers, others displayed the self-conscious shyness of an accountant press-ganged into the local am-dram production of *Cats*.

'In the name of the Great Stag in the heat of the chase,' monotoned one particularly bashful chap, reading from a folded piece of paper like a man examining his shopping list at Tesco, 'I call upon the powers of the south. May they bring inspiration and power.'

'In the name of the Salmon of Wisdom, who dwells within the sacred waters of the pool,' roared another, with all the gusto of a pumped-up Brian Blessed, 'I call upon the powers of the west – may they bring wisdom!'

There were repeated references to Britain as a land of forests, meadows and seas. The 24-hour garages, semi-detacheds and Yates's Wine Lodges more familiar to us failed to get a look in. All the same, I liked the notion of the Salmon of Wisdom. It sounded like a dish that my Aunty Judith might bring over on Boxing Day. 'Ah yes,' I could imagine my old man saying happily, rubbing his hands as he sat down for lunch, 'Christmas just wouldn't be Christmas without Aunty Judith's Salmon of Wisdom . . .'

'It is the turning point of the whole world,' Wakeman was intoning gravely. 'It is the time of nadir and rebirth. Long ago it was spring, and the year was young and full of promise. Now the winds of time bring darkness to our lands – let the darkness be felt within our minds and our hearts!'

I didn't want to feel darkness in my heart – I'd only just got to the point where I could go to sleep in it without having to leave a bedside light on – but so agreeably amateur was the ritual, so amiable the consecrated, that I'd completely forgotten about sickles and sacrifices. It wasn't just the way the Scottish Widow kept stroking the back of my hand, soothing though that was compared to the rough, calloused Dirs digits holding the other one, but the tiny details: the way several of the druids kept missing their cues, how a cloak would fall open to reveal stonewashed jeans and sensible brown brogues, and one Gandalf lookalike popping on a pair of black-rimmed Diesel glasses to read out his lines.

The first feeble rays of sun dipped onto the hillside above. 'Into us is poured the light of the one!' cried a blonde girl in the garb of Little Red Riding Hood. A younger man in pearly white robes burst into the circle, carrying a large glowing lantern and wearing an expression of immense excitement. 'I am the Mabon!' he shouted happily. 'I am the golden child of light. I bring you the blessings of the Sun God and his promise that he will ride his chariot ever higher in the sky!'

No matter that the weather forecast was predicting that the Prince of Precipitation and Sultan of Snow would be steering their own vehicles all over Britain for the next few months, or that the speech triggered an unfortunate memory in Ben's subconscious and made him quietly sing, 'Ooo, Mabon', in the style of the Danone yoghurt adverts. This was clearly the key moment of the ceremony, and the assembled druids reacted accordingly.

'The light has arisen from the dark!' shouted one. 'The new fire is with us!' exulted another. All around, the same solitary word was being sung, in deep, ringing voices, on a single note: 'Aaaan-whennn, aaaan-whennn, aaaan-whennn . . .'

The effect was both spooky and stirring. It was like being on a football terrace when the home side has just gone 5–0 up, or in the abbey at Pluscarden as the monks sang their Latin benedictions. I'd read about the pagan call to 'anwen', a universal force that flows through the world bringing inspiration and wisdom, and this was surely it. What was remarkable was how much it sounded like the Christian 'amen', or even the Buddhist 'om'. Here we were, on a freezing hillside at dawn, in a ring of one hundred druids knee-deep in a heathen ritual, and yet with eyes shut you could imagine yourself to be in an Italian Mass or Thai temple.

Sprigs of mistletoe were handed out, happy smiles exchanged. 'We swear by peace and love to stand,' the assembled throng began to chant in unison, 'Heart to heart and hand in hand. Mark oh spirit, and hear us now, confirming this, our sacred vow!'

With a spontaneous burst of applause the druids came out of their reveries and began to smile and sigh contentedly. Car keys were removed from folds in cloaks, mobiles pulled out and turned back on. Of stone altars and rudimentary organ transplants there hadn't been so much as a sniff. The only risk of a limb being sacrificed had been to frostbite.

*

BEN

Avalon was a little bit of a disappointment to be honest, much like the Roxy Music album of the same name. For years people told me it was Ferry's best work, but when I finally got round to ordering it on Amazon, it turned out to be make-out music for yuppies, something Aunty Judith might have on in the kitchen while she's knocking up a Salmon of Wisdom. And the Mabon wants to be a bit more careful – it's all very well coming over all Gielgud during the ceremony, but whipping out your Blackberry as soon as the show's over is like a bloke inside a mascot costume taking his head off in front of the kids: it shatters your belief.

Tom and I headed into the village of Glastonbury, which was gearing itself up for the festivities ahead. The mayor declared the Frost Fayre open, before a brass band belted out the national anthem. The Lady of Avalon rode by on her horse. It was all a bit of a hotchpotch. We took a stroll around the shops, fine if you're after some crystals. That said, Witchcraft Ltd will sell you a set of crow wings for forty-five quid and a jackal skull for just under fifty.

'What do you do with one of those?' asked Tom.

'Are you a worshiper of Hekate?' said the shopkeeper. 'It would make an imposing piece on an altar.'

TOM

We were late for the mid-morning session down at the town hall. Inside sat row upon row of attentive druids, changed now into more sober casual dress and looking expectantly towards the stage. Hanging along the walls were large cloth banners bearing the colourful emblems of the sects present – Sentanii, the Appleseed Grove; at the front, there were a couple of denim-clad blokes who had the air of Def Leppard roadies. Between then paced a man with the extravagant curly hair of a spaced-out Leo Sayer. It was Philip Carr-Gomm.

'After last year's debacle, the Melting Cups of Doom have been banned,' he said gravely, and I shuddered slightly. Was this where the nasty stuff began? A ponytailed chap alongside me leaned over.

'We tried using recyclable polystyrene mugs for the teas and coffees,' he whispered. 'They weren't up to it. Complete disaster.'

Philip was in full hypnotic flow. 'This Order is a foundry, a temple, a club, a fellowship,' he said in his mellifluous tones. 'On another level, it is a happiness factory. It helps people become extraordinary.' He gazed slowly around at the eager faces. 'Ancient lore speaks of the sacred land of Avalon, and of a cavern of initiation under Glastonbury Tor. Let us close our eyes and travel there together.'

There were sighs and yawns as people settled back into

their seats. Philip's voice had a mesmerizing quality. As he described the cavern in rich Dickensian detail, heads lolled all around.

'You see a light coming from the entrance. It is the light of the dawn sun. Follow that light. Feel the energy from the grass flowing in, connecting you to the whole earth.'

I half-opened my eyes and stole a look around. Chins were on chests, arms flopping loose across outstretched legs. A man who looked like the dwarf king from *Fellowship Of The Ring* was dribbling slightly onto his leather waistcoat. There was a distinctive rumbling noise coming from the chair to my left. Was Dirsy asleep?

I slipped outside for fresh air and found the chap with the ponytail drinking tea on the hall steps. 'I'm Sean,' he said cheerfully. 'You found much happiness yet? Can be a bit dull, the daytime stuff, but it should be a good knees-up tonight. You should see it for the summer solstice – 200 druids on the Tor, mead all night, then we all pile onto coaches and head up to Stonehenge for the sunrise. Quality.'

Sean, it transpired, was a builder by day, druid by evening and weekend. 'I've tried the lot,' he said. 'Started off Christian, studied Buddhism, lived in an ashram, became a spiritualist and ran healing groups. At forty, the scales fell from my eyes.' He paused to plant an ostentatious kiss on the cheek of a chesty druidess who had winked at him as she'd swung past. 'As far as I'm concerned, Christianity is just as valid as paganism, even though extreme Christians think we're Satanists. But I tell you one thing, pagans have the most fun.' He looked fondly at the druidess's departing rump. 'Unlike most religions, you certainly won't find much "shouldn't."'

'I'll tell you a shouldn't,' grinned a tubby chap who had come outside for a cigarette. 'You shouldn't buy any of that rubbish Jamie Oliver flogs through Sainsbury's. I bought a packet of his sausages the other day. On the back of the wrapper it said, 'Prick with a fork'. Sounds about right, I thought.'

Sean had joined the Order of Bards, Druids and Ovates several years ago and progressed through its teaching courses. 'The usual route is to start off as a bard, doing some poetry, then ovate – that's divination – and then move on to druidism. It's pretty time-consuming, though. You can't just fall into it.'

I'd read somewhere that druidism could be hard to define. There was no sacred text, no universally agreed set of beliefs and no written record of anything that the ancient druids may or may not have practised. 'It's like trying to grab a slippery eel,' confirmed Sean, as the well-tiered temptress sashayed past again and blew him a kiss. 'In fact, one of the few things we all agree on is that no one has a monopoly on the truth. Beyond that, most of us believe in the law of harvest – what you reap, you sow – that we're all connected in the universe, and that, when you die, you pass on to the Otherworld. You can also visit that in shamanic trance or meditation, which is what Philip's doing inside.'

A rare splash of golden winter sun shimmered on the rooftop tiles of the Georgian buildings along the street. A man dressed as Father Christmas walked by, leading a pony which had fake antlers and mistletoe tied to its head. 'Pagan,' said Sean and his mate together, and both laughed. Sean put his arm round my shoulder.

'I'll tell you the secret to happiness,' he said, suddenly serious. 'I found it written on a bottle of bleach.' I nodded, mouth open, pen poised over notebook. 'Stand upright in a cool place,' he whispered, and gave me a squeeze.

BEN

Over at the Lazy Gecko cafe we lunched with a chap called Mark, a former trainee Catholic priest turned staff-carrying druid. Mark lived in a wood with his dog near Salisbury, and his hour-long walk through the countryside every morning had been his route into paganism. 'I'd look at the sky and the sun and the trees and the stream trickling beside me, and I'd think, "there must be something behind all this, some divinity of nature".'

Mark then made a startling revelation, casually dropping in a grenade between great mouthfuls of chips. 'We make it all up, all these ceremonies and rituals. Anyone who tells you different is lying.' It turned out the Order had only been founded in the 1960s, before reforming, like some half-forgotten prog rock band, in the late 1980s. But what about the Mabon? The Great Stag? That chap called Arthur Alban? (Didn't he used to play for Man Utd?) 'They're all historical pagan divinities,' said Mark, 'but as for the ceremony itself, it's a modern construct. We've nicked bits from different religions, but then you have to remember that other religions, such as Christianity, lifted lots of their components from paganism. All this stuff about resurrection and rebirth and miraculous healings, that had all been part of the pagan tradition long before Jesus was born.'

We left Mark to finish his chips; there was a talk on Celtic deities I didn't want to miss. A bard who looked like Richard Harris in Gladiator *told tales of the Holly King, of the Bird King and a horse woman in golden apparel riding through a glen on a beautiful white steed. A lady sang a ballad about catching and cooking a wren, and we all sang the refrain, 'Said John the red nose.' It was the sort of thing Sting knocks out nowadays, except he wouldn't use a guitar like she did, he'd probably use a lyre.*

The chap in the red fox-hunter's coat from the King Arthur reappeared on stage, and it turned out that what we'd been treated to the night before was a spot of 'mumming', seasonal folk plays performed by troupes of actors. In one of the skits, Father Christmas was beaten to death by his wife, before being brought back to life by a quack doctor called Old Tosspot. And there was that scabby horse again, terrifying Tom and the children.

We were implored to carry on these folk traditions, as if our lives depended on it. But when you think about it, folk traditions never really went away. They just evolved into something else, things that resonate with people's lives in the here and now. Dizzee Rascal's a folk singer, it's just that his folk, modern folk, live in high-rise flats on estates, and most of them wouldn't know a wren if one dropped by for dinner. EastEnders is a folk play, but they'll never write a part for the Holly King, because you don't get his type drinking in Walford anymore and the audience just wouldn't believe it. All in all, folk just got a bit more complicated.

TOM

Back inside the hall, the bearded man from the previous night was back – draped in a white sheet, galloping round with the horse's skull on the end of a long wooden pole, snapping its elongated equine jaws menacingly in the faces of anyone seated within stretching distance. Most people were chuckling happily, but even that brief glimpse of another hollow-eyed skull had me in a sweat. Parting Ben from a stack of vegetable samosas in the pantry, I marched us out into the street and away up the hill to the top of the legendary Tor itself.

The views across the icy white levels down below were

sensational – rolling russet hills away to the north, the red roofs of villages winking in the weak sunshine, a spectral mist hanging over the marshes. I waited for Ben to catch up and gave him a few extra moments to cough his guts up in the lee of the stone tower at the peak.

We sat in silence, looking out at the winter countryside, reflecting how different it felt from that naked summer meadow in Kent, and how far we'd come since the initial meetings with Tarot Cilla and Big Russell back in the spring. Ben smoked a Marlboro Light philosophically and pulled a silver hipflask from the pocket of his trenchcoat.

'Here's a thought for you,' he said, gulping down the Calvados I'd given him for his birthday a few weeks before. 'We exist in a relationship with a series of boxes – waking up in a box, leaving it in a metal one to enter another one made of glass and concrete, in which we will stare into the little box of our computer before returning home in our metal box to relax in front of a television.' I gave him a look.

'You're changing,' I said. He sniffed.

'Not my words, but Philip's,' he said. 'I can't see myself dressing up like Professor Dumbledore – I'd get stabbed if I went out like that in Romford – but I reckon he's on to something there.'

'Try this one,' I said, taking my turn on the hipflask and taking my notebook out. 'It's from Philip's book. "Druidism appeals because it deals with the three most pressing problems of our age – the destruction of our environment, the alienation of individuals and the commercialisation of culture." I like that, too. Trouble is, they seem to be making it up as they go along.' I told Ben the tale of a Welshman named Edward Williams, who back in the eighteenth century had changed his name to Iolo Morganwg, swallowed an industrial portion of laudanum and invented the entire back catalogue of druidic lore. Despite his subsequent unmasking as a charlatan of wondrous imaginings, he was still the most influential source of material that the modern druids had.

Philip had been nonchalant about it when I'd put that to him on the phone. 'That apparent weakness is its greatest strength,' he'd said. 'The wide spread of beliefs, from atheists to polytheists. Religion goes wrong on the details – that's where it gets divisive.'

Ben shrugged. 'Brother Gabriel wins the history lesson hands-down. Thing is, who would you rather spend the weekend with – G-Dog and the Pluscarden posse, or the mead monsters down here?'

There was another quote I'd found, this one from G.K. Chesterton. 'The pagan set out, with admirable sense, to enjoy himself. By the end of his civilization he had discovered that a man cannot enjoy himself and continue to enjoy anything else.' Who was right – the learned, exulted Chesterton and Gabriel, or the earthy, sociable Sean and Jeanette?

Down at the village pub the pagans were undoubtedly on top. Enjoyment of all sorts was to the fore – of the guest ales, of the Man United v. Aston Villa clash on the big screen, of the mince pies and spliffs doing the rounds just outside. There were druids playing pool, ovates on the quiz machines and bards on G&T, not to mention an increasing number of empty glasses on our table. How much had we drunk? Why was Ben buying whisky chasers? Should we really be eating scampi fries when the Salmon of Wisdom was swimming free?

By the time we stumbled back into the darkened hall, my earlier misgivings had been sloshed away by a tidal wave of sauce. It had already been the strangest week of my life. I felt inured to anything else the night could bring. Up on the stage, a hairy bunch of musicians were rattling out some fierce Irish folk music. Glasses were being drained all around. It could have been my gran's eightieth birthday. I sat down with a bump and grinned.

There was something stroking my leg. I looked down and saw the Scottish Widow from earlier crouched at my feet, dressed entirely in skin-tight black velvet and making coquettish eyes. She was holding up a goblet of something golden. 'Drink this,' she murmured, her eyes never leaving my face. 'I think you'll enjoy it.'

Close up she was older than I remembered – late fifties, maybe, with an angular bob that gave her the air of Mystic Meg.

'What is it?' I asked.

She smiled mysteriously. 'We call it Druid's Delight.' Somewhere at the back of my brain, an alarm bell had started to sound. I paid it a moment's attention, and then thought of something else Philip had written: 'We see life on earth as an adventure to be undertaken, rather than a prison to escape or a bridge to cross.' I looked into the upturned face and then into the goblet. As they say in parts of Italy, I thought, 'Fuck it.'

'Smashing,' I said, and downed the lot.

Ben had reappeared clutching two carrier bags, and he set them down on the floor with a clink. 'Bingo!' he sang happily. 'I've grabbed us some mead from the offie. Dunno what vintage it is, but the bloke says it's the strongest he sells.'

Meg batted her eyelids and uncurled from her crouch. 'I'll get you another of those,' she said softly. 'And you will dance with me.'

Acts were coming and going on the stage like a pagan version of *Britain's Got Talent*. There were mandolins, quavering flute solos and ancient yarns of St Gawain and Rhiannon. A shy man almost killed the atmosphere with a self-indulgent poetry solo; the young blonde girl who'd earlier been dressed as Red Riding Hood brought it back to life with a storming set of her own.

Ben was in his element – brakes off, mead in, dander up. 'Brilliant!' he was yelling to Mark, who had changed for the night into the garb of an Amish peasant. 'That girl should be on telly. Fuck Victoria Wood. What's her name?'

The mead kept slipping down. It tasted like dessert wine mixed with lip balm. I watched Ben badgering the blonde girl and tried to keep the room in focus. Sean was waving from across the room. I waved in return and lobbed back another goblet of Druid's Delight. 'You having fun?' he shouted, and I gave him a wobbly salute as he came over.

'What's a good pagan dance move?' I asked, and he laughed.

'Anything you want!'

Time seemed to be simultaneously on fast-forward and reverse. This already felt like the longest day of my life, yet somehow it was still shy of midnight. At the same time, the three hours since 8 p.m. had slipped by in a succession of meady belches.

'Hello again,' whispered a voice in my ear. 'I'll show you happiness . . .' It was the Widow. Where was Ben?

The pagan folk music had reached a new crescendo. Submissively, I allowed myself to be led into the mêlée, and Mystic Meg twirled closer, twisting her arms above her head, staring into my eyes. Dirsy, where are you? . . . There was Mark, jigging past . . . 'You feel pagan yet?' . . . Philip, on the edge of the dancefloor, looking on like a benign headmaster . . . the mead and the Guinness sloshing together in my stomach, the whisky and the Calvados, the Widow coming closer and closer, black velvet flashing, the music hammering and jabbering and the lights flicking and flashing . . .

'WOOO-HOOO!' Ben was there in front of me, bottle of mead in one hand, fag in the other, arms outstretched. He turned to stare at Meg and then looked back at me, glassy-eyed and sweating. 'I'm off to pull a witch!' he roared, and dragged the Widow away into the crowd.

*

TOM

The first thing that woke me up was the cold. The second was a headache so calamitous I feared my skull had burst. After three attempts I managed to sit up, after two more to get to my feet.

I looked around. The patio door of our room was wide open, a spiteful midwinter wind ripping at the flapping curtains. My jeans were hanging off the television, my T-shirt on the bathroom floor. I was naked except for my socks.

At least I was there. Ben's bed was empty, his duvet untroubled and his pillows plumped and pristine. I staggered to the window and almost threw up on the windowsill. What time was it? Where was Ben?

Suddenly it all came battering back – the mead, the Widow, the madness, the dancing, the way Ben had snatched that woman away into the night and . . . No. Oh no. The witch. He'd made some sort of move, hadn't he, buoyed up on booze and excitement and adventure, and she'd been forced to cast a terrible spell . . .

I ran to the door, bile rising into my throat, and fell headlong over a bundle on the floor. It was Dirsy, asleep in his pants, the bathroom rug wrapped around him. He moaned and looked up in confusion. 'Wha?' he groaned. 'Why is this bed so low?'

BEN

Druid's Delight can skew a man's judgement, but getting stuck into Tom's elderly cast-offs? Come on, son, give me some credit, the woman must have been knocking on sixty. I'd actually been disappointed the evening hadn't been weirder. I mean, once the bards had been yanked from the stage, what were we left with? A common or garden disco, 'Oops Upside Your Head' with some chap called 'Two Horns' Steve positioned at the prow of a human boat. What was it Mark had said to Tom? 'Do you feel pagan yet?' Not really, I felt like I was at a wedding in Dagenham.

Still, I'd learnt a thing or two. First and foremost, the druids struck me as a down-to-earth bunch, with 'tolerance' very much their byword. Everyone we met seemed to have a slightly different take on things, with little tweaks and tucks creating their very own bespoke belief systems. But here they all were, revelling in the difference rather than rowing over it. Some saw druidism as a full-blown religion, others just as a way of life, but whether they viewed the world in theological terms or not, at the core of everyone's belief system was the reverence of each other and of nature.

'We are part of a great web or fabric of life that includes every

living creature and all of creation,' Philip had explained. 'Once you believe that you are part of the family of life, and that all things are connected, the values of love, and reverence for life naturally follow.' This struck me as a very humble way of thinking: us humans aren't separate from or more important than everything else on the planet, we're just another feature of the landscape.

We met Philip in the Lazy Gecko, which was dotted with druids, bards and ovates of all stripes and colours. They still looked strange to me, but as far as they were concerned, Tom and I were not much different to them.

TOM

'I think of happiness in three ways,' said Philip, pushing his scrambled eggs to one side. 'There's that peak moment, the one-off experience of bliss, the sort of thing I've felt trekking in New Zealand. Then there's that very deep feeling of satisfaction you get when you're being of use to the wider world.'

He looked at our hungover faces and sideways hair. 'Also, as you get older, there's a contentment. When you're young, you're very ambitious and adventurous. You're never in the place you want to be. That can change. The world is a troubling place – just watching the news is enough – but your spiritual path should help you achieve calmness.'

The cafe was filled with handshakes and goodbyes as the druids began to make their way home. Mark and Sean had already left, and the Dwarf King would join them as soon as he'd finished his full English.

'There's one thing in particular that works for me,' said

Philip, curly hair backlit by the morning light coming through the windows. 'When the cynical inner voice starts playing, I pop out that cassette and put another one in. I talk myself up.'

As we scraped our belongings off the walls of the B&B half-an-hour later, I reflected on what he'd said and what we'd learned in our tumultuous trip through paganism. Seen one way, they were all lunatics. More and more, however, I wasn't looking at the world that way any longer. The biggest fool of the lot was me, with my hang-ups and paranoia and petty preconceptions.

I thought back to a remark Steve had made when, with typical generosity, he had given me a lift all the way back to Bethnal Green tube station. 'For me, being a pagan is all about being free. Everywhere in life today they try to stick you in narrow little pigeonholes, and this is my escape.' He could have been Brian talking about naturism, or some of my triathlon mates talking about extreme exercise. Dressing up as a raven and eating foxes seemed bizarre behaviour, but was it really that much stranger than playing nude table-tennis with low-slung pensioners or climbing into a muddy lake at 6 a.m. with fifty blokes dressed in black neoprene?

Happiness through liberation. If it sounded like a course they might have taught at Berkeley in the late 1960s, or something David Beckham might have tattooed across his arse in Mandarin, it still had a certain ring to it.

Everyone we had met had been wonderfully welcoming. They all seemed remarkably happy. The solitary bad bone between them had belonged to the cock of Jeanette's hippo. I suddenly felt proud of the fact that I lived in a country where you could be a druid or a witch without anyone else giving two heathen hoots.

I went into the bathroom and sat down heavily on the toilet. Next door, I could hear Dirsy fighting with the TV remote control, flicking through the Sunday morning TV shows with ill-disguised fury. 'Fuck off!' he bellowed. Click. 'Fuck off!' Click. 'Fuck off!'

I sighed and reached for the toilet paper. We still had much to learn about happiness. The quest must go on.

7. COMPUTERS

'412 friends on Facebook and not one of them knew he was dead'

BEN

They say the darkest hour is just before the dawn. While bent over the back row of the Jerkwater Porn Cinema, a man going by the name of Dominic Donegal pounding me vigorously from behind, I'm in no position to disagree. Whoops-a-daisy, now it's definitely time for bed, he's finished himself off all over my back.

'It can be anything you want it to be,' was how *Second Life* was sold to me, although being cyber-raped by a burly computer character from the west coast of Ireland had been pretty low on my wish-list going into the experiment. Having seen the film *Avatar*, I had expected my first day in my new virtual world to be spent swooping through lush rainforests inhabited by strange, blue-skinned natives, skipping across the surface of crystal-clear lakes, virtual rain splashing off a virtual body burnished by a virtual sun. Let's just say I fell in with the wrong crowd. Two hours after becoming a 'resident' of *Second Life* and I'm strolling around the place looking like a two-bob tart who's fallen behind with the rent. Bum-skimmer, G-string, boob tube, slag wellies – all the gear and no idea. I've even bought myself a cheeky little tramp stamp for the bottom of my back. Oh, I almost forgot to mention, on *Second Life* I'm a woman. A psychologist would have a field day.

TOM

There are three main things I've learned from the internet: nothing is too rubbish to have at least one obsessive fan; nothing is so obscure that it hasn't been mentioned at least 1,000 times; and no orifice is too inconsequential to be explored by at least one pie-eyed pioneer. But the secret to happiness? I wished Ben luck. YouTube compilations of the greatest moments of Mélissa Theuriau (voted the 'world's sexiest news anchor' by a magazine noted for its coverage of sex-based news) were a fine way to while away a single bored afternoon, but would they be enough to sustain him over an entire week? I feared for his complexion. I feared for his flatmate. But most of all, I feared for his mind.

Anyway, I had plans of my own. An idea planted in my head at Fuck It had taken root while we'd been gallivanting about in Glastonbury – a combination of the pastoral and the tribal, with a little time-travel thrown in. 'Dirsy,' I said, as he shut himself away in his flat with a Namaqua wine-box, a notepad and pen and a family pack of Walkers Sensations, 'I'm just going for a short walk. I may be some time.'

BEN

'Hell is other people,' said that old misery guts Jean-Paul Sartre, and through the post-Christmas, post-New Year, post-'YES, I AM HAVING A GOOD TIME!' fug of early January, his words seemed suddenly rather apt. It is said that French peasants in the 1800s would hibernate during winter, retreating to their cottages and snuggling up for months on end with their livestock, stirring just once a day to stoke the fire and eat a hunk of hard bread. Some would argue the Gallic work ethic has changed little over the centuries, but as I stared forlornly out of my bedroom window at the snow forming a thick, suffocating blanket over the streets of Romford, I thought that perhaps the old-time Frenchies had it right.

Of course, if French peasants in the 1800s had had Tesco Express and *Dancing On Ice*, then they probably would have slept normal hours. And if they'd had the internet, they might never have slept at all (although, on the downside, they probably would have been burnt as witches). The World Wide Web means it is possible to withdraw from traditional society, i.e. real people, almost completely, while at the same time becoming active members of new communities, albeit from the comfort of your own home. Its impact on mankind has been nothing short of monumental, to the extent that it is difficult to imagine the world without it. Think of all the things the internet has impacted on or hounded to the verge of extinction since it became widespread in the 1990s, and you begin to understand its power: newspapers, encyclopaedia salesmen, bin-bags full of porn in the woods, record shops, book shops, dear old Teletext, cricket statisticians, telephone directories, Christmas cards, post offices, office know-it-alls, photo albums, bookies, television, travel agents, radios, Woolworths (apparently, although I would contend it went under because it was a load of old tat), road maps, libraries, Leslie Grantham. Every one of them ubiquitous only two decades ago, seemingly indomitable pillars of our cultural landscape, all now crumbling under the might of the World Wide Web.

Critics of the internet argue it is destroying more than concrete things and that it threatens the very fabric of society. While it is an almost infinitely deep pool of human knowledge, bringing enlightenment to the lives of billions, aiding communication, collaboration, the sharing of information, and the expression of thoughts and ideas, critics argue that, in perhaps mankind's cruellest ever paradox, the greatest social tool ever invented is eroding social interaction as never before, to the extent that in a thousand years' time, *Homo sapiens* could be a featureless, heartless species sporting fingertips the size of ping-pong bats and a USB cable where the old chap used to be. Humans, the anti-internet brigade have it, need to see, hear and touch each other, not while away their lives cultivating virtual relationships online. Relationships which are ultimately empty, ultimately unsatisfactory, ultimately virtual. But then I'd had my fill of humans for the time being. The Portuguese have a saying: you have five friends, the rest is just landscape. When you hit your mid-thirties, I swear things get worse. Most of the humans I know are married, most of them have kids, most of them never go out. 'Fancy a few pints up town?' 'Can't mate, I'm building a pagoda in the morning.' And in January, things get even bleaker. They're not building pagodas, but like most of the country, they just can't be arsed. So if there was nothing going on in the real world, it was time to try out a few new ones. Batten down the hatches against the snow, put a mental block on the bills and the tax returns, tune into my laptop and drop out of real life. I might even get a bunk-up. A virtual one at least.

Second Life was launched in 2003 and is a 'virtual world' inhabited by millions of 'residents' worldwide, all interacting with each other through 'avatars': animated, three-dimensional representations of themselves. Abdul from Costcutter reckoned you could do everything on *Second Life* from watching virtual gigs to playing pub quizzes to designing your own kitchen. He even owns a nightclub, with a recording studio, and earns money flogging virtual ladies clothes. Abdul, whose avatar is clearly more entrepreneurial than his real self, or he wouldn't be eking out a living flogging *Readers Wives* to schoolchildren, also had a second virtual career as a cage fighter, with twelve wins and five defeats on his record. And on *Second Life*, Abdul was half human, half cat. I promise you, Abdul is a decent man.

I have no idea why I chose to be a woman. Let's just say I was curious. What I do know is it took me three hours to design her, and although I say so myself, I definitely would. The detail is dizzying: as well as the basics like height and body thickness and hip-waist ratio, you can also dabble with skin tone, 'nose bulbosity' and 'nostril division'. Then there are the all-important breasts: crank the buoyancy up to eleven? Or let gravity, not to mention reality, have a say? For the record, I plumped for a not entirely unbelievable nine. Squeeze them together so they look like two billiard balls set up for a cannon? Or set far apart, so that you could drive a Routemaster between them? It's a bit like virtual plastic surgery, or playing God. If there is a God, I think I might have discovered why he's been letting so many natural disasters slip through the net: he's spending too much time down in his shed trying to conjure the perfect pair of norks instead.

The moon gazing on my midnight labours, I felt like Dr Frankenstein in his laboratory, except without the bubbling test tubes and surgical instruments, a laptop my only tool. I am, in effect, a postmodern Prometheus. A nip here, a tuck there, a tightening of the buns, this was one monster I was determined not to be ashamed of. And when my work was done, I came very close to falling to my knees and yelling through the skylight, 'It's alive! It's alive!' At first, like a protective father, I opted for conservative dress. Marks & Sparks-style undies, a sensible knee-length skirt, gingham shirt, pumps, whatever I had lying about in my inventory. Then, fully clothed, it was time to set her free. I only wish I had remembered those words of my own father, which he used to say when dropping me off for a new term at university: clamping my right hand tightly in his and drawing me in close, he would hiss portentously, 'Trust no one,' as if he was the head of MI6 and I was about to embark on a top-secret mission to Baghdad.

Ten minutes later and I'm supping virtual Guinness in a virtual Irish pub. When the Chinese land on Mars, they'll probably find a Scruffy Murphy's nestled at the foot of the Borealis basin. It was there that I met Dominic. He was handsome, well-groomed and polite. At first. After a spot of small-talk, he's telling me I need to buy a whole new wardrobe and 'sort out my hair'. I've been a woman less than half-an-hour and already I'm in an abusive relationship. He took me clothes shopping and made me look like a whore. Short skirts, stilettos, a fishnet top, he even insisted I buy myself a new 'skin': new face, new legs, new breasts, new walk. He told me it made me look 'like Jell-O on springs'. He asked if I wanted him to 'show me the ropes', and seconds later I'm being teleported to his house, a log cabin with a crackling fire and, if the sounds of whinnying horses are any indication, stables in the grounds. 'Nice place,' I type. 'Thanks, but I'm only renting it.' We get chatting some more. 'Do you want to keep your Second Life and your real life separate?' he says. 'Erm, I think that's for the best,' I type back. 'But you wanna have some fun?' he continues. 'Oh yeah, what did you have in mind?'

Next thing I know I'm in the Jerkwater Porn Cinema. This is not what I had in mind. There are a few other characters milling around, including a lady dressed in leather chaps with the arse cut out. She makes contact, and her words send a shiver down my spine: 'Don't offer friendship to someone you've only just met. Trust no one.' I'm almost certain it's not Donny Dirs, he's more of a V-neck sweater, grey slacks kind of guy. Even so, it's all getting a bit too weird. I step out onto the balcony and light up a cigarette, in the real world that is.

When I return to my *Second Life*, I can hardly believe my eyes. Dominic's got his kit off, and he's packing some irate looking wood. Before I have the chance to ask him how or why, he's put me in some sort of trance and I've lost all control over my actions. 'Get on that,' he types, and I fall to my knees before him, like a collapsed marionette. 'That feels so good, baby,' says Dominic, 'you don't have to say anything back, it's rude to talk with your mouth full.' Next I'm being bent over a chair and he's taking me roughly from behind. 'Hmmmm,' he types, and I start to feel a little bit sick. Then it happens, a thing no man should ever have to see happen: his cyber-wood starts gushing cyber-sap – he's cyber-ejaculating all over my back. And with that he's gone, disappeared into the *Second Life* ether. No 'goodbyes', no 'here's looking at you kid', not so much as a cyber-tissue flung my way. And then it occurs to me: at that very moment, somewhere in the real world, whether it be Anchorage or Aberdeen or Antwerp, there is a man shuffling towards his bathroom with his trousers round his ankles, tool in hand, fresh from deflowering a *Second Life* virgin. I was that *Second Life* virgin. When I tell my housemate Dave all about it, he's unequivocal: 'I'm pretty sure the internet wasn't designed for any of that.'

TOM

What would a healthcare professional say about Ben's decision to make his avatar a woman? One phone call to Richard Wiseman, the country's premier psychosleuth, was all it took.

'Is he in a relationship? He's not? Then it's even weirder, that's my professional opinion. It's not unusual for a man to choose himself a very good-looking avatar, but only a very small number indeed would choose to be the opposite sex.

'Sometimes there's a desire to see the world through someone else's eyes, to experience life from another perspective. If you ever spend any time with a particularly beautiful person, you begin to realize how much most of us judge each other on appearance, so it may also be that Ben is wondering what it would feel like to be attractive, to be viewed by others as sexy and desirable.

'There's another possible explanation. Ben may have an inner secret. Deep down, he might want to be viewed as a woman. It would probably take some very in-depth analysis to find out which of those two theories hold true, but at this stage I certainly wouldn't like to leave either out.'

BEN

Surfing the net, I discover that 18 January is the most depressing day of the year, according to some psychologist somewhere. But I'm determined to buck the trend, to prove this grey little man's grey little self-fulfilling equations wrong. I spend an hour punching celebrities in the face on puncha-celeb.com – Cristiano Ronaldo, Céline Dion, the bloke who played Beppe di Marco off *EastEnders* – before an email drops into my inbox: my mate Rob has completed my profile for the dating website My Single Friend. It needs some work – he's decided to announce to the ladies of Great Britain that I look like Bill Beaumont, and I'm guessing Bill Beaumont doesn't get the ladies frothing. I do a bit of research, and one quote jumps out at me and doubles me over: 'Internet dating is ideal for those who lack the social skills or the opportunity to meet people in more traditional ways.' It's that handsome sod Beppe di Marco I reckon, exacting sweet online revenge. Rob gives my profile a tweak, and from that point I'm on my own; just me, my laptop and tens of thousands of other social retards who don't have the opportunity to meet people in more traditional ways.

My mum met my dad in the Blind Beggar on the White-chapel Road. The pub where Ronnie Kray shot George Cornell, where East End 'faces', dandies and boxers rubbed shoulders with spivs, crooks and out-and-out villains. Where men were men and women were women, and if you were a 'poof', well that's all right, because Ronnie was one too. What would my dad say if he could see me now, scrolling through this online menu of ladies? 'The world's gone fucking mad,' or something along those lines. Truth is, I've never been that good at pulling. Come to think of it, I haven't pulled in a pub in years. It might have something to do with the fact that my hair's staging a race between bald and grey, and at the moment bald is winning. I go out with my mates from time to time, most of them married, and we get drunk and chat about nonsense. Ladies don't get much of a look-in, and to be perfectly honest, they don't seem that interested in us. At the time of writing, I've got 412 friends on Facebook. Some of them must be single? Some of them must want to go out on the pull? Aah, but of course, hardly any of them are actually friends. I could cark it in my flat and no one would know for days. And they'd say in the papers, '412 friends on Facebook and not one of them knew he was dead, just another statistic in broken Britain . . .'

There are a lot of 'sporty' women on My Single Friend, which is strange, because in real life I know hardly any. No one smokes. No one's fat, just 'curvaceous'. Everyone likes the countryside. And if I read one more time that 'she's just as comfortable dancing the night away in her stilettos as she is curled up on the sofa with a DVD and a glass of wine', I think I'm going to smash the place up. Still, a couple of hours in, and things are looking promising. All human life is here, from lawyers to doctors to ex-girlfriends to the girl who works down the corridor at BBC Television Centre. And either everyone's an expert in airbrushing, or there are some bona fide sorts. Maybe it's not that weird after all? I give the old typing fingers a stretch and take the plunge . . .

Helen, 32, from Hackney, she looks quite nice. A teacher, a 'pub lover', picture of her skiing, wallop, let's get involved. 'Dear Helen . . .' Fuck me Dirsy, you're not Mr Darcy. 'Hiya Helen . . .' Hang on a minute, when have I ever said 'hiya' in real life? 'Watcha'? Even worse. What about an ironic 'Yo!'? I make my living from writing and I'm struggling to get past the preliminaries. Right, she's draped in a Union Jack in one of her photos, make a quip about the BNP and move on to the next one. Tara, 30, from Wandsworth. Bit out of my way, but any port in a storm. 'Likes men with a sense of humour.'

Seriously, who doesn't? 'A hard worker.' Hmmm. Wait a second, what's this? 'So if you're tall, dark and handsome, why not get in touch?' Jesus wept, these modern women want the moon on a stick . . .

I haven't left the house now for fifty-six hours, so it's time for a spot of online grocery shopping. Bit of meat, some veg, some fruit, some of those Fox's Viennese Dave likes and . . . oh, I like the look of that Gaggia coffee machine. 300 quid? Done. Well, it's nearly Christmas. An hour later and I've bought a James Brown box-set, fifty golf balls and stuck a score on Ronnie O'Sullivan to win the Welsh Open snooker. I bloody love 'The Rocket', and William Hill loves me. Back on My Single Friend and there hasn't been a peep. In fact, no one's even opened any of my messages. I take a quick peek at Facebook: I see Nick's updated his status, he's just had a bag of salt and vinegar Hula Hoops. Terry's out with clients tonight, so will be back late, and Tim's single again, which is a bit of a shock, because when I last met him, about eight years ago, he wasn't even courting. Then I'm back on My Single Friend. Jane from Hornchurch has read my message! But she hasn't replied.

I dare to re-enter *Second Life*, but this time I play safe and stick a pair of jeans on. I play a bit of Zombie Meltdown on a virtual arcade machine, a spot of Whack a Mole, and then I'm a little bit bored again. Back on My Single Friend, and still no replies. This isn't happiness, this is death by a thousand knockbacks. Well, five knockbacks to be accurate, but rejection does make you melodramatic. I head down to a *Second Life* beach club called Cannibalism and get talked into doing a bong by a man called Nathanial before collapsing in the sand. Then it's time to take a break altogether and head over to Abdul's for some fags. You need a bit of escapism, he says, and he might have something for me: *Manhunt 2*. Banned', he assures me, 'in every civilized country.'

Funnily enough, only that day an online newspaper is reporting that computer gaming is being blamed for the rise of rickets in children. I can't help thinking this is a little bit unfair. Next they'll be blaming excessive teeth-brushing for an upsurge in tennis elbow. Down the years gaming has been blamed for a lot of things, from backache to diabetes to heart failure. In 2005, a South Korean man collapsed and died after playing a game called Starcraft in an internet cafe for fifty hours non-stop. Fifty hours in an internet cafe? How can they be sure it wasn't the bill that killed him? But we're not just talking physical problems, unless you count getting stabbed: also in 2005, a bloke in China was hunted down and killed after he borrowed a 'dragon sabre' in the online game *Legends of Mir 3* before selling it on to someone else for 7,200 yuan. The message from this story is clear: if anyone's flogging any dragon sabres down your local, be sure to ask if they've got a receipt. Meanwhile, the football game *Championship Manager*, which allows you to be gaffer of your favourite team, has been cited in at least three divorces, while computer games have also been blamed for everything from juvenile delinquency to social retardation to emotional immaturity to itchy balls.

While gaming used to be the preserve of spotty fifteen-year-olds to whom the waggling of a phallic shaped joystick for hours on end was second nature, the industry is now reckoned to be worth $50 billion a year, more than the film and music industries combined. That tells you something: the adults have taken over. While the idea of your dad whiling away his Sunday afternoons trying to top the 9,000 point mark on *Daley Thompson's Decathlon* might seem a little bit surreal (my dad usually had better things to do with his time, like tiling bathrooms, or sawing mysterious pieces of wood), it's easy to see why the big boys have got involved. In *Call of Duty: Modern Warfare 2*, players get the chance to play members of an elite military unit taking on a Russian nationalist terrorist group, while in *Championship Manager* you can sack one of your players for getting the tea-lady up the duff. I made that last bit up, but you can bet they've got their best men working on it. Grown men queue round the block in snow and rain for the latest releases, and now the women are getting involved, in droves. In *The Sims*, which its creator calls a 'digital dollhouse', you're the director of your own virtual soap opera, in which families act out their virtual dramas. And in *Café World* you can create your own menus, hire your online mates as waiters and get them to try out and rate your online food. No, I couldn't get my head round it either, and not wanting to get sucked in so far I might not be able to haul myself out, I decided to look up a man who can.

Professor Mark Griffiths of Nottingham Trent University is an expert in computer addiction, which he passionately believes exists, despite scepticism from other academics. Whether it exists in the purest sense of addiction or not, it is a fact that people spend hours on end lost in the online soup of wizards and trolls that is *World of Warcraft*; it is a fact that marriages have ended, jobs have been lost and trousers soiled because people haven't been able to drag themselves away from their laptops. And Prof Griffiths thinks he knows why.

'People engage in behaviours that are rewarding in some way, psychological, physiological, social and/or financial,' he explained. 'People get a mood-modifying experience as a result of engaging in their favourite games, either a feeling of intense excitement, a buzz, arousal, a euphoric feeling, or they get the exact opposite. They use the game to escape, to numb, to de-stress, to relax. We know that when people gamble, have sex or play video games, their adrenaline levels increase, endorphins are released, and that also gives a psychological high. People who design games are using the kitchen sink approach, they're throwing almost everything they can into a game in terms of increased realism, graphics, sounds, noises, skill levels, whatever. Some people might be rewarded through skill enhancement, others might be rewarded through playing with other people, or through beating their own high score. There are very idiosyncratic rewards which appeal to different types of people.'

Prof Griffiths recalls the story of how one American house-wife went from three hours a week on the internet to sixty hours a week in the space of three months. She would put in fourteen-hour sessions, stopped doing housework, stopped seeing friends and got depressed and anxious when not online. Within a year of buying the computer, she was estranged from her two daughters and separated from her husband. He also tells of a high-flying college student who would spend fifty hours a week playing *Red Alert*, in which Britain and its allies battle a rampant Soviet Union for control of the European mainland following the Second World War. The student would sleep all day, play all night and spunked all his food money on a faster modem. Not surprisingly, he wasn't a hit with his tutors and ended up dropping out. So surely the $64,000 question is this: this housewife, this student, that bloke whose ticker gave out in Korea, that fella who got stabbed over a sword that didn't even exist, Abdul from Costcutter: surely they're all just a little bit weird?

'No, not at all,' argues Prof Griffiths. 'It's just a different way of being. People have written about how we as human

beings seek out experiences that help us change our conscious-
ness in some way and what most of us like to do is change it
for what we perceive to be the better. That's why we drink
alcohol, smoke cigarettes, take drugs, gamble or play video
games all day. Of course, when it's taken to excess those short-
term rewards are overtaken by long-term, negative detriments.
But people who use online chatrooms, online role-playing
games, they like the fact they're engaged in a non-face-to-face,
non-threatening activity in what is perceived as a very anony-
mous environment. It lowers peoples' emotional guard, people
can truly be themselves online, they don't feel stigmatized,
alienated, they feel very secure. These activities allow people
to change their social identity, their persona. Effectively you
can become something you're not. People create these identities to make them feel better about themselves and raise their
self-esteem. And there are some behaviours people could
potentially do offline, but only do online because of this
disinhibiting experience, such as certain sexual practices or
peccadilloes.' What, like getting cyber-fucked in a cyber-porn
cinema?

This idea that 'people can truly be themselves online' seems
ripe for philosophical debate. You might say that crouched
over a laptop in your bedroom, communicating with others
while masquerading as an elf, you're not really being yourself
at all, and that someone's true self only becomes evident
when they are exposed to other, real-life human beings. Prof
Griffiths disagrees, contending that it all depends on what you
define as the 'essence of being and identity'.

'People react differently to different situations and how I
act in a room full of neo-fascists and how I react in a room
full of family members will be completely different,' he argues.
'When I first started looking into internet addiction, there

were lots of stories in the papers about these strange people who met on the internet and ended up getting married. People pathologized that behaviour, called them nerds and geeks and anoraks. But now when I look at my friends, especially those who are single, the main way they meet people is through internet dating. We are growing up with a generation of people who spend as much time online as they do offline, and peoples' online selves and offline selves may be different, but at the core you're still the same person. The internet has become another tool in people's social armoury and is normal and socially acceptable. Ten years ago the idea of having virtual friends was pathologized in the way a penpal was never pathologized. Because of the technological generation gap, people who don't understand the world we live in now tend to see that behaviour as strange and abnormal.'

When I get off the phone to Prof Griffiths, I've got a text message waiting for me: 'I hear you've got yourself on I Can't Pull.com. It's great they can do things for people like you nowadays.' Well, it doesn't look like they can: back on My Single Friend, I still haven't had a sniff. I spend the rest of the day downloading and watching Hollywood films, and the thought occurs to me: the internet, among other things, has turned me into a petty thief. At about nine, my housemate Dave appears in the doorway, and he's got a look about him I don't like. It's the look of love. It's a look that says, 'While you were watching *Newsnight* last night, I was conkers deep.' I think I know how to break his smug reverie: it's time we both went Manhunting.

When Tomohiro Nishikado created *Space Invaders* back in the mid-1970s, he first experimented with tanks, battleships and soldiers as targets, but decided it would be immoral to invent a game in which the aim was to extinguish human life, and so he plumped for aliens instead. Other developers had less compunction. In 1982 *Custer's Revenge* caused uproar when it depicted General George Armstrong Custer himself raping a bound Native American woman. The aim of the game, made for the iconic Atari 2600 console, was to steer Custer, wearing nothing but a hat, boots and a bandana and sporting a raging chubby, past hails of Injun arrows to the other side of the screen. Once there, Custer would have his wicked way with his large-breasted prey. One radical feminist claimed the game led to the increase of gang rapes of Native American women, while shops were forced to store it under the counter and sell it in brown paper bags. Whether Custer was out for revenge for his defeat at the Battle of the Little Bighorn, or whether he was out for revenge because his bighorn in the game resembled a piece of Lego, the makers never said. But one thing's for certain, seeing the game now, all the controversy seems rather ridiculous, because if *Manhunt 2* is anything to go by, things have taken a marked turn for the worse.

It's 1 a.m. and my housemate Dave, who's had a few scoops too many, is jumping up and down behind me and imploring me to 'chop his fucking head off'. The thing is, I don't have much of a choice, either I chop his fucking head off or I don't get to the next level. And anyway, he deserved it: minutes earlier him and his mates were kicking me to death in a nightclub-cum-dungeon whilst wearing pig masks and roaring, 'I'm a necrophiliac!' at the top of their voices. Once I've chopped his fucking head off, I've got to hold it up in front of a hatch and hopefully the bouncer, thinking I'm the necrophiliac whose fucking head I've just chopped off (probably with a Biro, although I can't remember exactly) will let me in. This place is how Studio 54 might have turned out if Fred West had been in charge of the guest list.

Mind you, I shouldn't have been too surprised. Within two minutes of starting *Manhunt 2* I'd had faeces thrown at me by a fellow inmate and been urinated and gobbed on. Oh, and I'd stabbed three psychiatric nurses to death with a syringe. If this wasn't harrowing enough, I was playing the game on the Wii, which meant I was actually acting out each murder, or, as I kept on reminding myself, each act of self-defence. For I was Ben Dirs no longer, but Danny Lamb, subject of a top-secret experiment at a hospital for the criminally insane. An experiment, evidently, that hadn't gone quite to plan. The premise of the game, and I have to keep reminding myself it is only a game, is this: it's all gone tits up at the hospital for some reason I can't recall, my cell has sprung open and I've got the chance to escape. Once out of there, I've got to hunt down and bump off everyone who's been involved with my incarceration for the previous six years, using anything from syringes to blowtorches to dildos (no, I'm not joking). It makes *One Flew Over The Cuckoo's Nest* look like a routine check-up with your local GP.

The attention to detail, especially for someone brought up on Spectrum classics such as *Manic Miner* and *Jet Set Willy*, is staggering. You don't just kill people, you kill people and drag them behind doors or into the shadows so no one else gets wind. You kill people and then, if you're particularly upset, you pull out another weapon and carrying on killing them. There are times when you don't have to kill people at all, just hug the wall, stay in the shadows and walk on by. But usually you end up killing them anyway, just to make sure they don't kill you. But more than the killing, it's the level of detail –

the labyrinthine levels with their hundreds of rooms, the many different ways of doing things, having to master the controls and improve your skills, the need to solve puzzles to reach higher levels – that reels you in. I hesitate to call *Manhunt 2* sophisticated – snuffing out a copper by creeping up behind him and sticking a plastic bag over his head is far from sophisticated – but you know what I mean. Sophisticated – and educational: I now know that if ever I have to fight off three assailants with a pair of garden shears, I'd be absolutely knackered. And I'd end up dead.

It's 3 a.m. now, and my housemate Dave is crouched beside me in the living room, whispering fevered instructions. I can almost hear his heartbeat as I stalk through a level entitled 'Ghosts', which involves a house full of spectral, screaming children and a stackload of homicidal maniacs wielding base-ball bats. *Pacman* this isn't. 'Hide behind the door,' whispers Dave, 'and when he comes round the corner, execute him with the shard of glass.' Aye-aye, Cap'n, whatever you say. Do you want me to stick this stale Ryvita up his jacksie while I'm at it?

Two hours later and we've completed 'Ghosts' and are onto a level called 'Sexual Deviants'. Bloodcurdling screams abound, and once in a while I poke my head inside a cell and witness men wearing white coats and pig masks performing indefinable acts, using a variety of instruments, on victims strapped to hospital cots. It's despicable, sordid, disturbing, but for some reason we can't tear ourselves away from it. I imagine myself and Dave still glued to the screen a couple of days later, both sporting vagrant's stubble, eating tins of mackerel and drinking each other's urine. But when Dave passes out on the sofa, a fallen comrade, I can't go on without him. I feel suddenly drained, dirty and a little bit guilty. It's not real, but it looks real. More disquietingly, perhaps there are those for whom it feels real. On the plus side, Dave doesn't look like he's in love anymore. Actually, is he still alive?

The next day when I wake up, I feel troubled. Not because I've still had no chat from anyone on My Single Friend, and not because it suddenly hits me that I've started sleeping with my laptop, but because I can't shake off the feeling that what me and Dave had engaged in the previous night had been a little bit wrong. Ten hours straight butchering baddies with buzzsaws, lopping off their goolies with wire-cutters and frying their faces in fuse boxes. But that's not really what's bothering me. I know I'm not going to creep up behind some old girl in Asda and smack her over the head with a can of beans because she's about to nab the last bag of Monster Munch. Of course not, with all those people around, I'd suffocate her with a plastic bag instead. Rather, and at the risk of sounding pompous, I'm troubled by how infantile it all seemed. Two grown men, playing computer games all night. What was wrong with having a sensible chat about gardening while smoking a couple of pipes? Never mind how 'sophisticated' it all was, and never mind how beguilingly grotesque it all was, it still seemed to me like so much kid's stuff.

Maybe I'm just on the wrong side of Professor Griffiths' 'technological generation gap'. Not so long ago, men used to go down the pub to play dominoes or shove ha'penny or darts, and I suppose you could argue they were simply playing less sophisticated games. But I would argue there was a social aspect to it, and that the games were merely incidental. Grown men mowing down Nazis or splattering aliens in their studies or 'dens' or 'romper rooms' while their kids are doing the same in their bedrooms upstairs, where's the dignity in that? If I'd ever caught my old man playing computer games I would have found it all a little bit unmanly, not to mention unseemly: 'Chop, chop Donny, get a fucking life and go and do some tiling . . .'

In five days I've made sixteen new friends on Facebook, twenty-eight new friends on Twitter, a fuck-buddy on *Second Life* and been custard-pied by a handful of women on My Single Friend who were, on reflection, miles out of my league. I've chatted about boxing and campervans on messageboards, and discussed with a bloke called DJ from Boston why the American 'finger' is to the British V-sign what the grey squirrel is to the red. I've discovered that the tallest mountain in the world is in fact Mauna Kea on Hawaii, not Mount Everest; that the winged figure outside Lillywhites in Piccadilly Circus is supposed to be Anteros, not his older brother Eros; that Marco Polo was actually from Croatia; that in Indonesia, the penalty for masturbation is decapitation; and that Wolves' Jody Craddock is Fanny Craddock's great-grandson. I've visited strange new lands, had a cyber-sex change and been cyber-raped. I've been cyber-shit-faced and cyber-stoned, been cyber-swimming and cyber-go-karting and I've cyber-thrown someone into a cyber-industrial mulching machine. I've been cyber-drenched in cyber-shite, cyber-urine and cyber-phlegm, not to mention cyber-man goo – I think I'll have to invest in a cyber-washing machine. By anyone's standards, a pretty eventful few days – so why do I feel so lonely?

Professor Griffiths argued that people found online relationships comforting, reliable and safe, but I missed the visceral thrill, the cut and thrust, the risk of interacting face-to-face; the risk of disapproval, of hurting someone's feelings, the risk of real-life heartache. Is there real emotional depth in a virtual friendship? Coming to it cold, I didn't think so, but then maybe that's the point: I'm thirty-four, I didn't grow up with the internet and, therefore, I am cold. Irony of ironies, maybe I haven't developed the necessary 'social' skills to thrive in an online environment, just as there are those who struggle to thrive in an offline environment. But if people are hiding behind computer screens because of an innate offline shyness, then how will they get over their offline shyness? If they are socially inept, how will they develop their social skills? How will they learn the real-life rules of communication, life's social mores? Perhaps, in the future, people will spend so much of their time online, such questions will become redundant.

I scroll through my 400-odd Facebook friends and I feel disgusted. I'm a social-networking narcissist, just like everyone else. No different from a child, running to his father on the beach, opening up his hands and revealing, with mouth open in wonder and eyes ablaze, how many pebbles he's collected. Wow. Like the father on the beach, we're all supposed to be impressed. It's to do with belonging, feeling loved, boosting self-esteem, all strong predictors of happiness. In centuries gone by, important people would commission portraits of themselves and hang them on their walls to show other people exactly how important they were. They'd make themselves look more handsome, they'd make themselves look humble or generous or oh so self-deprecating. Now we have Facebook, which allows millions of people of no importance to show other people how important they think they are. People of no status obsessed with updating their status. I toy with switching my Facebook account off, but I convince myself I need it, that I couldn't live without it. Just as people convince themselves they couldn't live without Jamie Oliver or their iPhone or their Dyson vacuum cleaner or tapenade.

The internet can educate and elevate and inspire. It's 'the great leveller', the greatest invention since Gutenberg conjured the printing press in the 1400s, smashing old orders, empowering billions. Everyone can be seen and everyone can be heard, from the bloke in Benfleet whose cat can play the harmonica to the freedom-fighter in Burma to the woman promising 'the best blowjobs in Brisbane'. It has been described as our 'new social campfire', where the people of the world can gather to argue, laugh, learn and presumably toast virtual marshmallows. If that is the case, then I'm one of the party-poopers who's happy, for the most part, to flee the campfire's smoke and hang out with real friends offline. For an old fella like me, the smoke can be overwhelming, suffocating and make me a little bit queasy: I'm not entirely in control, it feels like it's controlling me.

Give me a real handshake, a real hug, a real kiss, a real poke. Give me a real newspaper, real Christmas shopping, a real bollocking at work rather than an email one, real emotions, real blood, real sweat and real tears. Give me a world in which people don't feel the need to tell me their kid's just puked down their brand new jumper, that they're 'feeling frivolous' or 'about to watch *Corrie*'. Give me a world where when you get blown out by a woman, your mates are there to see it; give me a world where they'll laugh in your face and you can laugh with them. Eventually. Give me a world where I can escape from the world without being assailed by emails, texts and tweets. Give me a world where I can see people, touch people, hear people, smell people, properly gauge people's reactions: whether they're being sincere, whether they're lying, laughing, exaggerating, piss-taking, empathizing, sympathizing. Wanking.

Sartre was wrong: hell isn't other people, hell is buying a set of second-hand golf clubs online. Barely used my arse, I've got your number sunshine . . .

Author's note: There was no accessing of online pornography in the writing of this chapter.

8. THE WISDOM OF ANCIENTS

'We're not savages, you know'

TOM

Having to bat away the occasional Biro and elude the odd plastic bag? Dirsy didn't know how lucky he was. While he was gadding about in a pixelated world of imaginary assassins and sexually frustrated financial advisors from darkest Essex, I was facing down a rather more authentic challenge. It's one thing putting the horn into Hornchurch. It's quite another being confronted by twenty-five half-naked Maori warriors, eyes out on stalks, screaming of ancestral massacres and thrashing at the air in front of my nose with sharpened spears.

We'd both come a long way in our search for happiness, but this time I couldn't have travelled much further; three days of weary journeying, across continents and seas and time-zones, about as far from Ben's overheating laptop as it was possible to get. If New Zealand was the other side of the world, the East Cape of its North Island felt like the far beyond of the backend of nowhere, an empty, windswept stretch of deserted beaches, dark-green mountains and bush-covered headlands jutting out into the relentless rumble and spray of the South Pacific ocean. Our reasoning had been straightforward. While Dirsy careered through the internet age, seeking happiness in the fizzing possibilities of the future, I would go the other way – reversing through the centuries, back to the ancient wisdom and timeless traditions of the original Pacific peoples. 3,000 years of knowledge, 2 weeks to soak it up. If we couldn't find some answers here, we couldn't find them anywhere.

The instructions I'd been given were even simpler. Be at the tribal *marae* (meeting-house) at midday, ring the bell at the carved wooden gate and wait to be called in.

I'm not quite sure what I expected. A hot towel, perhaps, or a basket of fruit on my neatly made bed. When a solitary old lady appeared to lead me into the deserted compound I thought I might have the wrong peninsula. Only when a conch shell sounded a mournful hoo-hoot did I guess that someone else might be there too, and even then there was a bucolic stillness as she beckoned me round a corner.

'TUUUURI WHATIA! UUUMA TIRAHAAA!'

If you've never been confronted by a crack squadron of muscle-bound fighters, yelling and rolling their eyes, sticking out their tongues and making slicing motions across their throats as they advance straight at you with stomps that shake the ground, you've never felt truly alone.

That this was the Maori equivalent of the red carpet treatment was hard to keep in mind. To run, to fall to the knees or just to stand there and gape? I certainly had no tribal *haka* of my own with which to respond. If given sufficient advance warning, the Fordyce clan might be able to come up with something befitting our lineage – miming a competitive family quiz, for example, or the staging of a fierce game of beach cricket – but there was neither the time nor, I sensed, quite the same level of intimidation.

Instead, with a nod to previous visitors to those shores, I

plumped for what we might term the Prince Charles – standing awkwardly with hands clasped behind the back, smiling wanly and tapping a foot badly out of rhythm like a broken wind-up toy. 'Charming,' I almost said to one young buck, as he jabbed a spear towards my stomach. 'And what is it you do?'

With a final roar and slapping of chests the men jogged into the high-roofed timber hall. The old dear pointed after them. Inside were 150 seats, lined up in rows and filled with large, staring Maoris. Opposite was a single small chair. The chair for guests.

I took my place. The most senior among the gathering stood up and strode to the front. He spoke in a deep, booming voice of the tribe and its history, finishing with a flourish and beckoning me to my feet. My aged escort scurried over. 'Now you must tell them why you are here,' she whispered.

I cleared my throat. 'I am Tom Fordyce,' I began confidently, 'of the Fordyce family.' Probably an unnecessary embellishment, but still. 'Thank you very much for that reception. My friend and I are looking for happiness. Unfortunately he can't be with us today, but I speak on his behalf: we want to learn as much from you as possible. We want you to show us how to be happy. Thank you. You've been very kind.'

I'd made it sound uncomfortably like an acceptance speech at an awards ceremony, but it would have to do. En masse the men rose, and began to sing ancient songs of their ancestors' mighty deeds and battlefield triumphs. The voices soared and swooped, echoing under the A-frame roof and bouncing back from the whitewashed wooden walls. Dirsy, I thought with a lump appearing in my throat – you don't know what you're missing. The old lady leaned over again as the hall fell quiet.

'And now,' she murmured, 'you must sing a song in return.'

I chuckled and gave her a knowing wink. She gazed straight back. I stopped chuckling. 'You're joking?' She shook her head. I looked up at the rows of serious, expectant faces gazing patiently back at me. 'But what do I sing?' I whispered frantically.

'Sing of your ancestors,' she said, and shuffled off to the back of the hall.

If the chair had felt a little exposed before, it now felt like the most isolated spot in the southern hemisphere. I liked to warble a little Dusty Springfield in the shower, but an impromptu a cappella set in front of a hall-full of brooding Maoris . . . What tune could I possibly choose? My internal jukebox seemed bent on sabotage. 'Love Me Do'? Not to a bunch of tooled-up warriors. 'Dancing Queen'? Certain death. 'We Will Rock You'? Where did I think I was, Live Aid?

I got slowly to my feet. Think, Fordyce, think . . . What did Mama Fordyce used to sing to us in the cradle? What did my Irish gran used to pull out whenever an audience had gathered – apart from her teeth, that is, and in her declining years, her canvas-and-whalebone bra?

'This is a song', I began, 'that I learnt at my grandparents' knees. It has been sung by my family for generations.' I took a deep breath. 'It's called "Seven Drunken Nights".'

Thank you, brain. Supposed to be praising my ancestors and celebrating everything my family stood for, I'd plumped for a song about an alcoholic sop and his dirty cheating wife. Still, the set-list had been made public. There was nothing for it but to commit.

'As I went home on Monday night as drunk as drunk could beeee . . .'

Error number two: I'd chosen the longest song in the

world. It had a verse for every day of the week, each accompanied by a full chorus. We could be here for hours.

I ploughed on, arms fully outstretched, Prince Charles foot tapping, into the big finish, '. . . but a baby boy with his whiskers on, sure I never saw before!'

I beamed out at the upturned faces.

Silence. I cleared my throat and waited for the applause. Nothing.

On the back row, someone coughed. Someone, surely – it only needed one of them to start clapping and they would all gradually join in . . . It would be so Hollywood, the applause breaking out all round the hall, slowly at first, then building in noise and numbers until they were all at it, standing on their chairs, cheering wildly, hoisting me on their shoulders and carrying me roun—

I sat down mutely and stared at my toes. I'd bombed. I'd flopped. I was a dud, a turkey, a total washout.

'Jerusalem'. Why hadn't I just sung 'Jerusalem'?

BEN

If only I'd been there with him, I would have known exactly what to sing. There is only one option when Maoris start waving their arms about and stamping their feet: you have to go barber shop on their arses. You may well scoff, but I've seen it done. You see, back in the day, my old school played rugby against some Maoris, and forget what you've heard about rap battles in the hip-hop clubs of Compton, morning assembly before that game made Eminem versus Lil Wayne look about as fierce as a fireside duel between Val Doonican and Barry Manilow. The Maoris would end up winning the game, but with that rousing rendition of the old Al Jolson standard 'Toot Toot Tootsie, Goodbye', at least our boys escaped with their honour.

Years later, when I was on a tour of Australasia, I found myself in the firing line, hounded, harried and eyeballed along with the rest of the First XV before a match in the Solomon Islands. This meant war, this meant hats, this meant brollies – this meant 'Singin' In The Rain'. If only I'd been there with him, we could have sung it together. Me Morecambe, Tom Wise, thrashing about in imaginary puddles. At least he stopped before he got to Sunday: 'I saw a thing in her thing where my old thing should be'. Try explaining that *bit of family wisdom to the village elder . . .*

TOM

There is a lot to be said for the simple handshake. As I made my way out of the *marae*, 150 Maoris lined up to say hello in their own traditional *hongi* way – by pushing their foreheads against mine and squashing our noses together.

The difference between squashing noses enough for it to count and squashing noses enough that you accidentally kiss the other bloke is remarkably small. Certainly in the approach it feels exactly the same – the leaning in close, the staring into the eyes, the nestling together of the nostrils and the warmth of someone else's breath on your top lip.

The last man I kissed was my dad, when I was about eight years old and on my way to bed. Since then the closest I've come to a male mouth is in the dentist's chair, when Dr Sultan leans in close to examine my disintegrating fillings. Even then he'll be wearing a green sanitary mask. To be a mere stumble or weak nostril away from inadvertently snogging the local hardman seemed an inauspicious way to begin my immersion in the community. I had no idea what the locals' attitude to homosexuality was, but the East Cape struck me as a well-locked closet at best.

Waiting by the gate was a curly-haired teenager in baggy black jeans and a baggier black T-shirt. He was massive – around six feet tall but at least seventeen stone, his body a giant soft presence, a shy smile squished around his malleable features. 'Harzit bro?' he asked bashfully. 'I'm Henare. You're with me.'

He slung my heavy rucksack over his shoulder like a man picking up a child's toy, and we ambled out through fields of maize towards his family's bungalow. Away into the distance climbed wooded hills, wispy clouds drifting above their tops like hazy smoke; to the north, sloping plantations of kiwi fruit stretching down to the foaming sea. This was Maori heartland, the place where the great chief Apanui had landed his *waka* (canoe) hundreds of years ago after sailing across the Pacific from the mythical ancestral islands of Hawaiiki. Most of the land was still owned by his descendants, the *iwi* (tribe) of Te Whanau-a-Apanui, and there was no missing the sense of identity; Henare had Apanui's name tattooed in large green and red letters across his entire right forearm.

I wondered idly what the limits of my commitment were. I was keen to absorb as much Maori wisdom as I could. At the same time, stencilling 'FORDYCE' across my arm sadly seemed certain to invite mockery when I returned home. It would be like having your mum sew your name inside your pants, except one hundred times worse.

Henare's parents Ani and Richard were waiting on the porch. Richard had the bristling moustache of a Maori Merv Hughes, Ani the meaty physique of a woman who has spent more time hammering nails than having them painted.

'Some welcome, eh?' giggled Ani. 'Quite an honour to get a *haka*. Unique to our tribe, that one.' So it wasn't the one I'd seen the All Blacks perform? 'Nah. That's "Ka Mate Ka Mate", from the Ngati Toa tribe. There's hundreds of *hakas* – welcome ones, battle ones, ones for your birthday, ones to keep fit to . . .'

Ani disappeared into the kitchen to cook dinner. Henare took me down to the river for a pre-meal wash. When we returned, Richard was standing on the porch holding an eel the size and shape of a car inner tube. 'Caught it from the river while you were down there,' he grinned. Ani stuck her head out of the window.

'Don't listen to him,' she warned. 'He got it from the supermarket this morning.' Richard shrugged.

'Someone caught it in a river, anyway,' he said, and wobbled the eel's head so it appeared to nod.

That evening we ate out in the yard, a royal flush of stars smeared across the empty southern skies up above. If it was almost as quiet as Pluscarden Abbey, the menu was rather more adventurous – *kawa kawa* tea, waxy purple potatoes, *kamo kamo* marrow and boiled *kumara*. The eel, chopped into fat chunks and basted in horopito pepper, sat steaming in a wooden basket. Monks 0, Maoris 1.

'*Na tau rourou, na taku rourou, ka ora ai te manuhiri*,' said Richard solemnly. 'It's an old Maori saying: "By your food basket and my food basket, the visitors will be nurtured." Food is very important to our culture. We believe in sharing it and eating together. It is a way of bringing us all together.' For a garnish there were small orange fruits the shape of lozenges.

'That's *karaka*,' said Ani. 'Sweet taste. Don't touch the

kernel, though. If you ate that you'd go mad. Yeah. There's no coming back from that.'

She lobbed a chunk of eel backbone into a dish and looked around at the silent landscape. 'There's a feeling of belonging here. The family had been here for generations. We used to live in the town two hours away, but like a lot of Maoris we've come back to our roots. In the last twenty years we've all rediscovered a lot of the old traditions. It's isolated here, and it's a long way to anywhere else, but we're *tangata whenua* – people of the land.' Family, food and formalities with foreheads. The lessons were piling up.

That night I dreamt of Ben's head on an eel's body. Richard was trying to spear him with a jade harpoon while I danced an Irish jig alongside. When Henare woke me before dawn and led me out of the house and onto the dewy path down to the beach, I couldn't move fast enough.

Henare was clutching a broad knife, a rubber ring and a large black bag. Gone was the clumsy and withdrawn teenager of the day before. Now, hurrying through the grey gloaming, he moved over the jagged rocks with the silent grace of an obese ghost as I stumbled over the black boulders and fell into rock-pools like a man wearing a blindfold. Where was he? There – clad in battered Reebok Classics and a black jumper that was more gap than garment, splashing out into the shallows, looping the drawstrings of the bag through the rubber ring and diving down into the freezing briny.

I perched on a lump of bleached driftwood and waited, looking out across the black sea as it sucked and spumed over the fractured slabs of rock. Every now and then a plump hand appeared above the surface and plopped something glistening into the bag, followed by a flash of white trainer as he kicked back down into the depths. The sun peeped cautiously over the headland. Somewhere on the other side of the globe, Ben was locked in his bedroom, eating a Domino's Meat Feast pizza while adjusting the size of Avatar Ben's breasts. Henare returned, striding out of the waves with his clothes plastered against his curves, an inflatable Maori version of Daniel Craig in *Casino Royale.* The bag was bulging – spiky sea anemones, abalone the size of softballs and snapping, panicking crabs. As I watched he plucked one of each from the bag and threw it back into the sea. 'Maori tradition,' he said shyly. 'The first fish is always returned to the sea, as thanks for the catch.'

We sat in companionable silence. Henare cracked the abalone open with his knife, scooped out the roe and offered me a chunk of flesh on the blade. If it tasted like liver dipped in salt, it felt rude to refuse.

I thought back over the preceding months, to Russell and his flapping, theatrical hands up in that strange Snowdonia mansion, to Father Fuck It perched owlishly in his Bond villain dome, to Dennis inadvertently wiping his old chap across the forehand court of an old table-tennis table. So many different characters, so many different solutions. A year ago, sitting on the edge of the world with a seventeen-stone teenager while eating raw shellfish at dawn would have felt surreal in the extreme. Not any more. Get to grips with rhino penis-bone, as they never told us at school, and the world will open up before your eyes.

The day drifted by. Snoozes were taken on the porch. Even the guard dogs got bored of barking, and lay down listlessly in the dust to act as impromptu aircraft-carriers for the squadrons of mosquitoes flying sorties round the skies. I watched the long, marbled clouds form layers out over the sea and tried to stay awake.

I had a date to keep. In the aftermath of 'Seven Drunken' shambles, as news of my quest spread around the community, one name had cropped up again and again: Tuihana.

Grandmother, tribal elder, conduit for all the wisdom amassed over thousands of South Sea years. Tui was a sage, scholar and history lesson rolled into one. Born and raised on the Cape with her nine siblings, she had been sent away as a child, like many Maoris of her generation, to a strict Christian school where speaking her native language meant a strap round the legs. A lifetime later, with her own offspring all around, she had established a village school where Maori traditions were celebrated, not censored.

As afternoon turned into early evening I wandered over to the *marae* at Kauaetangohia, close to the banks of the river Whangaparaoa. Maybe it was a good job rural New Zealand was so sparsely populated, I mused; there simply wasn't room on the map for many more letters.

'It was all passed down verbally to me,' Tui explained, brewing us up a pot of tea and digging out some biscuits. 'I learned about the stars, about how to find my way, about when the big tides came and how to catch the moki fish when they came round the coast. I knew how to use fishing nets, and how to make honey from manuka blossoms.'

Tui was no frail old pensioner. Flinty of eye and jet-black of hair, she had the feisty, combative look of a woman who'd done more rounds than George Foreman. Professional boxing between grandmothers was illegal, and rightly so, but I couldn't help but speculate what the outcome might have been had Tui been matched in the ring against Dirsy's nan. In one corner a woman who had taken on the world and won; in the other, a woman with a temper like a crocodile and mouth like a trawler's toilet. Don King would have filled his boots.

We strolled around the *marae*, the wind tugging at her short black hair, and talked happiness and how to get there. Tui listened patiently as I described the road we'd travelled so far.

'There are five rules we have which will help you,' she said eventually, narrowing her eyes and looking out towards the Tihirau mountain at the river's mouth. 'First of all, don't be greedy. Share with others, and enjoy the sharing. Rather than saying, "This is mine," say "This is ours." When I was a child, each family would wait on the beach for a fishing boat to return, and when the catch was landed, everyone would be given a share. It didn't matter if you'd played no part in the fishing. When you did go out, you would do exactly the same.'

She led me into the tin-roofed dining hall. Stretching along the walls were stylized red and black drawings depicting the tribe's journey across the Pacific and its landing on the headland outside. 'Know who you are and where you come from. "Whakapapa" is the story of our people, and everyone here is taught their own. Keep that strong family base. Our ancestors taught us to keep our family together – even when they hunted, they did it as a family. Now there is too much pursuit of money, and not enough nurturing of children.'

She pointed to a mural above the door showing two men making peace with one another. 'Resolve your arguments with diplomacy,' she said firmly. 'Here on the *marae*, all disputes have to be sorted out before we enter this room. When you eat together, the argument is over.'

I followed in silence, scribbling furiously on my pad. We had reached the small classroom where she taught. Through the window the maize in the fields leaned sideways in the stiff breeze. 'Always remember there's someone coming after you.

You don't own this world; you are only looking after it.' She tapped me on the chest. 'Last of all, appreciate what you've got. I find that people take things for granted these days.' She smiled. 'You've got a lot more than you realize.'

*

TOM

Wisdom can be found in the most unlikely of places. I had been lying in bed at Ani's, mulling over everything Tui had told me, when I thought I heard the voice of Roger Federer. I shook my head and put it down to jet-lag, or the *kawa kawa* tea. It had been *kawa kawa* that Tui had served up, hadn't it, not that *karaka* stuff?

Roger spoke again. He seemed to be coming from the adjoining room. This was ridiculous. Had I swallowed the wrong kernal? Which was the one that sent you mad? *Kera kera* was the yellow ber— no, Kawakawa was the name of the tribe, that was it, and *whakapara* was the canoe— nope, *tehanare* was the canoe, and *moki-iwi* was the—

I pulled on my shorts and stumbled bleary-eyed into the lounge. Ani and Henare were perched on the edge of their seats, staring at a state-of-the-art 52-inch flat-screen television showing live coverage of the Australian Open.

Ani glanced up. She saw my expression and laughed. 'We're not savages, you know,' she chuckled. 'Have a seat. Andy Murray's up next.'

Ani, it transpired, knew more about tennis than most sports journalists back home. So did Henare, and Tui, and everyone else in the area. The East Cape was in the grip of tennis mania. 'There's a court up at the *marae*,' she explained. 'We played all the time as kids. Best game in the world.'

For the next two hours we watched Murray do battle with Marin Cilic. There was in-depth discussion of his relationship with Kim Sears, of his short-lived hook-up with Brad Gilbert, of Justine Henin's forehand, her remarkable return from retirement and whether she could generate the power to dethrone Serena and Venus later in the year at Wimbledon.

Sport had often made me miserable. My football team were consistently mediocre, except for the short spells when they were just plain rubbish; the English rugby side specialized in joyless drudgery, and watching the national cricket team was enough to give Dorian Gray white hairs.

I had often wondered if I should cast it adrift. What was the point of caring so much about something you had so little control over? Surely no one's wellbeing should be dependent on the success of a last-wicket stand between Paul Collingwood and Graham Onions. The Greek philosopher Epictetus had been sure of it: 'There is only one way to happiness, and that is to cease worrying about things which are beyond the power of our will.' I could imagine the old boy's eloquent fury in the stands as a Stoics Invitational XI collapsed to successive innings defeats against the touring Epicureans.

Here, in a small cottage among the kiwi fields, was an answer of sorts. Happiness was a serious business, and Tui's little pearls were priceless, but happiness could also be mucking about with complete strangers and feeling like you belonged. In many ways I had nothing whatsoever in common with Henare and Ani. Yet thanks to a mutual admiration of Andy Roddick's second serve, we would spend the rest of the fortnight messing about like old friends.

BEN

My head feels like a pinball machine, facts and figures ricocheting between nodes like ball bearings, my mental flippers being worked so hard it hurts. It's what they call being 'stuck in the loop', bouncing from website to website, from Outlook to Hotmail to Facebook to Twitter, and all for no reason my tattered mind can fully fathom. Concentration shredded, I'm unable to focus on one particular thing for more than a minute. Sometimes, I'll get halfway through reading an article on one website, think of something else I need an answer to, only to forget what I thought I wanted to know before I've had the chance to type it into Google. Crouched over my laptop, fingers poised, staring blankly into the oracle, desperately seeking answers to questions that haven't even occurred to me yet.

I was envious of Tom now, of his road less travelled. I pictured him paddling to the shore of a lake, a fish flapping between his teeth, one side of his face scored with a tribal tattoo. His mind clear of clutter, and when a question crops up that might need answering, his oracle comes fitted with a smile and a pulse. Or perhaps it's not quite like that. I've seen Once Were Warriors, *and not every Maori is a wistful font of wisdom. Maybe Tom has gone the other way? Now I picture him wearing tribal leathers, slumped at a bar, crushing beer cans between his hands and throwing them over his shoulder: Tom 'The Muss', not to be fucked with. But more likely he's living the simple life, perched on a log next to a fire next to a trickling stream, proving that happiness can mean doing nothing in particular. Not frantically thrashing around with his happiness net, just sitting still and allowing it to flutter down from the sky and perch upon him.*

TOM

I was slowly marinating in a rich cultural stew, but there was one big part of the Maori way of life that I was yet to experience: the rumble, the ding-dong, the fisticuffs. The slow-motion pace of life was a delight, the living off the land a pleasure, but to truly live as a Maori, I would have to go to war as one.

It was about more than mere male braggadocio. In a world of homogenous hip-hop culture, a Starbucks on every street and *The Simpsons* on every screen, traditional fighting skills play a huge role in maintaining Maori identity. I wasn't just learning how to impale a man, useful though that might prove next time I joined Ben for a night out in Seven Kings; I was being taught a fistic philosophy, a code of honour that had survived the centuries. If it came in handy next time someone started throwing chips around on the night bus, that was just a happy coincidence.

My tuition would come at the hands of a chap named Jamus. This was good news. Going by his size and handiness with *taiaha* spear, Jamus was someone you wanted on your side. He had arms that appeared to have been borrowed from Achilles and a set of slicing skills that would have done d'Artagnan proud. I'd seen people with scarier tattoos, but only in documentaries about death row.

'We have a motto,' he said, pulling various weapons off shelves in his garage. '"*Waewae taumake, kiri maki*" – heavy feet, wet skin.' I looked puzzled. 'Wet with your blood,' he said with relish as I stood rooted to the spot, the carved point of a stick flicking marginally past my left ear.

It was an enlightening time, and not only for the damage

I was taught to inflict with a greenstone *patu* club. Jamus was a man in touch with tradition. Schooling in the mortal arts ('Smash through at the temple and lift the scalp up like the top of a can!') went hand-in-hand with nuggets of time-honoured principle ('We say, "Bundle up the twigs, and they will never be broken." We are stronger together, weaker alone').

There were long sessions on blocking and defence, longer soaks in the sulphurous, sacred springs where warriors had come to recover after epic battles against the British in the past. Surrounded by reeds and flowers, the water up to my neck and steam rising past my ears, I felt as far from that Wetherspoons at Liverpool Street station as it was possible to feel.

One evening, at the end of a scorching day, I took off from Ani's and headed off along the coast, through the tangled brush and slanted trees and out onto the very edge of the peninsula. This was where, 250 years before, the Te Whanau-a-Apanui tribe and European man had first come face to face. Maori canoes had paddled out to within hailing distance of Captain Cook and his crew on HMS *Endeavour*. Nothing would ever be quite the same again.

'Before the Europeans came, we only had one word for men and women,' Jamus had told me after a particularly punishing routine with the greenstone clubs. 'Everyone looked after one another, but they split us up.' He had spun a spear through his fingertips like a Maori majorette. 'We're all about our families. We work to live. But look at those who colonized us – they live to work. What has their society produced? Environmental destruction, global warming, mass depression . . .'

I looked around, out to the thick wedge of white cloud sitting flush with the horizon, down to the churning Pacific a hundred metres below. Windblown fronds of the palm trees created a flickering strobe from the light of the sinking sun. There was no one else for miles around.

Cape Runaway, Cook had christened it. Hundreds of years later it felt just as apt. The Maori way was all about family, so what was I doing here, on my own, as far from my friends and relatives as anyone could ever be?

I shut my eyes and tried to block out the unexpected rush of loneliness. Sure, I was 12,000 miles from home, but wasn't this one of the most beautiful places on the planet? Wasn't everything in place – the sun, the solitude, the silence – for the perfect set-piece moment?

I stretched out my arms, held a *qi-gong* pose and waited for happiness to arrive. It felt suspiciously like a full bladder. With a silent nod to Brian and Dennis from the naturist camp, I pulled off my T-shirt, stepped out of my shorts and pissed nakedly into the nothingness.

The nothingness turned out to be full of a stiff Pacific north-westerly. Windblown piss stopped in mid-air, reversed and covered my legs.

I shook it off and shut my eyes again. Here we go – ecstasy, any moment now, a surge of— What was that song in my head? Dubliners? Nope. Handel's *Messiah*? No . . . Was that Blue?

Who the hell put 'All Rise' by Blue in my brain? I didn't own any Blue. I would never own any Blue. 'All Rise' wasn't even their best song. It was no 'One Love', that's for s— Why was I even debating this?

There was an unpleasant itching sensation coming from my arse region. What now? I craned my neck and looked down over my shoulder. Bang in the middle of my right buttock was a freshly drawn mosquito bite, bleeding slightly and with a small pink peak clearly visible.

I sighed heavily and pulled my clothes back on. If heaven existed, it was in stubborn mood. I started back down the path and began to sing, quietly at first and then gradually with increasing volume. By the time I reached Henare and Ani on the beach, the last sliver of sun had dropped away beyond the curve of earth. 'ALL RISE!' I bellowed inappropriately, and flopped into the sand.

Henare was carefully threading line into two fishing-rods by the water's edge, Ani building a big bonfire where the sand met grass. The silvery, flat sea extended away like an endless sheet of tin foil, pierced by occasional wonky triangles of rock. Water burbled onto the shore and slid across pebbles with a quietly admonishing shhshing noise.

I'd come all this way, and what had I found? That I missed my family, that I missed my ladyfriend, that I missed Ben. What was it Bertrand Russell had said? 'To be without some of the things you want is an indispensable part of happiness.' Bertie had written many wise things in his time, but he'd got this one wrong. You can find your way to paradise, I thought with a pang, but if your mate's at home pretending to stab strangers with a Biro, it will never feel like perfection.

The moon eased out from behind some torn-up clouds. I bent down to select the smoothest stones I could find. 'Come on Henare,' I said wistfully. 'I'll show you how to skim a stone. Did I tell you about the time I took part in the Stone-Skimming World Championships?' He shook his head mutely and handed across a bottle of beer. 'Easdale Island, the Inner Hebrides,' I said, glugging down a cold mouthful. 'What a weekend. Whisky, crab sandwiches and a bloke called Melon. One of the great trips away.'

We stood side by side, fishing-rods angled away in the

shallows. Dwarfed by his colossal bulk, I stared out to sea, waiting, watching the moon sit like a spotlight above the curtain of dark green trees on the headland.

Maybe I'd been wrong to expect a miracle moment of happiness. Maybe it wasn't a sudden flash of wonder, a one-off hit of holy revelation that filled you with golden joy. I glanced across at Henare, spinning his line in and then letting the reel go again. Maybe it was actually the absence of something – an absence of stress, of anxiety, of the constant need to seek something bigger and better and faster and more expensive just around the corner.

Henare gently took my rod, adjusted the line and handed it back. Behind us, Ani's bonfire crackled and spat as she drooped abalone into the flames and let them bake on their own shells. She'd already set up the comfy chairs for Andy Murray's Aussie Open final with Roger Federer later that evening.

There was something else I was coming to realize. Happiness was finding friendship and similarities where you least expected it. It was finding out that your preconceptions and stereotypes were hopelessly wrong. Witches could be designated drivers for disabled kids. Tribal Maoris knew the ground-strokes of Belgian tennis players inside out. Naturists were fans of Transit vans. Silent monks liked Whitesnake. There was delight and surprise all over the place. You just had to remember to search it out.

'Food's up!' shouted Ani, and the two of us plodded over. Henare picked up a fat fish in his enormous hands and pulled it apart, leaving the juicy flesh of the body in one palm and the slimy head in the other. Fair enough, I thought. He should get the best bit. He was a growing boy.

'All right if I have the head?' he asked shyly. I nodded, and he put it to his lips, gave a suck and sighed with delight as the eyeball popped into his mouth.

I'd been wrong all along. 12,000 miles to find that happiness was sucking a fish's eyeball. Not even Bertrand had seen that one coming.

9. LAUGHTER

'This is not me mumbo-jumboing you'

TOM

So many lifestyles, so little time. Almost a year had passed since our crisis meeting in Wetherspoons, and while the spirit of adventure still burned strong in our breasts, the patience of those around us was wearing thin.

Friends had got married to people we'd never met. Bosses were demanding to know why we were so seldom in the office. Brother Gabriel had probably worn out another pair of sandals disco-dancing round his monastic cell when no one was looking.

We had time for maybe two more forays – but where should we go? So many potential paths were fraught with danger. Our plan to enter a commune and share our few worldly possessions with our fellow collectivists was vetoed by the ladyfriend, who was still fuming that I had failed to put my Pluscarden vows into action. 'If you're not moving in with me, you're certainly not moving into a free-love squat in Harlesden,' she growled, with a face that suggested resistance was entirely futile.

Sometimes we stumbled on a dogma that suited one of us but not the other. Discordianism appeared so perfect for

Ben it could equally have been called Dirsyism – a religion based on a love of chaos and rooted in a fear of order and harmony. I liked the sound of its founder Malaclypse the Younger (also known as Mal-2 and, in less prophetic moments, Gregory Hill) as well as elements of its holy text, the Principia Discordia (sample quote: 'Tis an ill wind that blows no minds'), but there was room in our partnership for only one master of disaster.

At other times there were practical concerns. A plan to become hermits had to be cancelled when it was pointed out that the two of us, by definition, could not experience isolation together; a revival of John and Yoko's Bagism was lost to Ben's claustrophia. 'Bed-in yes, Bagism no,' was his stubborn vow.

It was with some relief, then, and no little excitement, that the pioneering work of Dr Madan Kataria was brought to our attention. Working with the unhappy and unwell of Mumbai, Dr K. had pioneered the idea of laughter as therapy – not simply for physical illnesses, but for malaises of the soul. Beginning with just 5 patients 15 years ago, he now had a network of 6,000 laughter clinics worldwide, staffed by disciples who had passed through his own stringent qualification course.

On his website he looked a little like Bernard Bresslaw in *Carry On Up The Khyber*, perhaps with a touch of Leo McKern in *Help!* The testimonials were glowing. According to the quotes, the Guru of Giggling could make your body 'release happy hormones', give you 'a sense of wellbeing and lightness' and boost your immune system 'by up to 40%'.

It sounded ideal. What else had sustained us throughout the year but laughter – during the evenings at Fuck It Towers, while stranded in the silent misery of northern Scotland

and during the nerve-shredding qualifying rounds of the British Naturism Table-Tennis championships? Ideal, with one caveat: our budget was blown. Even with recourse to overdrafts and advances on birthday presents from aged relatives, we still barely had enough to get to Heathrow, let alone fly to Rajasthan.

I scoured the good doctor's notes to find a franchise closer to home. Kerala? Too far. New York? Too expensive. Hold on – Rayners Lane?

Of all the places I'd imagined we might find happiness, a faceless north-west London suburb famous for precisely nothing was very low on the list. Northolt had the airfield, Harrow the school, Pinner the Elton John, but in the middle of them all, Rayners Lane stood like a beacon of mediocrity, and a very weak beacon at that. Despite that, it was home to a fully certified Katarianite devotee named Harish.

'I am qualified laughter therapist. I trained in Spain by doctor himself,' responded Harish to my email enquiry. 'We meet Saturday. All are welcome.' We were in. What was lost in mystic glamour would be made up for by the fact that we could travel there for a £2.20 Oyster fare.

I stepped off at the tube station that weekend to a familiar message on my phone from Ben. With a touch that would have warmed the heart of Malaclypse the Younger, he had confused Rayners Lane with Raynes Park and ended up fourteen miles away at a set of council football pitches near the Kingston bypass. We had changed in many ways over the past twelve months, but certain characteristics were invulnerable.

'Absolute shocker,' he puffed on arrival, an hour-and-a-half later. 'Tubes were all screwed. Had to get a bus.' Choosing to ignore the fact that the same screwed tubes had both delivered me on time and continued to disgorge considerable numbers of other travellers, I put my arm round his heaving shoulders and led him up the road.

The Quakers' meeting house fitted perfectly into its surroundings – red-brick, sober 1930s design, as ostentatious as a paving-slab. Outside, propped up against a frost-covered bench, was a whiteboard with 'Harrow Laughter Club' scrawled wonkily on it in red marker-pen and the words 'ho ho ho' dotted randomly about.

We pushed open the door and walked in. On wooden pews arranged in rows sat twenty neatly dressed Asians of various ages, from a tubby woman in her twenties to grey-haired dowagers clutching walking-sticks, plus a small pale chap with a bushy moustache and stern female companion. At the front, facing the rest of the hall, stood a middle-aged man wearing white cricketer's trousers, plimsolls and a cream T-shirt with 'LAUGHTER YOGA' spelled out in orange stick-on letters. He had dark wavy hair forced into a reluctant side-parting and soft brown eyes with just a hint of melancholy about them. Behind him, Blu-Tacked to the wall at a lopsided angle, was a printed sign advertising 'World Laughter Day'.

'Hello to all!' he said, suddenly beaming out at us. 'And greetings! My name is Harish – welcome to Laughter Club! Today, we talk benefits of laughter, we do laughter exercises, then meditation, then question and answer. Then, at finish, networking opportunities.'

He pointed to man with a clipboard at the back, whose naturally baleful expression was accentuated by a front tooth that jutted out diagonally between his lips like a small tusk. 'That is my Junior Assistant.' He reached down into one of the three plastic bags at his feet, rummaged around and pulled out a cloth monkey. 'And this is my Senior Assistant!'

The monkey was placed carefully on the seat beside him. Harish looked around with a Frank Spencer smile. 'He's good at laughter!' he said happily, before folding the toy's floppy legs over each other. 'And also yoga!'

Harish had a likeable air, his use of the definite and indefinite articles charmingly haphazard, his sing-song accent reminiscent of King Julien of the Lemurs in *Madagascar*. He poked around in a second bag and took out a copy of the *Beano*. 'See this? Know what it is? This used to be very popular with children. But now it's all killing on TV. And stabbing. This no longer exists. Well, exists, but look – now eighty-five pence! Used to be two-and-a-half pee!'

His big eyes slowly scanned the room, his face troubled. 'Life now has little room for laughter. At school it becomes serious. Then work is serious – going on the train, the hectic life . . . the laughter stops. Then you have health problems. When you baby, you laugh like nobody's business, yar? This we need to return to. I offer you my personal guarantee: I give you refund if you don't laugh today. It's like wirus – one person start to laugh, everyone start to do. I'm providing you with the full package.'

I glanced to my left at Ben. He had the haunted look of man who wished he was still in Raynes Park.

'I work as contractor in IT,' Harish was saying. 'Recently my boss tell me my contract is up. No more job, no more money. First thing I did was shake his hand. Then I went to the toilet, looked in the mirror and laughed and laughed. I felt so much better.' He paused. 'The boss looked very surprised.'

A slightly sombre mood had settled over the hall. Harish seemed to sense the change. 'Many people have uniforms. You respect policeman because of uniforms. The tie is a uniform.

It tells us about person wearing tie. If you went to work in nightdress, not sure it suits.' He delved into his third and final bag. 'So I have my own uniform!' He waved a multi-coloured Afro wig in the air and wedged it onto his head with a flourish. There was laughter from along the pews. 'See?' he said delightedly. 'It working already!'

His Junior Assistant trudged over with a bulging dustbin bag and upended it on the floor. A tidal wave of comedy headgear flooded out – plastic policeman's helmets, jesters' hats with bells on the horns, felt Santa ones with a strip of white fur around the brim. He threw them into the audience with relish. 'Already we feel different!' he laughed, open-mouthed. An old chap at the front wedged a cardboard crown on his head.

'It's working!' he cried.

Harish shrugged his shoulders in mock disbelief. 'And we haven't even done anything!'

BEN

To think people pay thousands of pounds to travel the world in search of the different when something so peculiar takes place most weekends in Rayners Lane. I yanked my jester's hat onto my head, making its bells jangle rather forlornly, and it felt more like a crown of thorns. I glanced across at Tom, who was fingering his green Santa hat and doing a very good impression of a confused pensioner in a care home on Christmas morning: 'Come on Mr Fordyce, why don't we put it on so you can join in the fun . . .'

Tom poked me and whispered: 'Look on the bright side, we could be in for a refund.'

Harish's Senior Assistant toppled sideways off his chair, causing

Harish to leap to his feet and start pointing and whooping wildly. 'Imagine you're a small boy again,' said a suddenly serious Harish, noticing I wasn't biting. When I was a small boy I rarely laughed. In fact I never stopped crying, so it wasn't the sagest piece of advice. 'Why you cry, Benjamin?' my mum's French friend Jacqueline used to say to me, and I never really knew why. At least this time I had a valid excuse.

TOM

Harish was an animated silhouette against the Art Deco bay windows, the wintry sunlight lit a halo through his curly wig. Around the edge of the hall, Junior Assistant was quietly laying bowls of crisps and plates of ginger nuts on trestle tables.

'We are here to laugh for no reason,' said Harish firmly, his expression solemn. 'There are two ways of laughing. Number one, people stand up and make jokes. But jokes don't work for everyone. Dr Kataria experiences this. When he is starting, they had problems with serious jokes. Some religious jokes. Some sexist. The clients are unhappy. They didn't like. Half are offended. Then sex jokes. Even worse. After six months, no jokes left, no clients left.

'Number two – laughing for no reason. Nobody is offended, everybody can do it. Don't need to be great comedian. Also, scientific fact: human body cannot tell difference between laughter one and laughter two. You get same benefit.'

According to unspecified researchers in the United States, ten minutes of laughter gives you the same health advantages as half-an-hour of aerobic exercise. This appeared to be better news for some than others. Maybe I'd been wasting my time entering the National Cross Country Championships; at this rate, Johnny Vegas had a better chance of winning Olympic gold than I did.

Harish discussed the example of the American author Norman Cousins, who claimed that watching Marx Brothers movies gave him pain relief more powerful than any orthodox drug. 'Norman was told he have three weeks until he would check out. You know check out? Not Tesco's check out – in the sky! Yet Norman lives for another twenty years. This is not me mumbo-jumboing you. He laughed himself better!'

The old dear on my right had nodded off. With the radiators on full blast and Harish getting close to top-speed, the heat in the room was stifling. 'Stand up!' barked Harish, and we jumped to our feet. 'All try to laugh – not for a reason, but for no reason.' A few nervous giggles broke out. 'Come on! We can do better!' Titters turned into peals. The old dear sat up with a start. 'HAHAHA!' I roared at Ben. 'HAHAHAHA!' he bellowed back.

It was a curiously disconcerting sound. The forced hilarity took on a maniacal air. Rather than feel better, I was starting to feel somewhat unsettled.

'You will notice whole body moving! Would you agree? If whole body moving, organs inside body moving too, yar! Kidney, liver, whole body gets massage. When they feel exercised, you feel benefits. Mentally too. It triggers endorphins. Like a feel-good factor.'

A pensioner down at the front was laughing like a Bond villain, throwing his head back and cackling. Suddenly he stopped, clutched at his throat and tottered through the door looking pale and shaky. 'Too much,' indicated Harish with a regretful frown. 'Has heart condition.'

He picked up the toy monkey and placed it under his arm.

'Laughter is very powerful. On World Laughter Day, my class marched straight out to Rayners Lane station. I could not stop them. So, if you have any illness – hernia, right? Back problem, okay? – you should know. Piles. You yourself know.'

He motioned us back into our seats and continued with his scientific discourse, his academic standing only slightly compromised by the lurid rainbow-striped wig hairpiece. 'Cells need the food of oxygen. Cells need a nice warm place, warm enwironment. Yar? Your body is very acidic, the cells don't like it. And when you are stressed, guess what happens – your enwironment becomes acid. Laughing gives a nice enwironment to the cells.'

The pale moustachioed chap nodded. 'Laughter, as they say, is the best medicine,' he agreed.

Ben made a face. 'That's what my great-great grandfather used to think,' he grunted, 'before half his kids died of tuberculosis . . .'

At a signal from Junior Assistant, the pews were pushed to the back and a space cleared. We formed a ring and began to circle the room. 'Ho ho ho!' sang Harish, clapping his hands in time with each words, 'Ha ha ha!' We followed suit, clapping and laughing along woodenly.

From the tubby girl at the rear came a rogue 'Heh heh heh'. Harish shot her a reproachful look.

We split into pairs. This time we were told to introduce ourselves to our partners and burst out laughing at the response. One of the dowagers offered me an outstretched hand in regal fashion. 'Heema,' she said. 'Northwick Park.' I chuckled indulgently, like a toadying courtier.

'Tom. Originally from Essex, but now from Hamme—'

'AHHAAA! HAAAA! A-HA HA HA!' I took a shocked

step back, and the gale ceased as suddenly as it had begun. 'Hammersmith, did you say? Oh, long way.'

I watched Harish as he dashed around the hall, urging his patients on, waving his hands about excitedly and rocking back with exaggerated mirth. While he had neither the charisma of Father Fuck It nor the showbiz sprinkle of Big Russ Grant, his unbridled enthusiasm was both endearing and admirable. At a mere £3 for an afternoon of his time, he also represented splendid value. I wasn't completely convinced by some of his more adventurous scientific claims, but it seemed cruel to burst his bubble. Harish, you sensed, sometimes found the world a troubling place.

'Media is so negative,' I overheard him saying sadly to Ben. 'Man walk to shops, have a laugh, nothing. Man walk to shops, stabbed at bus-stop – this they print. You don't believe me? Pick it up!'

The exercises continued – something he called Creditcrunch Laughter, where we mimed asking a waiter for the bill and then flash an empty wallet while howling with glee; and then Laughter Milkshake: pretending to slurp a drink so fantastic the only response was to almost soil yourself with pleasure.

At every turn there were sad-eyed asides, bittersweet laments for a world that had forgotten how to be happy. 'At the moment all is sales and debts,' he said distractedly. 'That is not funny. It is more money. The falling and the noise. These are the two fears we are born with. The rest is made up! So why so sad?'

He pinned an enlarged photo on the wall. It showed street kids outside an Indian railway station, dressed in rags and with smiles on their faces. 'These people have nothing, but they are happy!' He turned his palms upwards and shook his head in admiration before gazing reflectively out of the window. 'I took this picture from my own camera. Imagine if I did this here. I would be reported as paedophile.'

BEN

I jerked my head back and drained my Laughter Milkshake before splattering the raven-haired beauty standing in front of me with the remaining contents of my imaginary glass. She cackled riotously, slapping her thigh as she did so, until it was time to move on and our false hilarity came to a juddering halt. A wave of relief came over me, before I was collared by Harish and compelled to go through the same routine all over again. 'Wery good, wery good, yay!' said Harish, before plonking his empty imaginary glass on top of his head.

The thing is, I thought to myself, if Harish actually thought about what was in your average takeaway milkshake – mono-glycerides and diglycerides, amyl acetate, benzyl isobutyrate, hydroxyphenyl-2-butanone, methyl salicylate, and much more of that ilk – he'd no doubt come over all sad and utter mournfully, 'They don't make milkshakes like they used to . . .' The irony of Harish's endeavour is that it requires his students to view the world as a scary place to withdraw from, in favour of a parallel world of fabricated jollity. Surely it makes more sense to look for humour in the horrors and mundanity of everyday life? While 'stabbings and killings' aren't exactly the stuff of Christmas cracker gags, we might find humour in the overwrought and dispropor-tionate media coverage of stabbings and killings, and indeed paedophiles, whom we are led to believe are lurking in wheelie bins and under kerbstones on every street corner. Not forgetting the takeaway milkshakes our children drink, which used to be made of ice, milk, fruit and vanilla, but which now include as many as sixty different additives and ingredients – how preposterous is that? And for preposterous, read funny.

Harish made us waddle round the hall like penguins for five minutes, screaming and howling as we went, before introducing us to the Mobile Phone Laugh. One of the old fellas shuffled by before pulling out an imaginary blower, pointing a bony finger and dissolving in front of me, knees sagging, bent double, hands waving like Jolson. The laughter soon gave way to wheezing and for a couple of seconds it looked like he might keel over. Laughing so much at a laughter class that you have a cardiac arrest and die. Now that's what I'd call funny. A couple of days later, of course . . .

TOM

Harish was in statesmanlike mood again. At his feet, we munched ginger nuts and listened intently. 'Many things in life are very expensive. We're in a situation. Go and join David Lloyd club in Sudbury, £800 a month. Or bottle of perfume at Boots – £60. If it is free – oh, it's not worth it. We don't want.

'For laughing, you don't need any equipment. There is not British laughter like fish and chips, or American laughter like hamburger. It's common language – you don't need translator. Isn't it – you know? Happiness is on tap. Because the creator, the chap upstairs who runs Tesco – he has given it to us for free.'

He scanned the floor. 'I need wolunteer!' The chap with the moustache took a shove from his lady and climbed reluctantly to his feet. He was still wearing his red Santa hat. From the expression on his face, public performance was not something he relished.

Harish put his hand on his shoulder. 'The way you physically act has effect on your mind. And wice-wersa. Is a fact. My friend here – your name? David? – David will demonstrate.' He looked away and stroked his chin. 'Act sad!' he shouted, without warning. David jumped a mile. 'SAD!' He managed an awkward frown. 'Act happy!' He forced a smile. 'Sad! Happy! Sad! Happy!'

David's face was jerking around like a glove puppet's. The audience roared at his contortions. Harish was in full flow. 'Observe! Seeing David with the funny hat on – the contagious factor, like a wirus. Not mumbo-jumboing you, agreed? Okay! We are locked on here!'

'You can fake an orgasm but not laughter,' Bob Dylan once said. I wasn't so sure. The way Dr Kataria's patented exercises made you laugh felt more like panic than pleasure, more hysterical than happy. There was very little natural about it. At one point a chap in our ranks was revealed to be turning fifty in a few days' time. Rather than sing him 'Happy Birthday', we were told to gather round him and guffaw heartily. Encircled by wild-eyed clowns, pointing and screaming with forced laughter, he looked close to tears.

Was this really better than old-fashioned jokes or yarns? The hardest I had laughed recently had been when my friend Danny had split up with his live-in girlfriend – not at his misfortune, but the key incidents that had caused the breakup. Danny had a well-known (and entirely involuntary) habit of picking his nose, something which, over the course of a two-year relationship, had driven his girlfriend slowly insane. Do that one more time, she told him, and I leave. He had been unable to help himself. One night as he lay reading in bed, consumed with a burning desire for a nasal rummage, he had carefully created a small pillow wall between the two of them so that she could see nothing of his face. To double his defences, he then bunkered down behind an opened magazine.

Barely had digit gone up nostril than a scream came from the other side of the bed. 'The wall!' she had yelled. 'Look at the bloody bedroom wall!' There, blown up into unmissable detail by the bedside lamp beside him, was the vast shadow of his head, his nose jutting out like the prow of a ship, a single giant finger frozen deep within it.

I looked around the room. How well would that story play with this particular audience? Junior Assistant was grazing from a bowl of peanuts, his tusk gently rotating as he chewed meditatively on the dry-roasteds. Perhaps he would see only pathos in the tale, a confirmation that life was a never-ending series of cruel tricks and reverses.

By the window, the dowager was sipping from a plastic cup of apple juice. Would the travails of Danny bring a smile to her face? Hot on the heels of the nose/finger debacle, the under-fire bachelor had copped another, even more spectacular, body blow. Like many men, Danny suffered from occasional bouts of violent wind. Like all those men, he understood the calamitous consequences of releasing it anywhere near his girlfriend. One night, gripped by a particularly aggressive attack of flatulence, he had left the kitchen where the two of them were preparing dinner and tiptoed into the adjoining room to release the pressure. Calculating that the brick wall between them would shield his actions but the open doorways would do little to contain any noise, he had unbuckled his belt, dropped his trousers and, gripping a buttock in each hand, carefully pulled his cheeks apart. With joy he noted the near-silent phfeeeeewwww of escaping gas; with horror he spotted the mirror hanging on the hall wall just outside, a mirror ideally angled to give his girlfriend an uninterrupted view of his actions. The sight of her disbelieving, disgusted face would, he told me afterwards, stay with him to his grave.

I looked at the old dear, picking daintily at a small samosa. Maybe Harish was right. I couldn't see her cracking up to tales of windy-pops, not in public at least. Maybe, I reasoned, there was a reason for laughing without one after all, however unreasonable that might have seemed.

Harish began handing out mirrors of his own. 'Meditation time,' he announced, distributing them along the re-formed rows until everyone was staring at their own reflection.

'We learn to love us as we are. The first thing when you look in the mirror – you won't like it. First instinct is only to see problems – 'I don't like my nose', 'I don't like my chin'. What we do now is, don't obsess. When you see unpleasantness, move away from it. I demonstrate.'

He settled into his chair with his mirror on his knees and adopted an expression of exaggerated interest. 'Let me see. Ears? Not so hot. I move away from them. Eyebrows. Don't like, I move away. Teeth? Oh, wery nice!' He beamed out at us. 'When you find that plus-point, just laugh. I look at my plus-point teeth, I laugh. Ha ha!'

I studied my reflection. Did I look happier than a year ago? Next to me, Ben was groaning. 'Plus-points,' he muttered, before summoning an old New Order line: 'I hate that mirror, it makes me feel so worthless . . .'

'David!' said Harish. 'My wolunteer. What do you find?' The moustache twitched forlornly.

'The only thing I liked was my hat.'

Harish looked concerned. 'But you have to leave that.'

David sighed. 'It's not my hat,' he confirmed, with a downcast look.

Harish had an answer: his patented Happiness Cream. It came in large pots, enough for everyone to have their own, and caused instant laughter when applied to the face. It was also entirely imaginary, but the point where that mattered had long since been passed.

With a nod of thanks to Junior Assistant, Ben and I slipped away through the door and out into the crisp winter afternoon. We sat down on a frost-covered bench. Ben took out a cigarette and offered me the pack. I shook my head, pulled a banana from my coat pocket and split the skin with my thumbnail.

'Perhaps I know best why it is man alone who laughs,' wrote Friedrich Nietzsche. 'He alone suffers so deeply that he had to invent laughter.' Only a German, I thought could be so serious about something so light-hearted. I looked at Ben, puffing away happily. I grinned and nudged him in the ribs.

'Come on,' I said. 'There's a Wetherspoons by the station. I'll buy you a pint.'

10. THE GOOD LIFE

'It's forbidden, of course'

BEN

From the Harrow Laughter Club in Rayners Lane to Langue-doc in the south of France – now I knew how the American Indian chap felt at the end of *One Flew Over The Cuckoo's Nest*, running from the madhouse into the arms of nature. Tom and I had crossed the English Channel to suck the marrow out of life, to be at one with the land. To delight in the small things – what the French like to call *le plaisir des petites choses*. In a sense, it was the culmination of much we had already learnt, a testing ground if you will: good company, hedonism in moderation, the freedom to bend the rules or ignore them completely, something the French do best. And, as we would soon discover, the opportunity to scare ourselves shitless.

TOM

On the EasyJet flight from Gatwick to Montpellier, Ben snoring gently in the seat to my right, flakes from a Pret A Manger almond croissant tumbling off his chest with each rumbling exhalation, I thought back over various other creeds we had considered but ultimately rejected during the last 12 months.

As non-property owners, we'd thought anarchy might work out well for us. We even had the perfect battered van for demos, but Donny Dirs had other ideas. He hadn't spent successive summers stone-cladding the family residence in Brentwood to see it burned down in the flames of a class revolution. The same stern response met the notion that we become freegans, ducking out of the spluttering capitalist economy and meeting all our dietary needs by scavenging through supermarket dumpsters for needlessly discarded food. 'If Marian at number two sees you in her bins, we'll have to move house,' warned Mama Fordyce, and I knew from sore childhood experience not to risk that lady's wrath.

Not every promising plan came to fruition. A much-anticipated experiment in which I would try Ben's lifestyle and he would try mine foundered, variously, on cigarettes and luminous leg-warmers. While the smoking of a boozy evening I could just about manage, and the mid-afternoon gaspers proved surprisingly handy in whiling away the working day, sparking up before I had got out of bed in the morning proved a lung too far. It gave me a certain cachet down the local pool – not many triathletes precede a 7 a.m. 3,000m swim-set with three Marlboros and a fried egg sandwich – but also unpleasant levels of catarrh. Ben's transformation into a finely tuned athlete ended even earlier. Asked to enrol him into a suitable exercise class, I plumped for a street-jazz dance lesson at Soho's world-famous Pineapple Studios. While Ben had no problem being the only straight man in a class of twenty-five, his fellow hot-steppers poured cruel scorn on his outfit of choice: battered Hi-Tec Squash trainers, a pair of dirty mid-calf tennis socks and an open-necked golf shirt that was so long out of fashion it had almost become tasteful again.

Court action scared us off Scientology. Madonna put us off

Kabballah. Breatharianism sounded amusing until a single day trial ended with us so hungry we almost ate Marian, let alone what we could find in her bins. Could you really find perpetual satiety and succour in just the air around you? Not when you live within inhaling distance of the A12 expressway.

BEN

Tom had spoken of living what he liked to call 'the peasant life', but as we were shown round the converted seventeenth century convent that was to be our home for the next few days, I couldn't help thinking to myself: 'Some gaff. Some peasants.' Not only did our guide Chloe have all her own teeth, possess a 1,000 euro Louis Vuitton handbag and a coquettish giggle, she could have read out a list of serial killers and still had me phwoaring à la Bernard Bresslaw: 'Arold Sheepman, Myra 'Indley, Jack ze Rippair . . .' Oh, do stop it Chloe . . .

Still, if the old cliché stands that visiting rural France is like going back twenty years in time, then the village of Hérépian, slap-bang in the middle of the Languedoc region, is the land that time, and British tourists, forgot. Fifty miles inland from the buzzy Mediterranean city of Montpellier, Hérépian has a population of 1,500 and a pulse that barely registers. But that was rather the point: while Languedoc used to be a place pétanque-struck Brits bypassed on their way to Provence, it is now, if you will forgive me some marketing speak, the new Provence. No retired hedge-fund managers from Bucks banging on about how they '*love* the Provençal light, that clear yellow luminance that holds everything in its crystalline precision'; no paediatricians from Putney telling you about the tarte Tropézienne they picked up from a delightful pâtisserie in Palete ('Listen to this, Francis, Simon's never heard of tarte Tropézienne . . .'). Just French people, mainly, although that might not be the case for long.

Tom and I spent our first evening in the convent dining with Chloe, very much a case of a French Fancy nestled between two crusts of stale English bread. I realized I'd been a bit effusive, not to mention somewhat previous, in my praise of the red wine when Chloe stuck her nose in her glass, wrinkled up her face and announced it was corked.

'Because it smells a bit fishy?' offered Tom.

'No, because it smells of cork.'

But Chloe, an interior designer from down the road in Béziers, was willing to overlook our lumpen ways and soon she was cackling away like a one-woman hen party. Little black dress, teeth stained red, a Francophile's delight. What was it Brother Cyprian had said? 'There's certainly far more humour in a monastery than there is in a convent.' That's the thing about monks, they don't get out enough.

TOM

Long lunches. Short working weeks. A love of cycling. Booze at any hour. Breaking rules and simply shrugging. Smoking in public. A regrettable attitude towards ethnic minorities. While not everything about the French rural way of life was perfect, we knew from prior experience that there was still a great deal it could teach us about happiness.

When you've been born in Harlow and Barking respectively, it doesn't take too much to impress you; even now I find it hard to pass a Little Chef without a slight shiver of excitement. Yet the two months the pair of us had spent tootling round France in 2007, covering the rugby World Cup and about 4,500 miles in a luxury Winnebago that was everything our Champervan was not, had opened our eyes to an entirely different way of doing things. Like straw-chewing hicks arriving in the big city for the first time, we had marvelled how men could kiss each other on the cheek without it leading to fisticuffs, at towns devoid of a single Frankie and Benny's, at the way people could not only eat food sitting down but do so while conversing with friends rather than balancing their plates on their knees and shouting abuse at the contestants on Total Wipeout.

Then there were the women. It had started when I was sixteen with my middle sister's pen-pal, a teenage siren with smoky eyes, a love of retro reggae and the entirely inappropriate name Virginie. I still don't feel entirely comfortable discussing what happened (if I shut my eyes I can still hear Mama Fordyce's words as she threw me out of the house: 'There's animal in all of us, Thomas, but Jesus showed us that we can subdue it'), but the love affair had endured. French women possessed everything that Essex couldn't offer: a language that could make knives and forks sound like poetry, an aloofness with just a hint of possibility and a refusal to spray themselves orange and iron their hair before going out and getting battered on Blastaways and garlic naans.

To French ears, Chloe may have had an accent similar to Janet Street-Porter's. To Ben and me every sentence was an aural massage. 'Monsieur Benjamin,' I whispered fuzzily as she stepped outside for a pre-cheese-course smoke, 'could I bother you for a cigarette?'

BEN

I spent most of that night in bed on my hands and knees, suffering from a horrendous bout of heartburn. Whether it was the half slab of Roquefort, the wedge of camembert, the chocolate tart, the two bottles of wine, or any combination thereof, on the few occasions I was able to lie on my back it felt like the ghost of the convent's last-departed mother superior was squatting on my chest: 'For the love of God, woman, I never asked for this place to be turned into a boutique hotel!' As a result, I wasn't in the most robust condition when Chloe arrived to fetch us to the local charcuterie, where main man Michel was all set to show off the tricks of his trade.

Michel greeted us with a butcher's handshake, proffering a forearm to clasp rather than a bloody paw, before grabbing a pig's head by the ears, dragging it out of the vat and shaking it in front of our faces, all accompanied by squealing sound effects. It was Tom who was supposed to be uncomfortable around meat, him being a vegetarian and all, but while he appeared to be coping admirably with Michel's impromptu show of porcine puppetry, my stomach was slipping and slopping like a plate of tripe.

A charcutier deals primarily with pigs, using every part of the animal, from snout to tail. This results in a bewildering array of produce, from the basic cuts of meat you'd find in your local Dewhurst to more 'challenging' fair, such as brawn, or what the French call *fromage de tête*. Also part of the charcutier's repertoire are sausages, fashioned from seemingly every part of the animal, pâtés and more esoteric offerings, such as quenelles, terrines, roulades, galantines and the fearsome andouillette, a tripe sausage which resembles an alien giving birth when pricked with a fork and which smells, however good it tastes, a little bit like shit.

Michel talked us through his trade with the swivel-eyed passion of a Bible Belt Baptist, as if the loin, belly and leg of the pig were the father, son and holy ghost of the culinary world. This is not to say butchers back in the UK lack passion, but maybe their French counterparts are used to a more receptive audience: 'Trotters? Two bags of mince please, Keith, and stop fucking about.'

Michel's instruction was interrupted by the entrance of Christophe, the mysterious truffle farmer of Hérépian, a character, apparently, who commanded much respect around town. A toothpick lodged beneath a nicotine-stained moustache, Christophe didn't say a word, just placed a plastic bag on a butcher's block and parted it to reveal four or five nuggets of black gold, which, to the untrained eye, looked a bit like semi-fossilized cat turds. Christophe then made a sweeping motion with his arm and backed up a couple of paces, as if to say 'Behold,' before the rest of us edged forward gingerly, as if we were getting our first look at a new-born baby. Black truffles can fetch 1,000 euros a kg, so presumably Christophe, who's got his own truffle trees in his back yard, is doing rather well for himself. Certainly Michel looked impressed, holding one between thumb and forefinger and studying it closely, so that I half expected him to pull out a jeweller's loupe, lodge it in his eye socket and take an even closer look.

After Michel had humoured me and Tom by letting us hack away at a piece of pig for a few minutes (a piece of pig that was, mercifully, destined for the mincer), the talk turned to hunting. Chloe had already informed us that that week's boar hunt was off, which was unavoidable really, seeing as the chap who was due to take us out was being buried that afternoon. But Michel had other ideas, and following a conspiratorial huddle involving himself, Chloe and Christophe, he announced he would be taking a day off work later in the week to take us pheasant shooting instead.

'Don't we need a licence?' asked Tom timidly, 'Back in England we'd need a licence, for the shotgun.'

Michel turned to Chloe to confirm what Tom had said, before his head lolled to one side and he shrugged and smiled as if to say: 'That is England, this is France.' Later we found out from Chloe that shooting without a licence is indeed illegal, or what she preferred to call 'forbidden', which made it feel like less like a crime, more just a little bit naughty.

The following day Michel, who doubles up as a chef for the convent, was in our kitchen knocking up yet another four-course meal, my fourth in the space of two days. I've always considered myself to have a copper-bottomed constitution, with peas, beans and other small round savoury things my only known culinary enemies, but to that list can now be added Michel's black truffle omelette, a concoction as silky-smooth as cat sick and as rich as a battered Mars Bar. A squirt of brown sauce would have no doubt taken the edge off, but as far as the French are concerned, you might as well smother your omelette with Ice Magic. Plus, I was worried Michel, a big, gnarled former lock forward with more sharp edges than a piece of worked flint, might have come over all Zinedine Zidane and nutted me into next week had I called for some HP. So, feeling not unlike Monty Python's Mr Creosote, I left my starter unsullied and ploughed on through. My reward? A slipping and slopping plate of tripe.

After lunch I retired to my bedroom, not only to sleep off

Michel's gastronomic assault course, but also to psyche myself up for some wine-tasting, which had been arranged for later that day. I've always had problems exhibiting my emotions, whether the expression of elation, anger or excitement, and as a child on Christmas morning I would feel the need to take myself off for ten minutes to practise my post-present-opening reactions: 'Wow, a Chopper!' or 'Excellent, I've been running low on pants.' A lack of visible emotion is very much a Dirs, and indeed a Langfield, family trait, although as the years roll by, members of the clan grow more sanguine about their inability to reveal their feelings. Nan Langfield, for example, had a penchant for drop-kicking her presents, half-opened, back under the tree, before falling back into her armchair and ordering up another Guinness. No words needed, we all knew what she was thinking: 'Not another pair of fucking slippers.'

My stock reaction on tasting a particularly fine wine is to raise the eyebrows slightly, lift my glass and utter rather unconvincingly, 'Mmm, nice drop.' But when it comes to food and drink, the French are rather more sensual beings and an 'Mmm, nice drop' is the wine-tasting equivalent of staring at a painting in a modern art gallery and stating 'That's bollocks, I could do better than that.' If cynicism is the enemy of romance, then on this occasion I was determined to cast it aside, like a comfortable pair of pyjama bottoms, and cosy up to the wine fully nude.

'I'm going to throw something out there,' said Tom earnestly as we were gathered round the spittoon, casks piled up all around us. 'Is anyone else getting a hint of aubergine?' If I was tackle out, then Tom was snuggled up behind this particular drop nudging a fully fledged hard-on into the small of its back. For whatever reason, most of the French contingent chose to ignore Tom's observations, while Louis-Marie, owner of the Domaine de l'Arjolle in Pouzolles, flashed a sceptical smile before wandering off in search of another bottle of red. Still, Tom's enthusiasm, if a little off-beam, was infectious, and minutes later I was fixing him with a quizzical stare before hitting him with the line: 'Bit too youthful, needs time to develop some tricks.'

Languedoc has 700,000 acres of vines, making it the single biggest wine-producing region in the world, and as recently as 2001 more wine was strained from its grapes than in the whole of the United States. However, overproduction, a gravitation in taste away from the bog-standard table wine that was once typical of the region and the flooding of the market with cheaper imports from the New World have combined to hit many winemakers hard. Consequently, a simmering anti-globalization sentiment has boiled over in recent years, with the shadowy group the Regional Committee for Viticultural Action (CRAV) launching attacks on storehouses of wholesalers and trucks holding vats of imported wine, as well as bombing supermarkets and the ministry of agriculture. But while many winemakers have perished in this new climate, bewildered by change and too set in their ways or simply unwilling to innovate, Louis-Marie, in an irony as sweet as one of his bottles of red liqueur wine, has turned to the New World for inspiration, as well as economic salvation.

As we strolled across the lawn overlooked by the fifteenth-century Château de Margon, Louis-Marie let us in on the secret of his success: 'Our only standard,' he said proudly, 'is diversity.' Not so long ago, talk like this might have seen him drowned in a vat of Blue Nun by the locals, to many of whom tradition and continuity trump evolution every time. But Louis-Marie was dubbed the 'bearded wonder of Languedoc' by one wine writer for a reason, namely his willingness to accept that the traditional French ways might not necessarily be best. Unlike other regions in France, where the appellations (the legally defined and protected geographical indications used to define where grapes can and can't be grown) are almost set in stone, there is more flexibility in Languedoc, meaning Louis-Marie is able to plant grapes not synonymous with that region, as well as blend different varieties to create wines with less-complicated, easier to grasp tastes. Of the 500,000 bottles-worth produced on the Domaine de l'Arjolle each year, 80 per cent is exported, much of it to the New World, so Louis-Marie is selling to the Americans similar stuff the Americans have been selling to the French, similar stuff that is burying those Languedoc winemakers resistant to change.

This might give the impression that Louis-Marie is some super-slick marketing guru rather than a man who bleeds Shiraz and has vines for veins, but the truth is he's both. Louis-Marie, who along with brother Prosper started the vineyard in 1974, comes from a four-generation family of winemakers. However, unlike many of his inward-looking neighbours, he sensed the winds of change long ago and realized the New World, instead of being worthy of derision, might have something to offer. The result of all this very un-French open mindedness is a vineyard with a bewildering variety of yield: Zinfandel, Cabernet Franc, Cabernet Sauvignon, Merlot, Syrah, Sauvignon Blanc, Chardonnay, Pinot Gris, Viognier and Grenache Noir. And while Domaine de l'Arjolle wines are known to be light-bodied and flowery, that doesn't necessarily mean it's low-quality gear, with a bottle of 2001 Zinfandel Vin de Pays des Côtes du Thongue fetching anything up to £160.

It's easy for us Brits to scoff upon hearing stories of French 'wine terrorists' fomenting unrest across the land (I can't recall any underground movements being rallied when they did away with Watneys Red Barrel), but in doing so we would be failing to understand the seemingly primordial link the natives have with their soil, and with viticulture in particular, which stretches back to Roman times and beyond. For centuries, wine in Languedoc had little to do with business; it was almost a human right – like water, like bread – not a luxury to be spun and marketed. Until the 1970s, the average person in Languedoc drank 100 litres of wine a year, its consumption helping define what it meant to be French. So it is little wonder the small growers and family vineyards feel threatened by competition from elsewhere and look upon the new school, with their un-French ways of doing things and emphasis on fancy titles, presentation and packaging, as somewhat vulgar. This connection between the people and the land seems to have been severed a long time ago in Britain, where one child in four thinks bacon comes from sheep, one in three thinks oats grow on trees and the nearest thing to a delicacy you'll find in most local shops is a Barbecue Peperami.

Back round the spittoon and I'm throwing out words such as 'impish' and 'naughty' to describe a peppery red. I realize I have become what many British folk, suspicious of any display of emotion in connection with food or drink, would call a pretentious twat. But I couldn't give a monkey's. Look where cynicism and suspicion lead you: into a world where a hunk of bread, an oversized lump of cheddar, some pickle and a stick of celery is considered a national dish and where visiting a restaurant on your lunch break is viewed as maverick behaviour.

Oysters, what are they all about? One thing's for certain, Tom doesn't have a clue. After his passion-fuelled pronounce-ments on wine the previous day, he was now back in full

British mode, gagging on his first slippery globule before muttering something about being hit by a wave and swallowing his own bogeys. While listening to him lie through his teeth to the factory-owner about experiencing 'the taste of the sea' provided me with some short-term amusement, I soon realized I was going to have to compensate for Tom's actual distaste for the delicacy by necking his quota, as well as mine. And as the tenth oyster of the afternoon tobogganed down the back of my throat and splash-landed into the saltwater puddle at the bottom of my gut, I was no closer to knowing what all the fuss was about either.

'Back home we sometimes add a bit of Tabasco,' said Tom. Chloe giggled. Pascal the factory owner just looked angry.

Pascal had wanted to take us out on one of his boats, but Chloe reckoned the police in the tiny village of Marseillan might consider that just a little bit too forbidden, what with the Baltic temperatures, foaming waters and very real threat of drowning. So instead Pascal took time from his busy schedule to walk us through the different stages of mussel farming, which begins with juvenile mussels being literally glued to ropes with cement by what appears to be a pâtissier wielding a giant piping set and ends with fully grown mussels being packaged and dispatched to all corners of the globe. But Pascal soon grew bored of the tour and we retired to the company kitchen where he uncorked a couple of bottles of Picpoul de Pinet, cleaved open some oysters and handed out some cigars. A little bit more than a plate of digestives – know what I mean?

Over yet another impromptu feast overlooking the Étang de Thau, a large saltwater lake which is home to eighteen different types of shellfish, the wide-eyed Pascal told us of his brushes with various exotic British foods, such as Marmite and Bovril, in the manner of a sixteenth-century explorer regaling us with tales of strange monsters of the deep. He also told us about the time he was visiting Ecuador and drove 200 miles to the capital Quito simply so he could purchase a wheel of camembert: 'Bovril is liquid shit, but it might be better than plantains . . .'

Soon we were joined by Miguel Espada, a local entrepreneur responsible for both the conversion of the convent in Hérépian and our new home for a couple of nights, the magnificent Port Rive Gauche, not more than a hop and a skip from the otters frolicking on the coastal rocks of the Étang de Thau. Miguel began his career as an investment banker in Singapore and also worked in Indonesia and Myanmar, before founding a photography business on his return to France. But Miguel soon tired of the frantic pace of life in Paris and relocated his family to his native Languedoc, 'to live in harmony with nature and the animals – that's happiness'.

'Nature is like a woman,' continued Miguel, so that I half expected him to unbutton his shirt and start sliding oysters down his chest. 'Sometimes you open the curtains in the morning, look out and think, "Wow!" I had to come back to where I was from and it's very important that my children have this same relationship with nature. I can shoot breakfast off my balcony, I wake up, stroll out in my pyjamas and kill some rabbits, and my children can kill rabbits too. I don't find happiness in a big palace, I'm not sure the people who want to show their power with big houses and big cars are very happy. I feel sad for them. Luxury is eating oysters on the beach, reading and playing with the kids. Money makes life very complicated, you need to be wise enough to follow your own route. If someone gives you 45 million euros, is your life going to improve? The grass isn't always greener, happiness is often right in front of you, a lot of people just aren't aware of it.'

Miguel, who had the affable manner of a florist or the owner of a local gadget shop, spoke from experience, having been offered 45 million euros for his company only recently. 'They told me I was the youngest CEO on the stock exchange, but that was not very exciting to me. I thought, "Fuck that." People in France, in Languedoc anyway, are less motivated by their jobs than their lives. What they're going to eat tonight is more important than what they're going to achieve before they eat. Personally, I work too much, but not at the weekend. I always make time for my two children, my wife and dinner. The weekends are only for family and friends.'

Miguel, whose mother was a homeopath and father an architect, had grown up in the first solar house in France and was eating organic vegetables thirty-five years ago. His wife comes from an aristocratic family and her great-grandfather once offloaded 96 Gauguins to the Hermitage in St Petersburg. Clearly, Miguel is no stranger to money, but that only made his attachment to nature and *le plaisir des petites choses* even more admirable in my mind. Wildly successful, magnificently rich, but Miguel was wise enough to know that it's the things that come free that make us most happy.

Not that Miguel was detached from reality, as he also realized his money and his investment in the region, poor by French standards, could improve the lives of many. 'We've created 150 new jobs,' he explained. 'People grew up here and don't want to leave but there's no work. But we've got winemakers, chefs and oyster-catchers on board as part of our vision of sustainable tourism. I feel I have a responsibility to the people, a responsibility to the history of the region. I have

an animal relationship with the buildings, with the stone . . .
I dream of stone . . .' On the way back to Port Rive Gauche,
Miguel reminisced about his childhood in Languedoc, spent
larking about in fields, across meadows, through forests and
on beaches, not really knowing what happiness was, or wasn't,
and basking in his ignorance. 'You should come and visit in
the summer,' said Miguel. 'We could go hunting for sea bass
with harpoons. It's forbidden, of course . . .'

TOM

*It's generally a bad idea to make big decisions while half-cut.
Songs you claim to be the greatest ever turn out to feature the
vocal talents of Andy Williams or Jimmy Sommerville. Golf
buggies are less appropriate for the morning commute than the
late-night journey home. Bosses you decided to email seem reluctant to treat rants and resignations in the reversible spirit you
intended.*

*At the same time, as we whizzed through the verdant Langue-
doc countryside in Chloe's canary-yellow Peugeot 205, drunk as
lords on white wine as crisp and delicate as a frosted flower,
bellies full of truffle and ears full of foo-foo fa-fa Gallic pop, I felt
a warm sense of contentment oozing through my boozy limbs.
This was it. We'd found our true calling, our spiritual home.
Farewell, Noel Edmonds; farewell, Dixie Fried Chicken. Goodbye
forever, Cheestrings and the Wandsworth gyratory.*

*I glanced over my shoulder at the back seat. Ben was puffing
away with the serene contentment of a meditating Maharishi, a
toxic cloud of smoke gathered around the thinning summit of
his forehead, a dark splash of lemon juice staining the front
of his polo shirt. To my left, Chloe perched behind the wheel,*

seat-belt undone, smiling face half-hidden behind outsized sun-glasses and dark hair bouncing along in the salty breeze whistling through the half-open sun-roof.

It all seemed to make sense. Happiness was cigars on the beach at eleven in the morning. It was fresh air and hilly horizons and men called Miguel with generous cellars. It was bowling about with a beautiful woman and your best friend without a responsibility in sight, three sheets to the wind and two Picpoul de Pinets to the good. Who cared about the long-term? Who cared about next week?

We careered round a sharp bend. 'I feel a bit sick,' I said uncertainly. 'I might have to go back to bed.'

BEN

Michel came knocking at six the next morning, his two dogs bundled up in a trailer attached to his van, shotguns stowed in the back, and we were soon winding our way up through the gloom towards the Domaine de Calmels, a hunting estate adjacent to the hamlet of Le Cros – population 38, and falling. Not far from Le Cros is the town of Millau, home to the tallest vehicular bridge in the world and the scene of one of France's most notorious and symbolic acts of anti-globalization, the demolition of a McDonald's restaurant by a veteran agitator called José Bové, before it had even been finished. The McDonald's was eventually built, but in a magnificent piece of French insouciance, not to mention casual anti-Americanism, President Chirac later gave Bové a pardon.

Michel coaxed his van ever upwards, intermittently patting the dashboard as if it was the nape of a faithful packhorse, and suddenly we dropped over a crest and all was white before us, a rare south of France winter wonderland. 'Chloe and her crazy ideas,' mused Michel, before ruminating upon what the headlines might be in the British newspapers if he accidentally shot the pair of us. '~~Two English~~ and one French in the middle of nowhere . . . *c'était un accident?* I don't think so . . .'

We reached the hunting lodge at 7.30 a.m and by 8 I had half a bottle of red swilling about inside me, three espressos, three of Michel's Gauloise, half a wheel of cheese, a couple of sausages and two shots of the local firewater, which was so rancid that Eric, the estate manager, recommended I soak it up and ingest it via a sugar cube. Never mind an Ulster fry, this was a breakfast of pre-Revolutionary decadence, to the extent that I half expected Eric to pull a mirror down from the wall and start chopping up lines of cocaine. I wouldn't have minded, but unlike with an Ulster fry, I wasn't going to be vegetating on the sofa picking my arse after I'd done, I was going to be stalking the land packing two barrels worth of heat. My head was spinning as I surveyed the monumental open fire and high walls adorned with a dizzying array of animals' heads, the grizzly trophies of God knows how many hunting trips. Only two people were likely to get accidentally shot on this jaunt, I thought to myself, and one of them wasn't me.

When the time came to bid farewell to Eric and his toothless mate Gilles, who went by the nickname 'Killer Man', I was like Elmer Fudd after a night out clubbing, a delicate yet highly combustible combination of lack of sleep, alcohol, camembert and caffeine: 'Be vewy, vewy quiet . . .' Michel's gun tutorial took all of two minutes, consisting as it did of him telling Tom his shooter didn't have a safety catch and telling me to stop looking so worried and have another cigarette. Michel then emptied a couple of boxes of ammo into our pockets, turned loose his dogs and struck out into the snow, gun slung over his shoulder, whistling as he went.

Having never hunted in Britain, I'm not really sure what the procedure is. But I'm guessing forms, lots and lots of forms, I'm guessing licences, I'm guessing lessons, I'm guessing rules. I'm guessing that when you ask the bloke who's taking you out hunting if he has any advice, he doesn't turn to you, shrug and say, 'Don't shoot me?' before sparking up a Gauloise and disappearing behind a hedge. What the hell, being careful might keep you safe, but it doesn't necessarily make you happy.

It didn't take long for Michel's dogs, Amélie and Armand, to snuff out the first bird, and Michel was quick on the draw, pulling the butt of his gun towards his shoulder in one syrupy movement and blowing it out of the sky with a single shot. The pheasant had taken to the air as if on a borrowed set of wings, and he came back down like a jumbo jet performing an emergency landing, engine off, belly-flopping into the deck before being retrieved by the faithful Armand. Michel bundled the unfortunate victim into his knapsack and we trudged off into the hills, the crisp crunch of snow under oversized boots and the chatter of Tom's teeth the only sounds.

Michel's early success had led me to believe there would be a veritable infestation of pheasants across the land, but it must have been half-an-hour before the next one appeared, and he only had to ask himself one question: 'Do I feel lucky?' At that moment in time, with me and Tom in stone cold pursuit, there wasn't a luckier punk alive. Pheasants, male pheasants anyway, are the animal equivalent of Elton John, all gaudy iridescence and ornate adornments, a bird as designed by Versace. But they also aren't the gainliest, and watching one come staggering out of a hedge and take to the air put me in mind of a man who'd just been found in bed with another man's wife: stumbling from the scene of the crime, trousers round ankles, the desperate kok-kok-koking and whirring of wings sounding not unlike a getaway car stubbornly refusing to start. But hesitation is deadly when it comes to hunting, although not for the hunted, and as Tom and I stood transfixed, fingers twitching on triggers, our prey was able to make his escape, landing just short of a distant hedge before scrambling for cover. 'That's one drink each,' smiled Michel, 'and we're not going in until you've hit one . . .'

Having never taken another animal's life, other than the odd wasp or spider, I didn't really know what I'd feel, if anything, when the time finally came. The truth is it felt good: I aimed, I pulled the trigger and a ghost of a smile appeared on my face. No regret, no questioning of one's morals, and I liked the fact I wasn't a carnivorous hypocrite. Snap its neck, stick it in your coat pocket and take it home for dinner. It felt like the most natural thing in the world – more natural than pulling a chicken out of a supermarket freezer, however free-range, that's for sure. I sensed Tom, a long-time vegetarian, hadn't bonded with his gun quite as easily and looked upon the cold steel gripped in his left hand more as a sure-fire way of catching frostbite than an extension of his manhood. He appeared from the other side of a hedge, hands in pockets, grimacing from the cold. 'Can we go in now?' He shivered, his weapon hanging limply beside him. 'Not yet,' I answered, my eyes narrowing. 'I'm just beginning to get the taste.'

Desperate for Tom to make a kill, Michel's methods became more and more unorthodox. For unorthodox read farcical. For farcical read dangerous. At one point, he ploughed headlong into some brush, grabbed a bird which had been partially stunned by one of his hounds and launched it above his head, all the while imploring Tom to take a pot-shot, an offer Tom mercifully declined. But Tom did finally come good, latching onto a target which had been sent spinning by my first shot and blowing its head clean off. Tom crouched down before the decapitated bird, felt the warmth of its breast and grimaced some more, like a soldier just stumbled across a fallen comrade.

'Yes, you killed it,' said Michel, sensing Tom's unease, 'but he has not had to grow up in a cage . . .'

TOM

It was as cold and bleak as the Russian steppes out there, as far from the sun-tickled coast and Chloe's dream machine as Michel was from Mary Whitehouse.

As dangerous as the cartridges stuffed into our pockets was my partial grasp of French and Michel's sketchy words of English. While Ben feigned incomprehension of everything le chasseur *said, fearful of being dragged into a linguistic whirlpool from which there would be no escape, I pondered the irony of under-standing just enough to get us into serious trouble. Always a phrase or sentence in arrears, I could pick up the 'walk in front of the guns' but not the preceding 'under no circumstances'. Here lie Dirs and Fordyce, killed by a B in their GCSEs.*

That I was a vegetarian and Michel a career butcher only made things worse. In the eyes of our host it wasn't so much a moral stand as a direct attack on his pension plan. For the first hour I had contented myself with blasting barrels vaingloriously into the wintry skies, but it became increasingly clear that only a solo kill would keep him satisfied. No matter that I blew the head off the bird Ben had crippled (accidentally, as it happens – I'd been aiming at a spot five metres to the pheasant's right, when suddenly the doomed mono-wing spiralled sideways and took the full force in the chops); we were out here until there was blood on my hands.

In the distance, a lone pheasant was strolling around the farmyard car-park. 'Vegetarian,' hissed Michel. 'Zees ees yours.' He gestured me over and put a finger to his lips. 'Wizz me.'

Pheasants, it seems, are very stupid birds. Like an in-bred Edwardian dandy promenading along Rotten Row in all his Sunday finery, the bird strutted around with chest stuck out, head held high, oblivious to the two gun-toting men bearing down on his unprotected rear.

'Now!' whispered Michel. 'Shoot!'

I raised the gun to my shoulder. 'On the ground?' I queried. 'Without warning him?' Michel nodded furiously.

I pulled the trigger. Whoomph. There was an explosion of brightly coloured feathers and an echoing rebound of sound from the snowy hills on all sides. I walked over and picked up the fallen bird. There was none of the 'he could have been asleep' pathos of military myth; this brave soldier looked like he'd been opened up with a chainsaw.

'Enfin, mon petit vegetarian,' said Michel, appearing along-side me and slapping me hard on the back. He took the pheasant from my grasp, unzipped my jacket and shoved the bloodied carcass inside. 'Tout va bien, non?'

BEN

Call it karma, call it pheasant's revolt, but minutes later, Tom's victim very nearly had his revenge. As I've already made clear, Michel wasn't big on safety, and after a few hours in his company his cavalier attitude had clearly rubbed off. As we made our way back to the lodge, pheasant tails protruding from both coat pockets, I slung my unbroken gun over my shoulder, cartridges in both barrels, and decided I needed a cigarette hanging off my bottom lip to complete the insouciant look – a look that said housing estate gentry, a look that said high-street laird, a look that said BOOM! As I was patting myself down, trying to locate my twenty Gauloise, somehow the strap had broken free of its catch, the gun had fallen downwards and the jolt had set it off, scattering shot inches, or centimetres, or who knows how close, from my face. For the first few seconds I didn't know what had happened, but the ringing in my left ear and the sight of Tom gesticulating wildly, flat on his back in the snow a few metres in front of me, soon alerted me to the fact that it was my weapon that had accidentally discharged.

How would they have remembered me in years to come? 'Dear old Dirsy. Blew his head off. Hunting pheasant. South of France.' I liked the sound of that. My nieces, friends of friends, future members of the Dirs clan as yet unborn, all would have thought of me as some reckless romantic, a swasher, perhaps even a buckler, maybe even an urban squire, a throwback to gayer, more carefree times. If they'd known I was just rummaging around in my pocket for a fag when my shotgun went off, it might have taken the gloss off things. Double barrel. Could have been missing an ear, or half my face. Perhaps even a life. If anyone from the British Medical Association is reading this, do me a favour and add it to the long list of ways in which smoking kills.

Tom hadn't been hit and had merely been taking evasive action, but he was understandably a little upset. Which was more than you could say for Michel, who broke into a disbelieving smile and took a puff of his cigarette before turning on his heels and shouting over his shoulder: 'Chloe and her crazy ideas . . .' Who knew that almost killing yourself could be such a giggle?

*

BEN

Is there a more crashing bore than the man or woman who constantly rails against the perceived ills of his or her own country? Show me a man who thinks his own country is a load of old rubbish and I'll show you a man looking for an excuse. So I should point out, rather belatedly, that this particular experiment wasn't intended as one long veiled dig at Britain, but rather a reminder of where many of us around the world, enslaved by the fast pace of modern life, have gone wrong. For example, it might surprise you to discover that McDonald's, for so long the *bête noir* of French culinary traditionalists, is more profitable in France than anywhere else in Europe: those cheese-eating monkeys have seemingly surrendered and are being bent over the golden arches and pumped with so much gristle. Not only that, but by some estimates the French will be as fat as Americans by 2020, unless, horror of horrors, the Americans keep getting fatter. In addition, the average French meal, which twenty-five years ago lasted eighty-eight minutes, lasts just thirty-eight minutes today.

Still, the connection between people and food, between

people and the production of food, the unabashed appreciation of taste and ingredients, the 'animal relationship' between people and nature and their land, remains far more apparent in France than in Britain. Sections of the media try to kid the British public that while the French have let standards slip, us Brits have become a nation of farmers' market-frequenting gastronomes, but having a few Jamie Oliver recipe books on the top shelf in your kitchen, arrayed like culinary wank mags, or watching Nigella fellate a chocolate-covered wooden spoon does not necessarily make you a gastronome – far more likely it makes you a food voyeur. Of course, there are simple reasons for this lack of intimacy between the British and the fruits of their land – industrialization, urbanization, intensive farming, postwar rationing, the power of the supermarkets – but while culinary regionality might not be embedded in the culture in the same way as it is in France, that's not to say producers of quality regional food do not exist. The problem is there is an unwillingness on the part of consumers to shell out for this quality produce: look at those silly Frenchmen with their funny sausages and baguettes – I just picked up twenty bangers and a sliced loaf for £1.50. Every little helps . . .

The 'big shop', a British institution, epitomizes the joyless, soulless relationship many in Britain have with their food: bomb down Tesco, whizz round with your basket, pile it high, buy it cheap, and if you run out of anything during the week, not to worry, it's only fuel anyway, not meant for pleasure. You may be reading this and thinking, 'Not me, pal, I'm strictly organic,' but it's a fact you can buy a chicken for £1.99 in Britain's favourite supermarket, and while you may not be buying them, millions of others are.

To many in Britain organic food, free-range food, seasonal

food, is viewed as posh food, a swindle, the food of toffs and lefties and the middle classes, of pretentious twats, of some plummy bloke off the telly who eats berries and fungi but lives in a million-pound cottage. One of the most cosmopolitan countries in the world and what do we plump for as our national dish? Chicken tikka masala, which many would say is a triumph of multi-culturalism, but I would say is a triumph of bad taste, seeing as the chicken tikka masala served up in most high street Indians is mass-produced, neon-red, brimming with fat and so full of sugar it tastes like hot, molten Hubba Bubba.

Miguel's line will stay with me forever: 'What they're going to eat tonight is more important than what they're going to achieve before they eat.' Viewed one way, it sounds like a loafer's charter; viewed another, it's the recipe for contentment – because the eating is really just a pretext, an excuse for friends and family to sit around a table, to chat, to laugh and enjoy each others' company. In short, to be convivial. And if you're in a convivial mood, the chances are you'll want convivial food, and so the circle is complete. And so our visit to Languedoc was about much more than just food and sensuality and unabashed intimacy with produce and nature, it was also a lesson in how to take control of life rather than letting life manhandle you, a lesson in standing still to stop and stare. In addition, it was a lesson in how happiness can be acquired by swerving inconvenient rules. As Miguel put it: 'We in France sometimes have an interpretation of the rules – we're just a bit more flexible.' And as Katharine Hepburn put it: 'If you obey all the rules, you miss all the fun.'

On our final night back in Hérépian, Michel roasted up a couple of the pheasants we'd killed the previous day, wrapped in bacon, before serving them up with an apple and Calvados sauce. The food was majestic, the company top-notch. All in all, it was what you might call convivial. Then the conversation turned to the French economy, with Miguel revealing that behind the idyllic facade, Hérépian and much of the region was creaking: high unemployment, over-generous benefits, an ageing population, a bloated bureaucracy, too many regulations, not enough investment. 'Everyone thinks the slow pace of life in France is great,' said Miguel, 'but we're really a bit fucked.'

'Yes,' replied Chloe, slightly piqued, 'but fucked in a nice way.'

EPILOGUE

'We had rolled the dice'

BEN

At the time of writing, the World Database of Happiness lists 9,042 'happiness investigators', that is, scientists who have published on the subject of happiness in the last four decades. There was even a recent article in the Journal of Happiness Studies entitled 'Personality, Psychosocial Variables and Life Satisfaction of Chinese Gay Men in Hong Kong'. Hong Kong's Chinese gay men aren't exactly over the moon apparently, although compared to Hong Kong's Filipino lesbians they may well be, it's just that no one's asked them. Yet.

Sift through the findings of some of these studies and you will end up thoroughly confused. Costa Ricans are apparently the happiest people in the world, until you discover it's the Danes— hang on a second, this list here says it's the Finns, but how come they only came 59th on this other list? And spare a thought for the poor old Vietnamese, perhaps the most changeable people on the planet: only 95th on the Satisfaction with Life Index of 2006, but 5th on the Happy Planet Index of 2009. God they must have hated Gary Glitter: if only they'd been allowed to execute him by firing squad like they wanted to, all bets on the Happy Planet Index Christmas number 1 would have been off.

Sex is good, everyone seems to agree on that, unless you're in an unhappy marriage of course, but then apparently marriage makes you happy (even though spending time with your spouse merely ranks as 'OK' in one study) until you have kids and everything falls apart and you decide to get a divorce, which is sometimes a good thing because people feel happier after a divorce than they do beforehand. Work makes us miserable, unless you're in a satisfying job, but you can escape the grind by socializing with friends or family (that makes us very happy), just don't socialize with the boss (and definitely don't have sex with him, especially if you're a gay Chinese man in Hong Kong). Then there are the studies that suggest happiness is all down to age. 'There's a kind of J-curve describing happiness over time,' says Andrew Oswald of Warwick University. 'Your late 30s are the most unhappy period of your life, but then the older you get the happier you are. Life really does begin at 40.' Try telling that to the 40-year-old with young kids in an unhappy marriage. Maybe they should just move to Vietnam or Costa Rica. Or was it Denmark?

Then there are the studies that say a person's happiness is inherited, and that the pursuance of happiness is a waste of time if your parents, the selfish swines, have gone and lumbered you with the gift of miserable genes. And if that's the case you might as well just do a Morrissey and make the most of it, instead of making yourself more unhappy than you already are by hunting for happiness. Which, alas, is easier said than done.

One thing most happiness investigators seem to agree on,

however, is that successive prime ministers and almost every other politician in the world has got it wrong, and that the creation of happiness in itself, rather than increased GDP and economic growth and more 'stuff', which has been proved not to deliver greater happiness, should be a government's ultimate ambition. But then it would be a brave government that announced enhanced happiness rather than increased wealth as its goal. And what chance have we Brits got? David Cameron wouldn't know happiness if it dropped to its knees and gave him a blowjob.

I'm not going to begin to claim mine and Tom's adventures in happiness even come close to amounting to an academic study, but it's amazing what nuggets of wisdom you can pick up when you're playing table-tennis with your spuds out or sorting spuds at a monastery or serving spuds to the homeless or eating dauphinoise spuds with the French. And when you consider that an awful lot of academia is about confirming things most people already know, then you might as well dispense with the brain monitors and the clipboards and have some fun with it. That way you get to stay on a £400,000 boat in Dubai and meet characters like Stef, who'll gladly tell you, over several glasses of champagne, the pros and cons of having money and the happiness and misery it can bring. Or like Brother Cyprian, to whom happiness means being virtuous and good rather than making fifty grand in an afternoon. Or like Miguel over in Languedoc, who revels in *le plaisir des petites choses* and dreams of stone. Or Brian at the naturist campsite in Kent, to whom freedom, one of the key indicators of happiness, means simple stuff like filling out forms in the buff. So even though this is categorically not an academic study, we're going to throw some findings at you anyway.

And if you don't agree with any of them, at least you can be happy that these two happiness investigators didn't spend any of your tax money, unlike that other miserable lot.

TOM: Appreciate what you have

When I was four years old, my favourite book was Petunia Beware. It was the tale of a goose who decided the grass in her farmyard might not taste as good as the stuff in the meadow and mountain beyond, and so sneaked off through the fence to try it. After some unpleasant business with a weasel and fox (perhaps some of my initial fears with the witches now make more sense) she came to the simple conclusion: the grass at home was the tastiest of the lot. Either Stef, Tuihana and Philip the Druid had all read the same book, or Petunia was on to something. It tied in too with something the aptly named Professor Richard Wiseman had said when I'd been chatting to him about Ben's avatar issues: 'The easiest way to make yourself happy is spend a minute each morning thinking about one thing you did really well the day before.' Rather than constantly thinking about your failures, about what you don't have, take a little stroll on the bright side and try to enjoy the view.

BEN: Health, relaxation and *le plaisir des petites choses*

To John and Gaia on The Hill That Breathes, happiness and contentment was all down to qi and vibrations and saying Fuck It to everything. To me and Tom it was about lying about in hammocks all day in the sun. It was about eating simple Italian food and drinking wine. It was about playing

Victorian parlour games and toasting marshmallows on a campfire. It was about banter and laughter and talking nonsense,
what Miguel in Languedoc might have called being convivial.
It was about applying the brakes and parking up for a while,
winding down the window and breathing it all in. Let's not
fuck about here, it was about going on holiday. Both Stef
and freeconomizer Mark, although from different ends of the
financial spectrum, could see it: for Stef it was the idea of
popping round a mate's for tea and toast or taking a cycle
through the woods; for Mark it was simply being – sitting
next to a river under a tree in a beautiful valley, sucking up
the joy of what life has to offer for free. And for Henare and
the rest of the Te Whanau-a-Apanui, it was about realizing
that sucking on a fish's eyeball could be every bit as gratifying
as buying a boat.

TOM: Leave the judging to the old boys in powdered wigs

*Witches aren't wicked. They drive disabled kids around. Pen-
sioners who walk around with their old chaps hanging out like
Transit vans and table-tennis, not flashing or shagging in the
bushes. Maoris who go diving for shellfish for breakfast are experts
on Justine Henin's forehand. Nothing is ever quite as you think.
When we'd first met a lot of our fellow happiness pilgrims, it had
been tempting to write them off as outsiders with far-off ideas –
crazy dressers and undressers, as different from us as night and
day. It's almost an easier way to be: you look strange, I don't; I'm
right, you're wrong. Finding out how bandy our preconceptions
and stereotypes were was a sneaky joy. Who decides what's strange
and what isn't? Who cares? Unusual is good. Similarities lie
where you'd least expect them. Get drunk with a witch. Take tea*

with a naked grandmother and laugh yourself stupid with an IT technician from Rayners Lane. Listen to Whitesnake with silent monks. Just make sure you take your headphones with you.

BEN: Freedom and courage

Thankfully, we Brits live in a tolerant country – if Stef ever tries strolling about with no clothes on in Dubai, it won't just be his boat he loses. Brian and his mates at the naturist camp can do what they do because Britain allows freedom of expression, tolerates diversity, people doing things and holding beliefs of which other people might not necessarily approve or understand. For Brian, not being able to play table-tennis naked in a shed in the woods would be catastrophic, just as for Philip not being able to celebrate the winter solstice would cause unbridled misery. And while they may be free to lead life as they would wish, Brian and Philip still require the courage to do what they do, and so courage in itself is a form of happiness. And for those who might lack courage or have low self-esteem or are just a little bit shy, there is the internet, where they can be members of special interest groups and communities and can flourish without fear of being stigmatized or alienated. Mark put it best: 'One thing we all crave is to be able to do what we want to do when we want to do it.' And if the rules are stopping you, you might want to think about moving to Languedoc, where you can bend and even break them to your heart's content.

TOM: Don't do it on your own

As any teenage Dirs could tell you, onanism can only take you so far. The happiest people we found all had a support group around them, whether it was the descendents of Apanui out on the East Cape of New Zealand, brought up on the Whakapapa and standing shoulder to muscular shoulder with their tribal brothers and sisters; Cyprian and Gabriel in the cold stone rooms at Pluscarden with their rather different brothers; or Steve, the East End witch, finally finding a home in the world with Jeanette's coven and the Viking boys from High Wycombe. Even Dirsy's avatar amigos had lived their Second Life for the same sort of reason, although the main support Dominic Donegal seemed to require was Ben's back as he unloaded all over it. What was it Tuihana had said? 'Know who you are and where you come from.' You can wallow in all this 'we come into this world alone, and we leave it alone' doom and gloomery if you like, but the time in between feels a lot more pleasant if you surround yourself with people who can help you out and make you laugh and show that you, and what you feel, really matter. Would the last year have been as much fun if Ben had stayed at home in Romford? Safer, yes, more sober certainly. Better? Get out of it.

BEN: Keep yourself busy, and (if possible) find a job you love

If you ever find yourself wondering whether you're happy, the chances are you're not, for no other reason than you've got the time to ask yourself the question in the first place. Ask Stef, Miguel or Brother Cyprian, and they will tell you that happiness isn't some mystical, far-off place, it is part of the journey, the here and now: for Stef, his job is no longer about making lots more money, it's about the satisfaction of a deal and the sense of achievement; Miguel works hard because he feels an animal affinity with the region he grew up in and a responsibility towards it; Brother Cyprian devotes 24 hours of each day to God because he believes that it makes him virtuous and good. There's Michel, glorying in the humble pig, or Louis-Marie, with vines for veins. And what about Mark, who some people might say doesn't do anything at all, but others would say is doing more than most by being the change he wants to see in this world. And then there's Jake from the soup kitchen, who's not content to sit about playing World of Warcraft when he hasn't got lectures, he's helping others, like Wayne, because 'life ain't all about take, take, take'.

TOM: Scare yourself

It's much safer to stay with what you know, to say 'Stick' to the celestial croupier, to reverse back into the cave at the first sign of trouble. But oh, the liberation of stepping out into the unknown . . . I'd never wanted to expose myself on a campsite in Kent, or sing solo to 150 Maoris, but the fear was overwhelmed by the sense of freedom and confidence afterwards. Whether you need to almost decapitate yourself in a shotgun accident with a mousta-chioed butcher named Michel is more debatable, but a little adrenaline never made anyone unhappier – fighting off killer cats in a Snowdonian mansion, trading blows with a warrior called Jamus, racing down an Italian hill on a borrowed mountain-bike you will shortly sacrifice in a shamanistic ritual. If I'd turned down Jeanette's invitation to go back to hers, I'd have never touched a rhino penis, and if Ben had ignored Tarot Cilla's advice, he'd never have been abused in a Chinese restaurant by Tina. All right, it doesn't always work out, but it's better to have learned and lost than never to have learned at all.

BEN: Money isn't everything

It's not just bearded revolutionaries and hippies who are saying so, the top brass at the London School of Economics are saying so; a few years back an Israeli scientist won the Nobel Prize for economics for saying so. There's hard scientific evidence to back up the claims, with the findings of neuro-science supporting myriad social and psychological surveys. Not all of these happiness investigators are cranks, you see, some of the finest minds in academia are on it. Let's not be naive here, we all need a certain amount of money to clothe, house and feed ourselves, but after that it's all about comparison: people are unhappy because other people have more than them, but they don't stop to ask if the people who have more than them are happy. And so we work like dogs to get where they are, 'squeezing out the happiness' on the way, only to discover when we get there that we're no happier than we were before. Getting what we want and enjoying what we get are two very different things. So instead of killing yourself with overtime to pay for that home cinema you thought you always wanted, take your mum and dad out for dinner, become a druid, knock back a couple of Laughter Milkshakes, or maybe just pop round a mates for some tea and toast.

TOM: Keep on moving

A man should be careful of quoting Soul II Soul lyrics; for starters they were always more about the dancefloor than the dictionary. All the same, Ben and I could see meaning in Jazzy B's meanderings. At the start of our quest we'd been stuck in the wrong sort of groove, singing the same song year after year and bored to the back teeth of the sound of our own voices. You seem to get to a certain stage in your life and think, that's it – I know how the world works, I know what I like and I know how things will be for me for ever more. To find that you can change that stuck record is a wonderful feeling. Stef had lost millions but gained a new contentment after the house of cards collapsed in Dubai. Cyprian had waved farewell to the medical labs at Colchester General Hospital and said hello to Pluscarden peace, albeit very quietly. Sean the Druid left spiritualism and an ashram behind to find happiness in mead and the Mabon. In the process he'd also come up with my favourite single aphorism: stand upright in a cool place. I was thinking of getting a second tattoo.

BEN: Experience new things

I'm getting a little bit emotional writing this, mainly because it's taken over my life for the last year and I was beginning to think we'd miss the deadline, but also because it's not every day I finish a book. For me, this book in itself represents happiness (you might think differently, but then that's your fault, you shouldn't be sat around reading, get off your arse and go and do something useful instead) because it's a record of lots of stuff Tom and I have done over the past year or so, and made ourselves very happy by doing so. Some of the things cost money, but just because money doesn't buy you happiness doesn't mean money can't buy you happiness. However, much of the happiness cost us little or nothing at all, such as climbing Glastonbury Tor, strolling through the Appenines, crying with laughter over a game of charades, laughing at nothing at all with Harish (unless you count an imaginary mobile phone as something), an afternoon in the company of Russell Grant, being told I'm at the very bottom of the pit relationship-wise by a tarot reader called Cilla. Being cyber-raped in a cyber-porn cinema by a cyber-man from Donegal. Proof, if proof was needed, that happiness studies are far from an exact science.

TOM

'Rupert,' I said, 'thanks for everything. It's been great.' I looked around at the walls of the house, with their Cecil Beaton prints and pictures of rearing stallions. We shook hands, and I pushed my bike out into the insipid spring sunshine.

On the towpath, kids were throwing stones at floating cans. I weaved between the strolling couples and thought back over the last twelve months. Somewhere out there, Mark would be wiping his arse on a newspaper, Henare diving for abalone, Brian dropping his khaki shorts before stepping into his garden to take the air. What was Steve up to now he was a fully-fledged witch? Were the Pluscarden brothers actually utilizing those pea-sized potatoes we had picked? Had McEnroe ever found the doubles partner she'd been looking for?

We had rolled the dice, chosen twist over stick, and for what?

For friends, for adventure, for naked table-tennis and solstice celebrations on the wrong day, for raves in domes and dead pheasants and laughter yogis with simian sidekicks. And happiness?

I turned off the main road and pedalled up to an open door. The ladyfriend was standing there with a big smile on her face. 'It's all unpacked,' she said happily. 'I've got the keys. Bring your bike in.'

I leaned it against the three others stacked against the wall and walked to the stereo. A Dubliners CD sat on top of a speaker. I stuck in on and flicked through to 'Seven Drunken Nights'.

The doorbell rang. The ladyfriend looked up, confused. 'It's all right,' I said. 'I'm expecting someone.' I opened the latch and beckoned Dirsy in. He moonwalked to the sofa and plopped down with a contented sigh. 'I've brought some mead,' he said. 'House-warming present. Shall we?'

ACKNOWLEDGEMENTS

Our heartfelt thanks go out to the following, without whom the last year and a half would have been a lot less happy: Stef and his gang in Dubai (great days, I think . . .); Moneyless Mark (I don't think you're an imbecile, although I think I'll stick with Andrex); Cilla the tarot reader (they were Horror Top Trumps, right?); Tina and all the girls on My Single Friend (I'm still available, if any of you are interested); Russell Grant, his cats and celestial chat; Brian, Dennis, Andrew and all the nice folk at the naturist camp (ping-pong will never be the same again, although Tom is still berating himself for not winning the championships); John and Gaia and our fellow Fuckiteers at The Hill That Breathes (that tea was no PG tips); all the Brothers up at Pluscarden, especially G-Dog and Cyprian – keep keeping it real, kind of; Wayne and the good people at the American Church in London; Jeanette and Steve for taking the wicked out of witches; Philip Carr-Gomm and the other bards, druids and ovates (the taste of mead will always bring back memories); all those I chatted to in cyberspace (except that bloke who raped me – so not cool); the necrophiliac-pig dudes on *Manhunt 2* (what? They're not real?); my Facebook friends (dunno who most of you are, but still . . .); Professor Griffiths for providing a thin veneer of academic gloss; Nicole and the gang at Tourism New Zealand (if happiness isn't mountain-biking round Wanaka followed by a swim in the lake, what is?)

and Fiona Reece for her fine PR skills; Steve and Fenella at the Sublime B&B in the Waitaki Valley (late nights, good times); Henare, Charles and the rest of Te Whanau-a-Apanui for their hospitality and wise words; Harish and the other happy chucklers at the Rayners Lane Laughter Club; Chloe, Miguel, Pascal and 'the Bearded Wonder of Languedoc' for teaching us about *le plaisir des petites choses*, plus Garrigae Resorts for tremendous hosting; Michel and the chaps at the hunting lodge (killed any English people yet?); Abdul from Costcutter; my housemate Dave (I'm very happy for you really); Ian Belcher for endless ideas and unbeatable contacts; Bettsuci for reading and Jon T for titling; Jon Butler and the rest of the guys at Macmillan for all their help and enormous patience; our agent David Luxton, whose advice and time is always valued; and Murf for only occasionally complaining that Tom spends more time with Ben than her.

www.panmacmillan.com

Printed in Great Britain
by Amazon

54491453R00187